ALL BY ACCIDENTS
and other plays

ALL BY ACCIDENTS

and other plays

Ramesh Panigrahi

AUTHORSPRESS

Worldwide Circulation through Authorspress Global Network
First Published in 2023
by
Authorspress
Q-2A Hauz Khas Enclave, New Delhi-110 016 (India)
Phone: (0) 9818049852
E-mail: authorspressgroup@gmail.com
Website: www.authorspressbooks.com

All by Accidents and Other Plays
ISBN 978-93-5529-578-1

Printed in India at Thomson Press (India) Limited

For those who invite new drama in India

PREFACE: FROM BEHIND THE CURTAIN

Ramesh Panigrahi fascinates as much as flummoxes and befuddles his spectators/readers by sending elusive signals about himself through his plays. A surface gaze would identify him as a humorist, but in fact, seen through the depths he would emerge as a very serious 'black humorist' or at least an ironist. Panigrahi's dramatic statements usually involve the explicit expression of one attitude or evaluation, but with indications in the overall speech-situation, the speaker intends a very different, and often opposite attitude or evaluation. This generates a type of humour that includes the use of sarcasm, irony and dark humour to create laughter from uncomfortable situations. His jokes are about serious or depressing topics, such as hopelessness, suffering or death. He presents them facetiously and playfully occasionally exposing human hubris. Chakradhara Parida, for example, in *Waiting for the Bus* is a former minister and now, a struggling politician whose only pursuit is power. He cares little to recognize his school teacher Biswamohan at the village bus stop. Similarly Gunanidhi, a crude and inhuman police top brass in *All by Accidents* who acted like a lion, transforms into a goat after his death.

Widely known for his satires, Panigrahi's dramatic intentions are implicit. He censures, but the true end of his playful works is the amendment of vice. To put it in brief, his satires are like a glass wherein the beholders do generally discover everybody's face but their own, which is the chief reason for that kind of reception it meets in the world, and that so very few are offended by it.

Panigrahi, through his satires, is able to exploit more fully the difference between appearance and reality, and especially is able to expose hypocrisy. The hypocrite's skin is notoriously more tender than that of the openly vicious. The one has nothing to conceal, the other everything. His whole reputation is at stake on Panigrahi's stage.

Our predicament, however, is no joke. Jokes fall in the scope of rational explanation. His plays, therefore, are bemusing, but are almost comical collisions of metaphysics and mirth. His humour subverts the status quo, but the norms it does subvert may be ones we hoped to preserve.

A competing theory of humour as incongruity, was pioneered by him in a time when his senior contemporaries concentrated on psycho-social themes with emphasis on abnormal sexual behaviour (that was around mid 1960s directly influenced by the counter-culture movement in America). Panigrahi founded his jest in *The Emperor with His Pot* (1971) while Girish Karnard's *Tughlaq* (1964) was popular throughout India. Vijay Tendulkar's *Encounter in the Umbugland* also gained some popularity in Maharashtra. Panigrahi's emperor may be compared with these historical and allegorical power freaks. Panigrahi's emperor emerged straight from the pages of Odissi folk tales. This highlights a confrontation between the human need for reason and the unreasonable silence of the world. At times, Panigrahi's satire represents a momentary respite from the tyrannical legibility of the world.

His primary business, in all his plays, is to awaken human sympathy. There are a few things that shake people; a few, but the worst of it is, once people have used a fair number of times, they work no more. Under such stringent conditions the playwright feels the need of repeating the issue of invoking human sympathy. Its object, however, is truth, not individual, but general and operative, not standing upon external testimony, but carried alive into the heart by passion, truth which is its own testimony.

We have become used to technological engineering of culture and human beings. A terrible process of dehumanization has started imperceptibly and the spectator in the theatre auditorium has undergone the psychological process of demonizing the enemy, making them seem less than human and hence not worthy of humane treatment. This leads to increased violence, human right violation, war crimes and genocide. Under such pervading instances of dehumanization what sociological space would be left for the theatre, if it shall not concern itself with what is most human and most fragile about it: the human factor?

But Dr. Panigrahi would not paint human beings exactly. He would deploy allegories as his vehicle. His plays are peculiar, in which each character or event is a symbol representing an idea or a quality—such as truth, evil, death, our pursuits, power or a utopia. Thus all his plays garbed in comedy convey two meanings: a literal and a symbolic meaning. In other words, his allegories are general while his satires are particular—or so it might appear to the casual literary theorist.

Panigrahi's literary art diminishes and derogates a subject by making it ridiculous and evoking toward it attitudes of amusement, contempt at times, scorn or instances of pure imagination. But they differ from the comic in that comedy works laughter mainly as an end in itself while these plays deride; that is, the plays use laughter as a weapon.

But the modern readers seem to have lost touch with this traditional wisdom. Many have forgotten its original meaning and are quick to take offence. The world, on the contrary, is opening up around and yet our minds are closing. Are we really so thick-skinned that we would prefer to have progressed in a material sense, but we also seem have lost the ability to laugh at ourselves, or see the other point of view? Can't we highlight the unease of an author with the present political, social, religious, academic or behavioural narratives of our country? How can we, then, take the stock of the rapidly changing world? It would be suffocating to live in a world that can't enjoy the pleasures of change.

We are inhabitants after all, of a cruel world of beasts. The lion has fierce teeth and claws, the elephant has formidable tusks, the deer has been given the swiftness of legs, the turtle a protective shell and the sparrows are given the wings to drift in the sky. How can then the mortal bipeds pull on? A Christian legend informs that God answers: "I have given you the sense of humour."

Whether we reject humour and enjoy with sadistic pleasure the death of a hero by suicide is a different matter relating to our latent abnormality. But why do we laugh at all? What are we to make of the sheer variety of laughter, from braying and cackling to sniggering and chortling? Is humour subversive, or can it defuse dissent? Can we define wit packed with illuminating ideas? To some other group of critics these seven plays are truly unputdownable: entertainment and instruction in every play. That is how humour is considered as the heart of post-modernity.

Humour reappears as parody in post modern literature. It is not the ridiculing imitation of the standard theories and definitions that are rooted in 18th.century theories of wit. The collective weight of parodic practice suggests a redefinition of parody as repetition with critical distance that allows ironic signalling of difference at the very heart of similarity. We may take for example, the character of Vajrabahu, who appears as a prototype of the historical or demonic archetypal king in *The Emperor with his pot*, but with a difference. The archetypal one is parodied here and paradoxically he enacts both change and cultural continuity. It may be perceived as a random cannibalization of all styles of the past, as the play of random stylistic allusion. We can compare Vajrabahu's style with the work of postmodern architects like Charles Moore or Ricardo Bofill. To include irony and playfulness is never necessarily to exclude seriousness and purpose in postmodernist art. To misunderstand this is to misunderstand the nature of much contemporary aesthetic production—even if it does make for neater theorizing.

In order to understand why ironic parody (as in *Forty Minutes)* should seemingly paradoxically, become such an important form of post-modernist art's desire to reinstate a worldly connection for its discourse, we should remind ourselves of what the tyranny of high modernism has meant in the 20th century. There have been two kinds of reactions to the modernist hegemony: those from the artists themselves and those from the public spectators at large.

It is, perhaps, a loss of faith in the pseudo-serious modernist value that has led to the expendable status of the art of humour and parody. The practitioners of this new mode (Kurt Vonnegut Jr., Robert Coover, Richard Brautigan, Thomas Pynchon, William S. Burroughs etc) should form an eclectic grouping sharing only a sense of the past and re-design them with their refreshing tinge of parody, satire and humour. Modernism rejected the past both ideologically and aesthetically. Panigrahi moves past them to post modern terrains decking up his plays with wit and parody. The plays in this anthology once again remind us of the 17th. Century British playwrights, especially, Ben Jonson(1572-1637).

Panigrahi's humour-satire-irony-parody plays rewrite history through re-contextualization of the forms of the past. Surely, this is exactly what Jameson and Eagleton are calling for, but failing to see how it occurs elsewhere beyond England, America and Europe. The past, in Panigrahi's oeuvre, is always placed critically, but not nostalgically—in relation with the present.

Great satirists like George Orwell (1903-1950), Evelyn Waugh (1903-1966), or more recently, Tom Sharpe (1928-2013) believe that satire is the only operative genre be it in prose or poetry. Robert C.

Elliott is of the opinion that ours is a satirical age. Similar sentiments are voiced by Gilbert Highet (1906-1978) and Leonard Feignberg (1970-). But Indian scholars do not pay as much attention to contemporary satires as it warrants. They fail to analyse the devices, the rhetorical tricks and subterfuges, the particular symbols and displacements. Leonard Feignberg writes in his Introduction to Satire: "For more than two thousand years we have known satirists as those wits who expose hypocrisy and deftly stick shafts into our ballooned egos."

P. Sumitra Patro

CONTENTS

ALL BY ACCIDENTS

We need to construct a volumetrical theatrical space distinguished by dynamism and economical form. The stage is to be constructed as a metaphor for hell. Avoid painted curtains and a cyclorama. The imaginary hell has an invisible entrance gate at the up-left through which dead bodies are carried over shoulders of four corpse bearers. They keep the dead bodies on up stage left and exit through the entry gate. The procession is lead by one fire bearer holding a thick small rope made of twisted hay, lit by flame and emitting smoke. Another holds an incense pot and fumigates smoke all around to disinfect the surrounding air.

As the lights fade in the ritual drum beats for carrying dead bodies is heard and a corpse is brought to the stage on a stretcher-like carrier, it is down loaded and the team exits through the door they had come. A spot light holds the body. Back-ground music continues. The dead body stirs and gradually regains his sense. He gets up and feels as if he was sleeping for a while. He stands erect, stretches himself and discovers a large gathering at his front. By an old habit he starts lecturing at them:

Man: …So? What do you think of me? I am the best martyr of this universe, the bravest and most courageous martyr! Because I was elected as the Member of Legislative Assembly in open voting; I was selected as the Minister for law and order openly. All of you know it well that I openly violated everything that comes under law and order. You guillotined me openly on the busiest cross of this capital city. I stood there bravely hazarding the beheading machine. Why? Because there is nothing called *sin* in this world. I don't believe in hells of any sort! This is Bhagirathi Behera's conviction. Bhagirathi Behera, the Minister for Law and Order!!

Full lights are on. We discover Bhagirathi to be a man of mid-fifties. He stands erect and stretches himself. He searches for his cap, takes out a folded cloth cap from his Punjabi pocket and puts it on. He hollers for his orderly:

Bhagirathi: Orderly! Orderly!!(No one answers. Bhagirathi is irritated) Idiots! He has not kept even a jug of water here. (He searches for the calling bell, reaches the wall and switches it on. It does not ring.) Oh, shit! The calling bell is out of order. That too, in Ministers quarters! (Bhagirathi is angry) All the peons of this country are suspended! And the Electrical Engineers of this backward State! You are all dismissed! Go to hell. (He discovers a sign board hung over there. He reads it silently. In the meanwhile, the ritual band for carrying dead bodies is played and the corpse bearers bring a corpse and unload it on the specified space. They exit through the door they entered. Then the messenger of the hell enters. He is queerly dressed. There are two horns on his head. He is surprised to find Bhagirathi there. He enquires:

Messenger: Hey! You standing sinner! Did you call me? Since when did you come to your senses? (Bhagirathi turns toward the messenger.)Were you shouting at me?

Bhagirathi: Yes. Why didn't you respond when I called for you? Why are you attending to me after half an hour? (Threatens) Show cause why you shall not be fired right now from your job?

Messenger: What? This punk should be consigned to Hell number four; the *Kumbhipaka* hell. Let he dance there on the frying pan.

Bhagirathi: (He mutters to himself) what did he say?

Messenger: You deserve a room in Hell number Four – *Kumbhipaka* hell.

Bhagirathi: Ha, ha, ha, ha! Your attempt to frighten me will end in fatuity. There's nothing called hell! That's a psychological construct. I don't believe in hell. What do you think of me? I'm Bhagirathi Behera, Minister of Law and order. I can create a hell here out of nothing.

Messenger: You damned fellow from the wretched earth! You don't know; this is not your Ministerial office and I am not your orderly. I am the messenger of the hell, the abode for the damned! I'm the messenger of Dharmaraja Yama.

Bhagirathi: What happened to my government? Is it dislodged midway while I was asleep?

Messenger: Shut up you rascal, everything is dislodged here. (Bhagirathi looks amazed) we care little about your mundane governments.

Bhagirathi: You are forcing me to issue you a suspension order.

Messenger: You are not tuned to the atmosphere of the hell. Anyway, practice will make you perfect. Keep experiencing it now.

Bhagirathi: I have to. (speaks to himself) My orderly didn't have a pair of horns. Who's this creature with horns? (To the messenger) You seem to be an alien; a character from magic realism novels.

Messenger: Practice will make you perfect. Gradually you'll know who I am. Stay in this hell for some more days.

Bhagirathi: How did I come here? Yesterday I had been to Gopabandhu square to address a public gathering. They gave me a sumptuous tiffin, received me with a large flower garland; then I climbed up the dais. What happened after that?

Messenger: People killed you at Gopabandhu cross. Someone pierced a dagger into your stomach and you were carried to the hospital. The doctors declared you to be dead. We collected your carcass from the hospital, brought out your soul and here you are...a political punk.

Bhagirathi: I see. (He brought out betel from his pocket) They gave me a bundle of betel yesterday. I'll have to manage with this stock till...till when I don't know. So, finally they killed me; are you an eye witness to that incident?

Messenger: you were brought here while you were cringing with fear.

Bhagirathi: Why did you bring me here? Do you render health services?

Messenger: Dead people are not kept in the hospital. You are dead since yesterday

Bhagirathi: Aye! Who said I am dead? (He checks his own pulse; then asks the audience) Can you tell me Sir? Am I dead? Do I look like a dead man?

Messenger: You are already dead, you fool. You have landed in hell. How many times I'll repeat it?

Bhagirathi: (in a compromising tone) yes, yes, that's right. I might be in the hell. But how long shall I remain here?

Messenger: (He picks up a wooden packaging box lying over there and orders Bhagirathi) Sit down here. I can't answer your question.

Bhagirathi: (sits on the packaging box and looks at the Messenger) Why?

Messenger: How can I answer? The record of your stay is maintained by Chitragupta.

Bhagirathi: Oh!

Messenger: Chitragupta reported you had bamboozled many on the mundane earth.

Bhagirathi: He might be wrong. What does he know about Bhagirathi Behera? He might have talked about some other Bhagirathi. Anyway, leave it Messenger! My past tense is blown away with the wind. Ah! This sitting place is uncomfortable. It's disgusting. Don't you have any alternative furniture here? (The Messenger nods in negative) So, I have to manage here with this broken box. Okay!, After all, I am a public servant, I can manage with even the people from the lowest rung of the ladder; doesn't matter.

Messenger: Manage with it now. Gradually you will get used to it.

Bhagirathi: Getting used to hell will be dangerous. I shall never be able to get out of here.

Messenger: You can never go out of this hell.

Bhagirathi: Then bring my suit case where ever it is. I've to change my clothes and get prepared for a week-long stay. How long shall I have to stay here?

Messenger: Please keep your mouth shut. Don't gaggle, I shall go berserk. Why should I go to Chitragupta and ask him about you? Who do you think you are?

Bhagirathi: (With equal force he orders) Go and fetch my suit case first! (He shouts)My suit case!!

(The messenger leaves the stage and disappears in one corner. Bhagirathi turns and finds that the messenger has disappeared. He's slightly flabbergasted. He searches for the messenger. The light focuses on the dead body placed on the platform starts moving. He stands erect. Back ground music. He is Gunanidhi Chhotray. He has put on a goat's mask. Bhagirathi enters and goes closer to the new entrant standing now)

Bhagirathi: Hello! Welcome to hell number one. When did you come? When did you gain your senses?

Gunanidhi: (He is under severe pain) Ah! Five minutes back. (He turns toward Bhagirathi, looks at his face and suddenly stands erect in attention position and salutes him.)

Bhagirathi: Er….excuse me, are you Mr. Chhotray, Mr. Gunanidhi Chhotray?

Gunanidhi: Yes, I was Superintendent of Police when you were our Home Minister. I got a promotion during your tenure. You know my daughter Swati. I am Swati's father. (Again salutes)

Bhagirathi: Keep those salutes away Gunanidhi. What is there in a salute? We've finally arrived in the hell, both of us, but (he points a finger towards Gunanidhi's face) what has happened to your face? (Bhagirathi laughs)

Gunanidhi: What's wrong with my face Sir?

Bhagirathi: (while laughing) It has transformed into a goat's face. How could it be possible Gunanidhi? While in service you moved like a lion. You were a terror for the young criminals and the Nuxalites.

Gunanidhi: That's true Sir. I flogged the students mercilessly during the strike, because I was afraid of them, but anyway, I am a wreck of my former self now. (Bhagirathi is absent minded) What are you so dolefully thinking about Sir? When did you come to hell?

Bhagirathi: No, I was just wondering how you recognised me in this hell-that too just at a glance!

Gunanidhi: I was an eye-witness to your execution Sir. I was alive by that time and I was on duty at Gopabandhu cross. I ordered the police to charge on the mob, but they surged up and somebody pushed the dagger at your chest. It was difficult for the ambulance to reach the spot and you died before it carried you to the hospital. It was unfortunate we could not save your life. I wonder how you endured the pain till death.

Bhagirathi: I have to endure Gunanidhi. Otherwise, how could I be declared as a martyr?

Gunanidhi: That's true! The government has decided to install your standing statue on the cross.

Bhagirathi: What will happen to Gopabandhu's statue standing there?

Gunanidhi: Gopabandhu is not a martyr! He's a freedom fighter. His statue will be removed.

(The sound of the ritual band for carrying dead bodies fades in slowly. Bhagirathi is alert.)

Bhagirathi: Listen, this is the band for the dead people. Somebody is coming from the mundane world, a new comer. Let us hide here and see. (They disappear in one side of the stage. The dead body of Saubhagya Das Mahapatra arrives and it is kept on the platform. He gets up and sleep-walks while gabbling but holding an imaginary steering of an imaginary car. He acts as if he is driving his car at a very high speed)

Saubhagya: Speed….Speed…..80 kilometers per hour … 100 kilometers and now hundred five…hundred ten, hundred fifteen, and now 120 kilometers on the winding mountain road …I won't take a turn…I'll go headlong and precipitate down the mountain (the sound of a speeding car rises high in volume and there is an abrupt sound of a car falling down the steep. Soubhagya Das Mohapatra is taken aback with a jerk. He stops as if in a dream)

May be, I got up too early in the morning (looks at the wrist watch) the watch has stopped. All watches are stopped here. It's stopped since yesterday. Time stands still here; cannot move ahead; it's eternity at your disposal Mr. Saubhagya Das Mahapatra! Ha, ha, ha! (The emerging sound of the ritual band cuts Saubhagya's laughter. He stops looking at a masked messenger carrying a woman on his shoulder and down loading her on the platform. The messenger exits and Soubhagya looks at the woman intently. He is stunned for a moment and then a cruel smile widens his lips. He takes out a pistol from his pocket aims at the woman's head and talks in a wicked whisper as he proceeds toward her aggressively.

Saubhagya: Swati! In my earth and the hell…in my joy and grief…in my breath and belief…wherever I am going you are goading me. I'm amazed. Will your shadow go engulfing me all my life? (He trembles with excitement, takes out a pistol from his coat pocket and points it at Swati's forehead.

Swati: In my mundane life and hell, in my joy and agony, everywhere you are present. How can I dismiss the nightmare that mocks me through your lips? Can you tell what floods of lust can do to cool the hell that brands your heart within? My dear perennial pit of folly and fault! I notice how far the all consuming serpent slithers. (Back ground music builds in) I killed you in your bed room yesterday. How could you find your way to this hell where I have driven my car to this point? Will you permit me to eject one more bullet from my pistol? Your mouth will be still for all the time to come.

Swati: (She regains her senses, opens her eyes, looks at Saubhagya and screams in fear) Ah! You? Why have you dropped me again?

Saubhagya: (whispers menacingly) you are chasing me Swati, in my dreams and nightmares… You seem more like that creeping serpent of lust. You are a civilised whore!

Swati: And you are an uncivilised brute, son of Marques De Sade!

Saubhagya: Are you going to create another scene of violence?

Swati: You are creating a scene here. Why are you goading me up? What do you want from me?

Saubhagya: Nothing my dear. Never did I want anything from you. I have everything in my possession: buildings, farm houses and cars, everything and to add to it, a ferrosilicon factory.

Swati: I married you Saubhagya, not your ferrosilicon factory! So, better live alone in your artificial paradise, why have you traveled up to hell to track me?

Saubhagya: We're always in hell, were always in, and will be here for eternity!

Swati: True, the devil pulls on all our strings and ultimately I discovered that you are that devil. After that in most repugnant objects we find charms; each day we're one step further into Hell. Aren't we devils?

Saubhagya: Content to move across the stinking pit. I revolted against it and killed you

Swati: A demon rioted in your brain and when you breathed, death flowed into my lungs. Then I escaped. Now we are no corporal beings, your designs for inflicting physical pain on me won't work now, my dear! Sure, I had married you. But you made me the wife of your ferrosilicon factory. That strategy didn't work. The banal canvas of our woeful fates never changed; they would never change.

(Back ground music suiting the mood of the play. Swati goes to the swinging chair and sits there hanging and swinging. Saubhagya moves around and discovers a hanging board on the wall and reads it out loudly. Swati answers to those loud readings as if what Saubhagya reads are questions to be answered. The lights change. Saubhagya stays in one light zone and Swati swings up and down on the swing in the light zone)

Saubhagya: Swati! Swati!! Swati!!! You are in my earth and you are in my hell… You are in my joy and grief…in my breath and belief…wherever I am going you are goading me. I'm amazed. Will your shadow go engulfing me all my life? (*He trembles with excitement takes out the pistol from his coat pocket and points it at Swati's forehead again. (Music) Gradually Swati gets up and sits calmly, rubs her eyes and looks at Saubhagya clearly. She is shocked and suddenly frightened. She screams loudly*)

Swati: Ah!

Saubhagya: No! (*Puts his pistol back in his pocket*)

Swati: Who are you here?

Saubhagya: Are you not getting me dear? I am Saubhagya Das Mohapatra (Laughs) your husband.

Swati: Brute! You should be in some reserved forest!

Saubhagya: And you? You are a whore! You should be in some brothel.

Swati: Shut up.

Saubhagya: Are you going to create a scene here?

Swati: Who's creating a scene here? You are hounding me wherever I go! Why? What do you need from me?

Saubhagya: Nothing. Nothing I need from you. I have never asked anything from anybody in my life…I've everything with me…buildings, cars, farm houses and bank balance, everything.

Swati: Then? Why have you come here?

Saubhagya: Once I have discovered you here in this hell, I felt as if we were always here!

Swati: What else could be our life except a hell?

Saubhagya: After I killed you I thought it'd be easier for me to live alone with peace. But that was not possible. Your police father, that Deputy Inspector General, Gunanidhi Chhotray goaded me with the whip of law, impelled me to commit suicide. Your dead body was lying there in the bed room, that bloody father-in-law sent two cops to enquire about you...there was no other go…I flummoxed them somehow and they left. There was no alternative. I wanted to escape from the drudgery of my ferrosilicon plant…I drove off at full speed…the plant road ended…thereafter the steep, winding roads…I pressed on my accelerator…I was at 90km per hour…I pressed it to hundred, then to hundred ten, then to hundred twenty on the steep mountain range and then the vehicle whisked off and precipitated down to the trees and rocks below… over! Finally, it was over!

Swati: The tortures you inflicted on my body and the sexual assaults you made had already forced me to lie half dead. What you saw me outside was a meat ball of a carcass, and you pounced on me like a brute, like the disciple of Marques De Sade.

Saubhagya: Might be, but it was fatuous…You stand here as a new sting, after all mundane pains are over.

Swati: Look Saubhagya, we are dead now, miles away from jealousy and love and hatred. Can't we live here with little peace?

Saubhagya: What else I have given you all my life?-nothing but peace. That I married and accepted you as a wife; lived with you for such a long time; is it not enough consolation?

Swati: Was it an act of kindness and grace that you married me? What the hell you think of yourself? A business tycoon, a ferrosilicon mine owner? You had some stinking bank balance and one day you bought me as your wife because I was beautiful. You wanted me to sell me in the market; you bartered my meat at Bhagirahi Behera's quarters. Mind you, you couldn't have dared to send me there. That you could do because my father was very close to the Minister. You should be grateful to your father-in-law Mr. Gunanidhi Chhotray, my respected father; he sacrificed his life to protect the Minister's life! He should have been given a medal by the revered President of India for his act of bravery.

Saubhagya: But he died a disgraceful death. A leftist cadre boy shot him dead. Anyway, I have given you the right to put this vermilion mark on your forehead. You should be grateful to me.

Swati: I hate you Saubhagya, I feel like spitting on your face; that's why I call you a *brute*! You have lots of money, lots of bank balance – of millions and a ferrosilicon plant…But I married you Saubhagya, not to your factory. How did you dare to have retailed me in the market?

Saubhagya: (Calmly) Ah! Snap it off! Getting too much excited at the slightest pretext is a sort a' tragic flaw with your family. Your mother died because of that! Take it cool baby! You are talking of retailing. I retailed you in the market as a promoter of my business. Tell me frankly, didn't you enjoy the game?

Swati: I said I married you, not to your business projects. Do you get me? Why did you send me to that dirty minister-Bhagirathi Behera?

Saubhagya: Don't shout Swati, others would think you belong to the class of chaste women, like Sita and Savitri

Swati: You cheat and hypocrite!

(Saubhagya goes to the wall like structure where a poster is hung.)

Saubhagya: (Reads from the hanging notice) Rules for existing in the hell.

Swati: Rules are made to be transgressed.

Saubhagya: (Reads from the hanging poster:)"Rule number one: Smoking's prohibited here!"

(He laughs, takes out a packet of cigarettes from his pocket, smells it deeply and keeps it back into the pocket. (Heavy background music for 10 seconds and silence)

Swati: Loneliness, terrible loneliness engulfs me.

Saubhagya: (Reads) "Society, friendship and love / divinely bestowed upon man"

Swati: Such a massive mansion you've built – and there's no one in it except some maid servants. You'll go to the factory at 9 A.M and won't come back before midnight.

Saubhagya: (reads from the chart) "to lie is to commit a sin!"

Swati: Do I tell lies?

Saubhagya: I'm not asking you any question. I'm reading out from this chart. Why are you answering me like a confessing culprit? (Back ground music of nostalgia. Swati gets down and acts romantic)

Swati: Let's make a plan to go for an outing to Puri. We haven't gone for outing since our honeymoon to Switzerland. That was two years ago.

Saubhagya: You've changed the Honeymoon into a poisoned moon there with your tantrums. I hate you for that Swati.

Swati: The world is weary of the past; Oh! Might it die or rest at last.

Saubhagya: It is a woman's business to get married and go for honeymoon as soon as possible

Swati: And a man's business is to think he's unmarried as long as he can.

Saubhagya: I made a mistake in the selection of a wife. It's like a bad project in war. I erred only once but was left undone forever.

(The back ground music is serious. Saubhagya feels fatigued at heart. He walks with heavy steps past Swati who is still sitting on the swing. She twists her lips cynically and tells loudly)

Swati: Mister Saubhagya Das Mohapatra! Nobody grows old by merely living for a number of years; people grow old only by deserting their ideals!

Saubhagya: I can't tolerate pseudo-intellectual feminine dominance under the umbrella of ideals. (He exits)

Swati: Years wrinkle your skin dear, but to give up 'enthusiasm' to live a life would wrinkle your soul. (Swati gets down from the swing and charges Saubhagya) You chased me up to this hell. I'll chase you back to that earth, to down-to-earth life, to reality!

(She runs after him. The lights remain unchanged. Then Bhagirathi enters with Gunanidhi Chhotray. It is an ordinary day on the mundane earth. The scene takes place in (Bhagarathi Behera), Minister's government quarters)

Bhagirathi: Come in, Come in Mr. Gunanidhi Chhotray! Please sit down!

Gunanidhi: How do you ask me to sit here Sir? You are my honorable Minister and I am just a petty police superintendent. I can only salute you. (He salutes Bhagirathi)

Bhagirathi: You've helped my followers and party leaders in a number of cases. You are a great help to me and to the state; you are almost a friend to me.

Gunanidhi: But I haven't got my promotion for the last three years. I should have been promoted to the cadre of a DIG of police by now.

Bhagirathi: I see. (Takes a pause and thinks) So, Swati is your daughter?

Gunanidhi: Yes Sir.

Bhagirathi: She's a great Odissi dancer. I discovered her in the last Konark festival.

Gunanidhi: Yes, Sir.

Bhagirathi: Send her today in the evening. She'll remind me about your promotion and get the work done for you. Send through her a small petition, stating your problems; I'll ask the Home Secretary to bring your personal file. Your job shall be done. (Bhagirathi exits)

Gunanidhi: Thank you Sir!

(Lights go off. As the lights come back Swati appears in a costly costume, fully decked up and searching for her father)

Swati: Dad, give me the application you have written to the Minister. Have you typed it out? I'm going to meet the Minister in his quarters at Forest Park.

Gunanidhi: (Gives the petition taking it out from the pocket) It's already 8.30 in the evening, when shall you return?

Swati: I don't know; depends when the work will be over. Can you lend me your jeep?

Gunanidhi: Go by your scooter, I have to go for the night patrolling (The ringing sound of the land phone is heard) Let me attend to the phone first.

(Gunanidhi exits through mid-left wings. The lights change and the back ground music indicates a change over in time, space and character. Swati is little coquettishly loitering from left to right to the tune and rhythm of the back ground music. She inspects the night sky keeping her back to the audience. Bhagirathi enters, discovers Swati and talks apologetically)

Bhagirathi: I am sorry, really sorry Swati, I kept you waiting. The orderly informed about your arrival, but I was undone. I was taking a shower in the bath. Now tell me dear dance queen of Odisha, what treatment I shall give you!

(Swati turns and laughs)

Swati: I am Swati Chhotray Sir, (Takes out an application and hands it over to Bhagirathi) Gunanidhi Chhotray's daughter. Baba has given me this application. (Bhagirathi takes it and says like a true politician)

Bhagirathi: I know dear, I know. You are one of the top most dance stars of the state. It's my duty to treat you properly and to do every work you order me to do. I'm at your disposal young lady. I respect artists.

Swati: Baba's officers have blocked his promotion. He should have gone to the level of Deputy Inspector General before three years.

Bhagirathi: That's true. I enquired about Gunanidhi in the vigilance department. He has a direct nexus with the narcotic drug peddlers. Instead of arresting them and seizing the narcotic material he sells the narcotic in the black market. The vigilance has thrashed him. The process will take a long time. Shall you wait?

Swati: Yes.

Bhagirathi: I'm afraid, it'd be midnight. That Vigilance DIG is not free before midnight. We get our private works done during the night. Of course I will ask my private Secretary to arrange a dinner for you.

Swati: I will stay for the night Sir, it does not matter. After all, you know my father intimately

Bhagirathi: I should also know you intimately. (He holds Swati in an embrace and kisses her on the forehead. Swati feels awkward, but does not protest). Your body feels like the sculpture of Konark.

Swati: (Still within the embrace of Bhagirathi) you are just like my father Sir! You should not compare my body with those nude sculptures of Konark.

Bhagirathi: The erotic motive is in your mind, my girl, it's not in your body. I just wanted to know you intimately. You've rightly said, you are just like my daughter. Come inside, you shall take something first! Daughter or not, you are a star material, a famous dancer of our state. When you shake your hip you look quite erotic. Come in. You will offer your body and I will just learn dancing few steps with you.

Swati: Sir, I respect you! I can't take you as a pal and a partner.

Bhagirathi: You are fidgeting and behaving like a cat on hot bricks; come on, I'll unwind you. (*Bhagirathi embraces Swati with an erotic posture. She feels twitchy and uneasy, then cringes and blenches and finally succumbs and compromises. The spot holds them in a compromising position. The back ground music builds up and lights dim out*).

The back ground music rises in volume in the darkness. The light comes after some time, it grows more intense through the dimmer and Swati is found sitting on the ground in a disorderly state with hair disheveled and dress creased.

Gunanidhi: Swati! (Pause; he surveys her) Are you... I mean, are you alright?

Swati: Yes, of course! What's the matter? (Gunanidhi is silent. Swati gets up) Dad!

Gunanidhi: Where's your mom gone?

Swati: Nelly auntie's daughter Rigma is getting married.

Gunanidhi: I'm also searching for a groom for you. When do you have your exams?

Swati: Next Fri day.

Gunanidhi: How's your preparation?

Swati: It's not satisfactory. (Back ground music)

Gunanidhi: Why?

Swati: (in a weeping tone) I can't sit for the exams. (weeps silently turning her face)

Gunanidhi: What's wrong with you? Why don't you tell it out frankly?

Swati: The morning will break before the night ends. (Forcibly checks the vomiting sound) May be, my belly will grow heavy with a child by the time I appear the exam

Gunanidhi: Why? Why should your belly grow heavy with a child? Who's the man? Is it Bhagirathi Behera?

Swati: (nods)

Gunanidhi: That was my mistake. I didn't know that fisherman would be so fishy. (The sound of the wall clock is heard. Gunanidhi becomes contemptuous and derisive, but could not speak it out.)

Swati: But Bapa, you use objectionable words! I've executed your promotion case with lots of sacrifice. It has been done. Be happy with your career hike Bapa. Bhagirathi Behera has taken the responsibility. He will bear the nursing – home expenses for me. You need not beat your head for the abortion. I shall wash my belly with Ganga water. I'll regain my chastity. Mom would reprimand me. I know. I will convince her. I am sufficiently grown up now Daddy, to solve such tiny physical problems.

Gunanidhi: (A deep sigh of relief) that's alright, but I must meet the Minister and talk to him about this. Go and prepare for the examination. You must be a graduate before I find a groom for you. Go. (Swati exits. Gunanidhi becomes serious and he loiters thoughtfully from left to right (the ticking sound of the wall clock is heard and Gunanidhi waits for the Minister. He discovers Bhagirathi coming towards him. Gunanidhi salutes him though the Minister is not visible. Later the minister gets in and tells:

Bhagirathi: There's nothing to worry Chhotray. Everything will be alright.

Gunanidhi: How can I stop worrying Sir? I'm the cursed father of a pregnant daughter.

Bhagirathi: What? Pregnant?....Oh! We'll consider her pregnancy as an emergency file.

Gunanidhi: Sir, I'm a poor police officer, have mercy on me. My daughter's future will be ruined.

Bhagirathi: No. She shall shoot into prosperity and fame. I've recommended her name for a senior fellowship from the department of Culture, New Delhi, telephoned the EZCC authorities of Kolkata to send her to Kualampur for a dance program. Besides, I've talked to the doctor; she will be alright by the end of this week. (Back ground music) Go, celebrate the occasion. Ask your daughter to be in touch with me. I'll find a very good groom for her. Go! Go with a free mind! (Bhagirathi pushes Gunanidhi out of stage. He comes to the mid stage disgusted with Gunanidhi) Disgusting fellows! Rascal, your daughter enjoyed few moments with me and harvested all benefits for you. Now you became a DIG and are asking my help for abortion? What do you think of a Minister? What do you think of Bhagirathi Behera? I know two things to aim at in life: first to get what you want, after that, to enjoy it. Only the wisest of mankind achieve the second. Now whether you send her to me or not, Swati will come to Bhagirathi Behera's bed room hereafter. No Gunanidhi Chhotray can stop her. (Laughs) This is Behera's public relation mantra.

(A calling bell rings. Behera shouts)

Bhagirathi: Come in whoever you are!

(A handsome young man in a winter suit enters and salutes Bhagirathi)

Subhagya: *Pranam* Sir! I'm Saubhagya Das Mahapatra, the Managing Director of the Ferrosilicon plant at Srirampore!

Bhagirathi: Oh, you are that person?

Saubhagya: Yes Sir!

Bhagirathi: I'm sorry, I can't help you.

Saubhagya: I'll be ruined Sir!

Bhagirathi: I can't help you Saubhagya. The government money cannot be thrown into gutters.

Saubhagya: But that's the trend sir, nobody repays the government loan. The opposition will shout to waive it off.

Bhagirathi: How much you have taken?

Saubhagya: Five hundred millions.

Bhagirathi: That's a big amount. How can I waive off such a substantial amount?

Saubhagya: If the Honorable Minister desires, everything can be done.

Bhagirathi: But that's illegal. How do you take us for granted? Its democracy and things are transparent these days. The opposition party sneaks into all private affairs. And Bhagirathi doesn't like to be black listed. Leave it. What is your argument in favor of waiving your loan? Why couldn't you repay the loan?

Saubhagya: There was a fire accident. The whole factory was ablaze. It was an accident.

Bhagirathi: The Industry Minister says it was a lame excuse

Saubhagya: You can come and visit the spot Sir! I swear it is not a lame excuse

Bhagirathi: You are a young man. You've spoiled your life so soon. Your father was a great organiser in our party. C.M. knows that because of your father. Hence he allowed you to draw such a big amount. You should take care of your ferrosilicon plant. Get married soon.

Saubhagya: My parents are no more living. Who'll arrange a bride for me?

Bhagirathi: I will arrange. The C.M. will arrange. That'lI not be a problem for you. You are a reputed organiser of our party. The thing is you should trust us, trust our selection. We are political people, servants of the people. We know people from a wider section of the society. Alright I will select two/three girls for you. You should respect our selection.

Saubhagya: Certainly I will. It will be a great favor. Thank you Sir! You will be my mentor for all my marital matters.

Bhagirathi: There is a beautiful girl, a renowned dancer. She is a celebrity in the city.

Saubhagya: Who's she?

Bhagirathi: Swati Chhotray! Have you heard of her?

Saubhagya: Yes. I have seen her in the Lions' Club function.

Bhagirathi: But her father can't give you any matching handsome dowry.

Saubhagya: I have no demands. I need no dowry. My entire requirement is a beautiful girl. But can I demand waiving off my loan?

Bhagirathi: That's not my department, you know. Still I will look into your case and try. Come inside, we'll see the girl's photographs in an album her father has given me. (They exit through the right wing. Lights dim out for a short while and glare up again. Gunanidhi is in civil dress and is at home. He is in tension, and moves in quick steps from left to right calling for Swati.

Gunanidhi: Now, tell me. Is everything ready? Swati?

Swati: (enters with a garland of jasmine flowers fixing on to her hair) Yes Dad! Your constable has brought sweet packets.

Gunanidhi: What about chicken fry and fish chops?

Swati: He'll fetch them after some time. I will put them in hot case. I've ordered for some garlic breads and mayonnaise to serve them as starters. Mom has cooked the soup

Gunanidhi: Where's your mom?

Swati: She is in the kitchen, frying fish.

Gunanidhi: Go and ask her to give you a good make up.

Swati: That's out dated Dad. I'll go to the Beauty Parlor for a ring ceremony make up. That's my responsibility. If time permits I will do some *mehndi* work on my hands

Gunanidhi: That's alright. But hurry up! They will arrive at 5.30 in the evening; it's going to be four. I don't know which way I will be able to help you.

Swati: Oh!, common; You are unnecessarily tensed up Dad! You need not bother. We will manage the event. How many members will come to interview me for the marriage? Come in and see what we have done! (Swati leads Gunanidhi inside. Lights dim for a moment and come again abruptly. Sound of an uproar outside with slogans about Bhagirathi. But what is said is not distinct. Bhagirathi gets in and is found tensed up by the riot outside. The sound of the corpse bearer's procession fades in.)

Bhagirathi: (shouts) Messenger, Messenger!!Mutters to himself) Not to be seen around, where has he gone? Messenger! Messenger!! May be, this hell is large and spacious, spread over an enormous space with thousands of cubicles and the messenger has vanished somewhere! Besides, there are seven hells… (he counts) no, twenty one hells …no (recounts) twenty eight hells... *Devi Bhagavata* says one thing and the *Vishnu Purana* says another and the *Garuda Purana* says something else. I have to ask Baba Kamananda (He takes out his mobile phone from his Punjabi pocket and connects Baba Kamananda) The mobile of Baba Kamananda is out of range. This dingy room of hell is cut off from all communications. Let me go to the open space. (He exits. The corpse bearers bring another dead body and place it on the mid stage platform. After doing some funeral rituals they exit silently. Baba Kamananda enters through down stage wings holding a mobile phone and talking to Bhagirathi)

Kamananda: Yes, yes, we solemnly announce that we are behind you; Baba Kamananda is behind you all the time. You fool, why you don't understand that you are under Baba Kamananda's protection? Do you know that?... What?... You are already dead? Impossible. We never read news papers. We read nothing that is not written in God's language. Why should I read newspapers? Why should I read news manufactured by mine owners? I'll manufacture my own news. The name of my future newspaper is *Kamananda Times.* Ok, when did you die and from where you are talking now? (Pause) What nonsense! You have already gone to hell? How can Minister Bhagirathi Behera land up in hell? You must have committed heinous crimes. I sent my lady disciples to you for some petty favor and you ensnared them. You impregnated innocent teen-agers. By the way, Bhagirathi, what's your caste? Fisherman? Okay, Okay. That's why you are fishy and foxy, both. (He is irritated) What? You want me to send for you some more lady disciples? That's why your wife has deserted you. No backward lady disciple has come to the hermitage today otherwise I would have sent one to you. But be careful. You are running through a bad patch of time. You are likely to be bulldozed. But you won't die. I've checked up your horoscope. (Change over) What? Oh, yeah, you are already dead. Alright, I'll try to come and meet you personally. What is your exact address? Which hell are you consigned to? *Raurava Narka* or *Kumbhipaka Narka*? No, no, no, no, no… how can I go to the *Naraka* to meet you? I'm a virtuous soul, holy and divinity incarnate; you know that of course. (Change over) OK, OK! Have patience. Bear with it, I'll reach you by *tantra* flight; well, there's nothing to feel skeptical about it; I'll whizz past the layers of earth and water, oil and fire and land up in your suite. You should be able to recognise me from my voice, otherwise, I'll be invisible to you. (Kamananda exits. Bhagirathi enters from the opposite side holding the mobile and saying:)

Bhagirathi: Thank you very much, Baba, I bow down, I genuflect. (He genuflects and says with delight)I will build a guest house in your hermitage premises, devotees from far and wide will come for your *darshan* and they will stay on Monday and Saturday nights in the guest house. I will recommend to the third floor government about the magic you are manufacturing. They will come and camp in *Kamananda Hall of Divine Residence* in the four air-conditioned rooms I will construct (Bhagirathi exits. The stage is empty. Lights go dim with the change of back ground music. A young boy of twenty four enters. He is Sagar Behera, Bhagirathi Behera's son His feet totter. He is drugged

Sagar: Who's going to build four air-conditioned halls here? Oh! My great Dad? Because he has lots of money and he does not know even how to fritter away them. Ha, ha, ha, ha! Dad, I pity you. I pity your political wisdom. Why have they made you a minister, for what purpose? These common folks are fools. Listen, I reject you as a Minister of this state. I, Sagar Behera, Your only son, your only successor, Sagar Behera rejects you as a father. I reject your air-conditioned halls. Did I ask you to build for me an air-conditioned room? Listen, I need a small thatched cottage for myself, but it must fill my empty heart with love. The cottage of love should keep a room reserved for my mother. I need my mother back Dad, my mother. She has committed suicide for your disgraceful, loathsome dealings. (A spot light holds his face. Back ground music builds up) Hey you idiots! Don't focus light on my face. I hate to be on the spot light. I am Sagar Behera, Bhagirathi Behera's only son, the minister's only successor. I love to stay behind the screen. I'm a back ground man. I don't come to lime light, not even to my father's quarters. I hate him, I hate his political associates. My mother committed suicide because my father. He is a debauch. Mr. Bhagirathi Behera has earned a great property. But the way he has earned it isn't okay. He says it is for me. It's not okay! Because I hate money, I hate affluence. It is better to commit suicide in Bindu Sagar tank than to stay in Bhagirathi minister's house. I won't go there. I will sleep here. Let me see what he will do. (He sits down... He takes out a syringe and injects himself with some drug. He fails to control himself. He yawns and falls into heavy sleep. Back ground music. The sound of car horn buzzing repeatedly is heard. Sagar does not stir. Swati gets out of the car, comes irritated to the sleeping young man and says)

Swati: Aye, who are you? Why are you sleeping here in front of my gate? (Stirring him) Hey mister! (She stirs the sleeping man. Sagar gets up and rubs his eyes.)

Sagar: What did you say?

Swati: Why are you blocking my way here in front of my gate? Leave me my space and let my car go inside. Now, get up'.

Sagar: What do you mean? Is it not Bindu Sagar? Can't I sleep here?

Swati: No! This is Mr. Das Mohapatra's bungalow!

Sagar: Oh! What a nice place!

Swati: Please come to sense and see where you have slept. Here is a public sewerage drain beside you. A pariah dog is sleeping beside you; it's a dirty, grimy place.

Sagar: So, it's not old town?

Swati: This is I.R.C. village.

Sagar: This injection is wonderful. If one injection transforms old town into I.R.C. village, what magic shall take place if I take five injections? I'll need no brown sugar hereafter.

Swati: Are you an addict?

Sagar: Yes, I have rejected the mainstream; freed myself from social restrictions and chosen my own way. I find new meaning in life. The brown sugar and drug-injection put me in alternative state of consciousness. I find new meaning in life through narcotics.

Swati: And your Dad allows you to be a victim. Is it so? Your Dad must be a great man.

Sagar: My dad is a bastard. He has killed my mother. I protested. He did not listen to me. So, I hate him. I never go to his house. I hate his air conditioned rooms. So, I slept here, in front of your gate. I found it to be a better place; at least, I was close to nature. I slept here like a true Nature's child (Pause) I love to live this bohemian life, free, pagan life; what Rousseau called the "state of nature".

Swati: What's your father doing? Who's he?

Sagar: He's Bhagirathi Behera, some Minister in the State Cabinet, a pet of the C.M. You must know him.

Swati: Come inside dear! There is no one in this mansion. I am alone. Mr. Das Mahapatra has flown to Delhi. Come with me for half an hour (*Swati holds Sagar's arm and leads him inside*) we'll chat for sometime over a cup of tea.

(They exit and the light dims. The eerie outlandish orchestra relating to the hell is played. The messenger of the hell arrives and surveys the cabin)

Messenger: Strange! The cabin is empty. Where have these wretched people gone, the criminals of the wretched earth? The hell is getting over-crowded these days. Every newcomer to the hell is a criminal. I ponder all day long in my cabin about what kind of criminal atrocities are committed in the Earth against innocent people behind the brick walls, behind the closed doors and blind windows. All those murderers have come into our hell. They have started rioting in the hell and fighting with each other-trying to blow off my head. Let me call them all to this lounge for a get-together. Let all of them sit together and decide for themselves. (*He reads out from a scroll*) Saubhagya Das Mahapatra, Sagar Behera, Swati Chhotray, D.I.G. Gunanidhi Chhotray and over all of them, Bhagirathi Behera. You are all required to come over here and decide for yourself what sort of life you want lead here.

(Each of these characters comes with his/her complaint)

Saubhagya: Why should you summon me to this place at this hour? Do you take me for a criminal?

Messenger: What else shall I think about you? You are a murderer

Saubhagya: No. I have killed myself. This is my life. I've a right over my life.

Swati: That's okay. But why did you beat me until I fell dead?

Saubhagya: How dare you bring murder charges against me? I am Saubhagya Das Mahapatra, owner of the ferrosilicon plant. I'm your legal husband Mrs. Swati. D.I.G. Gunanidhi Chhotray is my father-in-law... Why should I be compelled to show reasons for what I've done? Am I a sinner?

Bhagirathi: Saubhagya! Have a control over your tongue. A ferrosilicon mine does not empower you to kill your wife. You are puffed up with your ego.

Saubhagya: Excuse me Sir, we are all dead now; you can't constrain me to obey your orders

Bhagirathi: But I was the only negotiator for your marriage. You can't deceive me now. I am like a guardian to you, a mentor

Messenger: You are nothing, you political punk, you are nothing but a cheater! You compelled Das Mahapatra to commit the sin.

Sagar: Nothing to think serious about it Mr…whoever you are! I find no difference between virtue and sin. They are relative terms. That which is virtue for me may be a sin for you. So, ladies and gentlemen! Come down from your pedestals, come down to this earthen floor and sit here like a humble farmer of India.

Saubhagya: And what shall we do here?

Sagar: We will do some *keertan-Hare Krishna Hare Ram keertan*.

Gunanidhi: Order! Order!

Sagar: I'm not prepared to obey your police law, DIG Sir; I'll only speak the truth and won't care for any consequence! That's Sagar Behera.

Bhagirathi: A rascal! Hmm. This fellow has gone off the track.

Sagar: Dad, we are all consigned to hell. The hell has its own law. If I have gone off the track, where have you gone?

Gunanidhi: Hear, hear me, this may be hell. But, we have to abide by certain rules we are after all, civilised people.

Saubhagya: Ugh, it's awful. The hell emits scorching heat!

Swati: What can I do? There's no A/C here. I was searching for a dressing table in the entire hell. There's none. How can I dress my hair?

Sagar: Desire is at the root of all your sufferings. Thence thou Prince of Kapilavastu! Say goodbye to your throne, and come down to this bodhi tree. Yes, one and all.

Messenger: Hey! Keep your mouth shut you young culprit! Now it's time for you to go to the court of Dharmaraj Yama.

Bhagirathi: What you do to us in the court?

Gunanidhi: What's the necessity of a court here? Can't we settle our own cases here?

Messenger: No. You were given a chance here to solve your problems. You have messed up everything.

Swati: They are all brutes. They have to be treated as brutally as possible, at least for the sake of dharma.

Gunanidhi: Swati! Have you lost your head or what?

Swati: I hate to address you as my father.

Bhagirathi: Gunanidhi, allow that girl to speak. Why do you intervene? After all, she is too young to manage herself in the hell.

Sagar: Do these dead old bodies have something called shame?

Swati: Sagar Samantaray! Hold your tongue! He's your father.

Sagar (looks sharply at Swati and stands up. He feels some kind of discomfort in his head and calls.)Messenger! Messenger! Why are you parading here like a drill sergeant? Do some favor to me.

Messenger: I know you are a clumsy troublesome guy. You won't leave me free for a moment. What do you want now?

Sagar: Five grams of brown sugar. My head is jammed.

Bhagirathi: It was already time for this rascal to arrive in the hell

Gunanidhi: If he'll smoke brown sugar at this tender age....

Sagar: I don't need much uncle, only five grams to unwind the mind.

Bhagirathi: Shut up! Don't you feel ashamed to beg five grams of brown sugar, that too in front of your father?

Sagar: We are no more bound by the limitations of mundane relationship dad; we are in the hell you know! Old order changes here giving place to new. But you don't change. You've deprived me of all my rights as a son. And now you give a package of advice. How can I take it?

Bhagirathi: What have I deprived you of? You are my only son. Whatever I've earned is your money. The bungalows at Bhubaneswar, Puri and Berhampur belong to you.

Sagar: I needed a kiss of my mother, dad, I needed a slice of moon in my vegetable bag…I needed a package of dreams to write poems.

Bhagirathi: Why are you asking for illusions? You know your mother is dead...You know moon is not a vegetable, and dreams can't be purchased in the market. Why can't you behave like other guys in the neighborhood?

Sagar: I belong to the sensitive minority of the city. I am allright with my illusions, if you call them so

Bhagirathi: But you are in serious trouble. A world that can be explained even with bad reasons is a familiar world. You are somewhere in an alien world.

Sagar: This is generation gap. You can't look into me and share my problems. That's because after you killed my mother, you have lost your creative courage. But you've failed to take upon yourself the loneliness, the experience of inner splitting of the self and the horror harvested by your sin. You are unable to bear the meaninglessness of your existence.

Bhagirathi: Stop your philosophical babbling.

Sagar: Yes, you can call me a philosopher, because I couldn't be a politician.

Messenger: Listen! Listen! Here's an announcement! Narcotic drugs cannot be supplied to philosophers.

Sagar: Is it a law you are going to promulgate here?

Messenger: I'm constrained to promulgate the law, Professor!

Sagar: Why?

Messenger: You have already created a pandemonium here. If I allow you to consume brown sugar, the turmoil would be uncontrollable. Ugh! I wonder what kind of sinners have come this time to the hell. Everyone is an island by himself/herself and has little connection with the other. Everyone is quarrelling with the other. Who are you all? Hey! All of you! Stand on a straight line and introduce your selves. We'll begin with this goat face. (*He asks Gunanidhi*) Who are you?

Gunanidhi: I was a Deputy Inspector General of police.

Messenger: What kind of thoughts did come to your mind?

Gunanidhi: I don't know my mind. I am only a physico-legal force. I'm only a uniform with power.

Messenger: Why don't you turn yourself into a mental force? Bring good thoughts into your mind: Sow good thoughts in the society and empower your mind.

Gunanidhi: The Honorable Minister took me once to Baba Kamananda. He was talking something like this. He asked me to live with honor and not to care for money. He said "A few get honor, but many get money. Life is short earn merits many, better to die than to be mean and puny". I got by heart what he spoke, but understood nothing.

Bhagirathi: But you were intelligent and you possessed a good memory when you got into Indian Police Service. The experience of this hell fleeced you off your wisdom. They gave you this goat face instead.

Gunanidhi: I was puffed with power and power killed the virtue in me. Baba used to tell, "where evil is alive and virtue is dead/that is the place people call hell."

Messenger: (to Bhagirathi) what was your crime record?

Bhagirathi: Crime? What did you think of me? Am I a criminal? (In an excited tone) I'm Bhagirathi Behera, Minister of law, order and home department

Messenger: That's alright! You've informed this several times. But why did you posted to hell after your death?

Bhagirathi: I did not die a natural death. I was brutally killed while addressing a public meeting. That was obviously a political murder.

Messenger: Then it was the consequence of public hatred. The killers, whoever they were, hated you. Why? What kind of thoughts you nurtured for them? Was it pure hatred?

Bhagirathi: Yes of course, it was pure, unadulterated hatred. What else could I have given to those brutes? They attacked me from the back, unawares. Otherwise, I could have been equally fatal. I acted like a matured politician. Baba Kamananda used to say: "The body is a tool/to keep the mind cool/Never to be used like a bull/to destroy peace and happiness of those who work under its rule." I didn't have the will power to put his sermons into practice. I was never good at studies I dug the pit for my opponents and now I am inside that pit.

Sagar: After he killed my mother, he was frantically searching for pits and now he has started living in pits. That's his destination, the South Pole!

Bhagirathi: (annoyed) Sagar!

Sagar: I reject you as my father. Go to your south pole.

Bhagirathi: You are the hell! Really the hell for me!

Sagar: You are my hell.

Messenger: (to Sagar) Hey you young hell! Why did you intervene in the middle?

Bhagirathi: He's a gone case! He has become an unruly hippy!

Messenger: (to Sagar) What's wrong with you? Why have you come to hell? Explain your sins and faults that impelled you to visit this *Kumbhipaka* hell. What are your faults?

Sagar: (Like a confessional poet) My offence? There are many. Offence number one is that I have kept long hair, Offence number two I smoke brown sugar and hashish; Offence number three: I keep away from my father's affluence, offence number four: I want to be a postmodern Buddha..I've renounced the throne of Kapilavastu and have settled under an insignificant banyan tree searching for enlightenment. I waited for the Alternate State of Consciousness to dawn on me. It did not come and I used hashish and brown sugar, and finally one day I negotiated my revolver and blew my head off. With that the conscience of the world was blown off. That was the end of the short spiritual journey of Sagar Behera through brown sugar fags. Amen! (*There is a small gap of silence and then Sagar says*) Alright inmates of the hell! So long for your parliament of the penitents! Let me slip into my own island of privacy. I can resist everything except temptations! I have a great fascination for the prohibited, great pull in the bizarre and amorous things of this world of Maya. Now I'll go to Swati Madam, (*He goes to Swati*), pulls her by her arm (*He pulls Swati by her arm; Swati volunteers to go with Sagar*) and absconds (*He moves out of the conference. Everybody looks agape.*)

Saubhagya: Aye, Messenger of the hell! This maniac has abducted my wife. This is a psychological assault Sagar has inflicted on me. And you are a witness to it. Note it. I may be very rude in future.

Messenger: Is he hobnobbing with your wife?

Saubhagya: I suppose so. Would you allow me to go and peep into to my previous life for a while?

Messenger: You mean, you need a short flash back? (Saubhagya nods)That'll be better.

(Saubhagya gets up and leaves the stage in the direction Sagar and Swati have gone.)

Gunanidhi: This son-in-law of mine is a jealous guy. I think all possessors of beautiful wives are jealous.

Bhagirathi: That is another form of love, Gunanidhi, not jealousy. I've selected the groom, that too, with the help of Baba. Nothing adverse can happen now, I can assure you. They are bound to live a warm conjugal life.

Gunanidhi: Where has he gone now? Let me check for a while. (*Gunanidhi follows Saubhagya*)

Messenger: (to Bhagirathi.) Whom are you waiting for? Go somewhere. I am waiting for an empty hell since last two hundred years. It's never empty.

Bhagirathi: I've booked a seat in the hell long before, when I was a Minister and I did all that with an ambition to settle here permanently.

Messenger: In youth you believed many things that were not true; in old age, now, you should doubt all truths if at all you encounter them. (He pulls him by hand) Come, I'll leave you in *Raurava Narka.*

Bhagirathi: Why? Is it a picnic spot?

Messenger: You are transferred to *Raurava* hell. Stay there hereafter, don't come to this side. (The messenger pulls Bhagirathi's hands and leads him inside. After they exit, the stage becomes empty. The light dims and becomes dark. The background music increases in volume. In few seconds full lights brighten the stage. Sagar Behera and Swati are seen entering the stage laughing wildly)

Sagar: (Laughing) I never knew you had so much of strength! You lifted me up at one embrace and I apprehended a fall. I didn't because we are running through the Valentine week. Today is the hugging day. Did you know that?

Swati: That's what I was doing. You think girls to be soft and light like flowers? Why can't they be hard? Look, how I hug and lift you again. (Swati lifts Sagar and the posture is obviously erotic. She holds Sagar in embrace and rotates. Saubhagya enters and is surprised to discover them in this position. They now change positions in stop – block frames and the back ground music is played in *mardal* some classical Odissi dance beats. Strobe light flickers)

Saubhagya: Swati! (*Swati does not listen. She is aggressive and she goes on implanting kisses on Sagar's body. Saubhagya intervenes. He pulls out Sagar from Swati's grip*)

Swati: (*irritated.*) Who are you here to pull us apart? Get out from here, you woman hater! I don't want to see your face. You were spying at us. Go. Bury yourself under a truck load of currency notes.

Saubhagya: Yes. I will. I doubt your integrity, Swati Madam, you are an infidel. Who's this young bull? Where have you picked him from? (In a cool coaxing voice) Who are you young man?

Sagar: I'm Sagar Behera, a first year graduate student in City College. You must know my father; he is Bhagirathi Behera, Minister for law and order.

Saubhagya: Oh! Come on Sagar! (*He shifts his mood abruptly*) Why are you wasting your time here with this old lady? You should be somewhere in the Axis Mall tasting Chinese or Italian cuisine in some modern restaurant. Or you should be buying diamond presents for your girlfriend from Tanishq. This is not the place for you. I know your father. How is it that he doesn't give you money for your pocket expenses? (*He brings out his wallet and takes out some bundles of currency notes*) Take this fifty thousand and find a green girl friend from your class. Come on, (he touches his shoulder in one hand and leads him the way to the exit point of the stage) You can find plenty of girls to accompany you when your wallet is warm. Ha, ha, ha! (*He leaves Sagar outside. Sagar starts his bike and dashes off. The off-stage sound is heard. Saubhagya comes back. He looks cool, but stern. Then suddenly he becomes furious and he bursts out:*

Saubhagya: What were you doing here you tart? How dare you auction my family prestige in my absence? Why were you toying with that young bull? (*He takes out his belt and starts lashing Swati.*) Tell me you whore, give me an answer!! Why were you making advances? (*He starts lashing at her brutally; Swati screams and then falls down and rolls on the ground. Saubhagya goes on lashing Swati incessantly like a maniac and mad man in anger; till she faints and dies. The screaming stops but Saubhagya does not stop beating. Then he stops beating and checks in a grotesque manner whether she is alive. He uses pantomimic acting style to the sound of heavy music*)

Saubhagya: Swati! Swati!! (*He shakes her. Swati's head drops to one side as a confirmation of her death. A crash is heard in the background music.*) That's your fate, unfortunate woman, that's your destination. You are as pale as your undergarment, now. When we shall meet at the judgment seat, this look of yours will hurl my soul out of heaven and the devils will catch it. You are cold my girl, even as your chastity is. O devils drive me off from this blessed sight. Fling me about in the winds. Consume me in hell. Steep me in the precipitous gulf of the liquid fire of hell. Who are you afraid of Saubhagya Das Mahapatra? (*Saubhagya loses his mental balance*) Who can rise above the fate? Go to hell! (*Saubhagya exits. The light focuses on the dead body of Swati. Music denotes murder. The stage is dark. Spot holds a new comer named Jayanta Mohapatra, a young man of twenty seven with well-cut beard on the face. He enters like a thief, with caution and watchfulness, proceeds past the lying body of Swati, comes back, stops near her body and calls*:

Jayant: Swati! Swati!! It's already evening. Why are you sleeping till now, that too on the floor? Swati! Swati!! What's wrong with you?

(Swati gets up little later and asks)

Swati: Um!... Who are you?

Jayant: I'm Jayant. Jayant Mahapatra.

Swati: (gets up): Oh! Jayant bhai! How come, you are here at this odd hour?

Jayant: I am in trouble; in severe trouble! The government has declared me a terrorist and your father has given shoot-at-first sight order. They have gone to my slum colony quarters. Your father leads the proceedings. They might have broken the door of my house to have an encounter.

Swati: And you came to my house? Are you alright, Jayant bhai? Is your head working properly? My father will shoot you at first sight and you have come here for a shelter?

Jayant: What can I do? I am totally flabbergasted, couldn't find an alternative. I thought this would be the safest place for me. Now tell me where shall I hide?

Swati: Come here. Look at that almirah standing there. There is some space behind it. Go there. Of course it'll be little suffocating, but that is the safest place. Come, we'll try that place. Dad won't be able to locate you.

Jayant: Okay, I'll hide there. (*Before Jayant moves Gunanidhi, in his police uniform, barges in. They encounter each other. Background music, crash sound. Gunanidhi cunningly acts normal.*)

Gunanidhi: Aye, Jayant! When did you come? No. Why are you startled? I know everything…You are a well wisher of my daughter Swati.

Swati: Not only a well-wisher Dad, he is like my elder brother! You remember our last college election, Dad? Ruffians from outside came and attacked me…Jayant Bhai rescued me and helped me to reach home.

Gunanidhi: That's right. Then why were you trying to hide him? It's good luck for us that he has come to our house, so mo to. Feed him with some good snacks. Good pieces of chicken were there in the fridge, why don't you fry some chicken? What do you say Jayant?

Jayant: That'll be right sir. But Swati will have to take some pains

Swati: That I won't mind! What I wanted to say was that you've to wait for half an hour for chicken fry.

Gunanidhi: Ok, we will wait. What do you say, Jayant? (To Swati) Go and prepare it Swati. Let Jayant know what cuisine we can make at home!

Swati: Okay dad, I am ready to prepare chicken fry. Both of you may sit and gossip. People outside will be amazed to see both of you gossiping – a police DIG of crime branch talking to a Nuxal leader. Swati laughs loudly and vanishes inside)

Gunanidhi: You shut up, Swati! Everything is possible these days. The attitude of the police has changed. The police are trying for some kind of unison and harmony between the department and the citizens. Yes, we can spend this half an hour in any way we like. Okay?

Jayant: Yes Sir!

Gunanidhi: That's like a good boy!! Ha ha! How have you come? Have you brought your "pulser" with you? We would have gone to some lonely place…OK, I've got my office jeep free. Come with me

(Both of them walk in pantomime action to upstage area. The lights are put off and the characters are held in spots. The sound track builds up the effects of a dense jungle with sounds of roaring tigers and other forest based animals)

Where have we come, Jayant? It seems this mysterious place is known to you!

Jayant: Yes. Some of my friends stay here in this jungle hide out.

Gunanidhi: Where?

Jayant: Come, we can't cross the stream here. There is no bridge. The villagers have put two log woods here to cross the stream. You can't cross this in this dark night. But you can see from here those distant lamps and smoke emitting out of those cottage roofs.

Gunanidhi: That's a tribal village. Isn't it?

Jayant: No, that's our private settlement, a snuggery for us, though a cottage

Gunanidhi: You mean a small kind of hide-out where you make hand bombs?

Jayant: (*He looks at Gunanidhi sharply*) who told you?

Gunanidhi: (Smiles) You are asking the question to the Deputy Inspector General of vigilance department. We have full information about your hide outs. Take me to that settlement. (Thinks for a while and then declares) I'll pay you one million rupees. Take me there! I will recruit you as a Police Sub-Inspector. Take me once to your hide out.

Jayant: Why should I? That too taking a bribe from you? Look 'ere Sir! I come to Swati and now I have accompanied you to this remote jungle at this odd hour of evening; that's okay! But I am not a traitor. Neither do I sell my party secrets to police officers, nor shall I be able to treat you like a guest here. After all, you are a police cat--number one enemy for my comrades. You can't be a guest in that cottage. Some comrade may fire you or blow your head off. Again, as far as I am concerned, I've a very solid commitment to my cadre, to my society and to my people.

Gunanidhi: What sort of commitment?

Jayant: A commitment for changing the society; to transform its socio-economic and ethical structure. Everyone here shall be given equal opportunity to study in equal standard of schools and compete for a given responsibility, for a post of job. I'll see that this shall be done in my life time. Come, whatever may, it may cost my life, but I shall translate my dreams into reality. I'm struggling to reach my goal and a section of selfish people try to maintain statusquo. They are afraid of change. They'll block our way and we will barge in; they'll use brutal force on us and we have to retaliate with greater force. Anyhow, I have to translate my dreams into reality! If it be done by deployment of terror, we are ready to execute it through violence and terror. Anyhow! I'll have to translate my dream into reality.

Gunanidhi: And to translate your dreams you will have to import RDX from Pakistan? What sort of logic is this? You will bombard and explode bus stops and railway stations, shopping malls and government police stations-killing innocent people. You are terrorists. And you think the police will let you free and sit silently? Impossible!!

Jayant: (Sternly) what shall you do to me? What can you do? I know the government has declared me a terrorist.

Gunanidhi: Not only that. The home Secretary has given the orders to shoot you at the first sight.

Jayant: Why don't you shoot me, then?

Gunanidhi: You are my daughter's elder brother; almost a son to me. I have brought you here as a well wisher Jayant! To take an initiative for talks that could not be started before.

Jayant: That's why I misled you and brought you to my operation area. I am aware of the government orders. I know you are pressurised to catch me live, for a trial, if it is possible. I am aware of the government orders: that you will shoot at me at the first sight. Still I've risked coming with a police. Look 'ere Sir! (He raises his hands) I am at your disposal. Do whatever you like and get a promotion. Take me as a surrendered case. But I won't agree to one thing: I won't be rehabilitated by the government. My mission is different.

Gunanidhi: You have already brought me to this dark and lonely place. Now show me your den, where you prepare bombs'.

Jayant: Must you go there? Come. Can you cross that stream through these two logs?

Gunanidhi: Yeah, I can go. I have not yet grown decrepit and invalid. Now, where shall we have to go after crossing this stream?

Jayant: Just a furlong on this jungle route. But reconsider Sir, I am giving you an opportunity. You are not acquainted with the area, with my comrades, and you are in police uniform. If somebody from our cadre shoots at you, your dead body would rot and contaminate the water of the stream. The carcass cannot be delivered to your family members for conducting death rituals.

Gunanidhi: Are you inducing fear into me? (He laughs cynically, then with new force in his voice)Of course, to finish you forever I needed this secluded place. I couldn't have shot at you in my house. Now, get ready! (Within a second, he takes out the pistol and fires at Jayant. Jayant somersaults and leaps to one side as quickly as possible; then from the fallen position takes out his pistol at shoots back at Gunanidhi. Gunanidhi immediately falls dead. But before he dies, he returns a shot to Jayanta and he is dead.)

(Lights go off abruptly. Silence for a moment, then music bangs in group violin strokes and gradually full lights come on the stage. With that the Messenger enters the stage pulling a reluctant bearded saint of about 45 into the hell. The middle aged Saint uses force not to enter into the hell. This continues for about a minute. Then finally he gives a heavy push to Baba Kamananda from the side wing and he saves himself from a fall and shouts at the horn-headed Messenger:)

Kamananda: Hey, you unholy man from the hills! What do you think of me; a prisoner or, something? I'm not destined to be here. Saint Kamananda, is the only god man available around this part of the earth originally belongs to the Paradise. I am the number one Baba of the twin city, Delux Baba. I was on deputation to the mundane earth only for a short time. Otherwise, my abode is paradise. (*aggressively*) Why have you brought us to the hell? (High pitch voice) Answer me right now. Give your explanation.

Messenger: (shrinks and retreats) I didn't go to that bloody earth to bring you here! I am only a messenger here, an orderly to my boss-Yamaraj. Okay I will verify from Chitragupta about your antecedents.

Kamananda: Do that early. Yes. I am a spiritual rebel. Some people call me a holy rascal. I used to tell the temples were corrupt politically, economically and socially. I questioned the temple Priests: Do you care about the issues facing people of low caste? Do you allow women Priests to worship in the temple? Come to my Ashram on the banks of river Mahanadi. We allow both the genders to serve god with equal rights, and equal dignity. Come to our Ashram and checkup. We have a branch at Bhubaneswar. We go beyond 'isms' and ideologies and live in the world as a liberating force of justice, compassion and joy

Messenger: Your earthly name was Kamananda. Right?

Kamananda: Why do you ask my name?/I am not a child of man/ I am the child of God, he sent me to the world only with an instruction: "Son, you are my child, don't forget the truth; my name is divinity sent to this world/ only to serve humanity/ to know reality and not to get lost in majority."

Messenger: The report says you are a homosexual, a passive one. The nearby villagers arranged a homosexual gigolo to satisfy your sexual hunger. After that you used to practice sodomy with young boys in the Ashram. You gave shelter to narcotic drug peddlers and in lieu of that they bought you two full bottles of whisky and some chicken-rice every evening.

Kamananda: That's none of your business. Who has told you about my private affairs? Must be some of my enemies. My enemies are jealous of my Ashram's prosperity and the number of cars that are parked in front of my hermitage every day at Bhubaneswar inflamed their hearts. Secondly, I am a spiritual revolutionary in a time of despair. I live in a time of political hopelessness and division. You know that? People abandon God and come to me for all kinds of solutions and even salvation.

Messenger: That's because you camouflaged yourself to be god, you performed tantric miracles and ensnared the blind devotees. You behaved like a hooligan and demanded money from everybody who came to meet you.

Kamananda: But we also distribute money to the poor people every day. We can create money out of empty nothingness, we can hear what you think if you are under my grip; we can increase and limit your life span, I can tell whether a man will survive or not. With such spiritual power what shall you call us, if not god?

Messenger: We also listen what you think. It is called thought reading. Chitragupta must have studied the evil imprinted in your mind. That's why I was deputed to bring you to this part of the hell. You will stay here for how many years I don't know. But don't play your earthly games here. You have to live like other sinners. Everybody is treated here alike. You cannot claim here to be a god-man.

Kamananda: Why? Do I not look like a god man? Look, this is my beard, this is my pigtail; it's a huge pig tail. I won't mind if you call it "horse tail" because its size is like that. I've put on a saffron dress. What more proof do you need? In my previous life I was Osho. In this life I am Kamananda. I preach people to understand the value of the body's South Pole. You are allowed to experience your South Pole perfectly and then gradually you take small leaps toward your North Pole; you get the first ever glimpse of *Samadhi* of meditation during the time of lovemaking, nowhere else. It is only in moments of love-making that human beings realise for the first time that so much bliss was possible. Those who meditated on this truth, those who reflect deeply upon the phenomenon of sex, of lovemaking saw that the moments of love making, at the climax, the mind becomes empty of thoughts. For a moment, all thoughts disappear. This emptiness of the mind, this disappearance of thoughts is the cause of showering of the divine bliss.

(As Kamananda was sermonising, Gunanidhi, Bhagirathi, Saubhagya Das Mahapatra, Sagar Behera and Swati come and act as Kamananda's disciples.)

Bhagirathi: Hail to Baba Kamananda for his invaluable speech on sex! Ladies and gentlemen! If you think your roots are dried up and the flame of life is dimmed, come to Baba's feet. He will rekindle your spiritual creativity and increase the power of your critical thinking. Baba, I touch your feet. (*He touches Kamananda's feet*)

Kamananda: Oh, Bhagirathi Behera! You didn't telephone me since long. What happened to your soul? I felt the urgency of coming over here to repair the battered hearts of my disciples.

Gunanidhi: But, Baba! A holy rascal of your stature shouldn't have come to this Kumbhipaka hell. How could it happen? Who forced your highness to come to this dirty inferno? I will investigate the case personally. This is unforeseen; a saint in the hell!

Swati: Why do you generate a new polemic Dad? What investigation will you make against a holy saint? Do you know, you wedded me with Saubhagya because of Baba's grace. Better you don't open your mouth.

Kamananda: Calm down dear girl, there's some politics against me in the hell, might be. (Pointing at the Messenger) My stars were not favourable. This horn headed fellow dragged me forcibly into this hell. He might know the reasons. But what happened to you? How did you die?

Saubhagya: I have beaten her to death. She is a civilised tart. She copulated with whosoever she found in her lonely hours.

Kamananda: (Irritated) Withdraw your words young man. What do you know about women? Prior to Satya Yuga there was Samhita yuga and in Samhita Yuga the society was matriarchal. The woman selected her male partner according to her choice. The practice continued till Tretaya Yuga in the hill-dwellers' community. Take the example of Surpanakha desiring to copulate with the Aryan brothers. Your wife is a primitive woman, a pure woman.

Swati: He is a masochist and he enjoys abusing me emotionally.

Kamananda: He has already reaped his consequences.

Swati: I've forgiven him Baba! I was trying to move past hurt and pain, and the other day he flogged me with his belt till I was dead.

Kamananda: That rich fellow is jealous of you. He was intolerant of your dynamic personality.

The Messenger finishes his rituals to wake up Jayanta Mohapatra and then comes near Kamananda. Messenger: So, this pseudo Saint already knows your insides; what do you say, sinners? Like Guru like disciples. Manage your quarrels yourself. Don't bring your case to this saffron saint. He seems to be an intriguing person. I am going to check his records with Chitragupta. (*The Messenger exits, goes up to the wings and turns to advise the sinners*) may be, this quaint Baba knows something. You settle you matters with him in the meanwhile, I am coming: (*He exits*)

Kamananda: Aye Messenger! Can you arrange some *Prasad* from Jagannatha temple? We are not used to eat outside.

Messenger: This is not a Dakbungalow nor a guest house, a hell it is. We don't provide food here.

(The band percussion of a dead body being taken to the graveyard is played in the back ground. The Messenger goes to the dead body, performs some bizarre rituals and Jayant Mahapatra gets up, looks at the other members and asks:)

Jayant: Where am I comrade? This seems to me an unknown place! Who are these people?

Messenger: You are in the hell, now.

Jayant: Why? Why am I brought here? Is there a leftist party running the government?

Messenger: You are a murderer. You have killed three police officers while they were on duty. Stay here till you realise what sin you have committed. (He exits)

Jayant: I had no other way. The government officers declared me a terrorist and they had planned to blow me off.

Bhagirathi: Helo Jayi! How come you are here?

Jayant: You are my first predecessor to experience the hell, Sir! You have changed your party and occupied the position of a Minister. But what happened at the end? They guillotined you on a public square. That was your entry point into the hell. If senior politicians of this country are consigned to hell, what will be the fate of the youngsters like us?

Kamananda: Come here, young boy. Tell me, what crime have you committed?

Jayant: Who are you after all to take the stock of my crimes? I don't admit religious people into our socio-economic wars. They are spiritual culture jammers…force us to nurture blind belief. Religion is a kind of opium for the people! You can't differentiate between a crime and a virtue.

Kamananda: We are different people dear boy! We go beyond 'isms' and cults and pantheons. But you need to have a faith dear boy; you may abandon God, but not faith.

Jayant: I have faith in social justice and equality. I have faith in *Das Kapital.* You religious people, people connected with temples are indifferent to corruption. We are not. I know people of your kind. You will help only the ruling party Ministers – Bhagirathi Beheras of the country, not the poor hungry folks.

Kamananda: Political power is also economic power young man. How can you run an Ashram without money? So, I need a rich patron like Bhagirathi. But how can we check corruption? People say Power corrupts and absolute power corrupts absolutely.

Bhagirathi: Not always Gurudev! These beggars are always jealous of my money!

Jayant: All money is theft. We revolt against theft and corruption Sir; it's not jealousy. It's a demand for justice! He has nothing so precious to be jealous of. Rather we hate him. He is a traitor; he changed our party and joined the ruling party only to become a minister and loot the country!

Kamananda: You power-mongers of politics are always fighting with the ruling parties and creating a hell for others. Why can't you be little tolerant, and little friendly with the other? We think beyond these political ideologies and try to bring a supra-mental consciousness unto the world so that people would keep away from all kinds of corruption automatically!

Sagar: Well said Baba! That's what I preach: the message of love and friendship. Get down from the ego-studded throne of Kapilavastu, O Power-holders! Come down to this banyan tree and chant: *Buddham Saranam Gachchhami/Sangham Saranam Gachchhami.*

Kamananda? Are you an anti-Hindu and Hater of idolatry?

Sagar: I don't understand religion. Do you have ganja or hashish with you? If so, we will smoke and dance with *Harekrishna Hareram* chorus. That'll enrich the eco-system of hell. What is there in religion?

Kamananda: Why do you depend on external inductions for nurturing an alternative state of consciousness? Why Ganja and Hashish for the expansion of consciousness? We detest such liberalism because of its equivocation and service to the social status quo. Liberalism misleads people.

Sagar: I know Jayant Mohapatra. He is not in favor of social status quo! He is very dynamic.

Jayant: All these Masters of Religion are traditionalists Sagar. They are conservative people. They will refer everything to the Vedas and Vedanta philosophy. And we are down to earth people, Marxist radicals. So, we are poles apart. We can't afford to run our party without a code, without a discipline. Sagar is a junior to me in the college. He belongs to a group of hippies. Bhagirathi Behera has killed his mother and he has no other energy except sex, but he cannot transform it into higher energy. So, he has no control over his son.

Bhagirathi: He is a gone case, a hippie he is. Jayant is a rascal; moves around with a pistol in his pocket. Such terrorists should not join politics. *(Jayant was about to attack Bhagirathi, Kamananda intervenes)*

Kamananda: You are wise, Jayant. You talked sense. It seems you have studied these characters rightly. Sagar is also wise but he is a liberal. Thus, he has a dangerous perception. He finds madness in all wisdom and folly in all knowledge.

Sagar: Gurudev! You are making the hell heavy with philosophy. Do some miracle for a change.

Kamananda: What miracle?

Sagar: Create some ganja and hashish from out of the blue! We will smoke it taking the name of Lord Shiva and feel lighter. (Pause) What is your source of power Baba? Your disciples say that you are blocking the sex energy like a wall not allowing it to flow. What power is that? This is nothing but ego, the feeling that "Only I am powerful". Your knowledge and wisdom are your weapons to dominate, mesmerise and hurt other's ego. This creates a hell for you. Why can't you get rid of your stupendous ego? Why can't your inner 'I' become smaller so that you gain the capacity to become one with anything?

(The messenger of the hell enters with his magic staff and he claps in appreciation of Sagar Behera's words)

Messenger: Well-said, you young sinner! The Ego is at the centre of the hell. You fight and kill each other because of your uncompromising ego. World wars and devastations take place because of this ugly ego. The desire to kill engenders in the deep core of your ego. This petty politician, this industrialist, this police officer and this terrorist…they suffer from possessing puffed up ego centers. They fail to descend down for a compromise, for syntheses.

Kamananda: Look here! Kamananda has visited the hell to repair the battered souls of his disciples. Jayant Mohapatra doesn't trust religious Masters. Let him not trust me. But he must adopt *ahimsa*, the removal of the desire to kill. Deconstruct your desires, don't kill.

Jayant: How can it be possible Gurudev? There are so many harmful creatures who want to kill me. So, I may be compelled to exterminate harmful creatures.

Kamananda: But you are not under a similar compulsion to feel anger or animosity.

Sagar: All men and women, living or dead, should understand this truth by overcoming the passion for destruction. After all you are in the land of Lord Jagannatha, a deity that preaches nothing but nurturing a friendly love for others, imparts the message of fraternity.

Jayant: I agree with fraternity. It's a kind of ethical relationship between people which is based on love and solidarity. But Sagar! Fraternity has been put at the service of nationalism and cosmopolitan humanism – it has been used to support both traditionalist and revolutionary visions. If the other treats me as a brother, I would respond.

Bhagirathi: That is easy to lecture on fraternity and love, but difficult to put the ideology into practice, Jayant.

Gunanidhi: Impossible! How can a police Officer love a terrorist? His duty is to exterminate them to run the society safe.

Saubhagya: I prefer not to give any opinion on the philosophy of fraternity. It sounds lofty, but how can I love a leftist and terrorist like Jayanta? He thinks industrialists are his arch enemies.

Jayanta: You are a terrorist Mr. Saubhagya Das Mohapatra. You have murdered Swati for nothing. You are crueler than a terrorist.

Swati: Yes, he is a sadist. He enjoys when others are tortured. He does not understand the meaning of love. His heart has become a vast desert. His concern is with the arid emptiness.

Saubhagya: These people hate me because of my richness and material affluence. How can I treat them as my brothers? Its better to stay aloof. So, I prefer a lonely life.

Swati: You are lonely because your heart has turned a desert. Your inner desert extends from private loneliness all the way to your environmental desolateness. Your loveless desert infects the green emotional fields of humanity.

Kamananda: (Laughs) Thank god, you have learnt a lot staying in this dingy hell.

Messenger: You holy rascal! You are little different from what I thought you to be! These incorrigible sinners were beyond repair. Somehow you have cast a magic spell on them and by the time I return you have changed them. What more you want to suggest holy sinner? I want these sinners to be free from the bondage of hell

Kamananda: May I advise you one thing? Believe on your body young generation; believe in your south pole. Religions aim at becoming absolutely free from sex. But Kamananda says that repression of sex creates madness. The more you fight, the more you suppress, the more sexual you become. Then sexual energy moves deeper into the unconscious. It transforms you into a beast; then you rape a girl in the town bus and become a news item next day. I strongly assert members of this *Kumbhipaka* hell: transform your sexual energy into a higher form. The higher it moves, the lesser and lesser sexuality remains in it. There is an end peak where it becomes simply love and compassion. This ultimate flowering is the divine energy, but the root remains sex prone. This energy cannot be killed; energy can only be transformed.

(All the disciples clap. The messenger asks them to stop. They stop. Then he asks Sagar:)

Messenger: What have you learnt from his teachings, young sinner?

Sagar: I cannot remain young for eternity. Old age will come upon me some day and I cannot avoid it.

Messenger: What about you, Mr. Industrialist?

Saubhagya: Some fatal disease will come upon me some day and I cannot avoid it.

Messenger: And you political freak? What have you understood?

Bhagirathi: Death will come upon me some day and I cannot avoid it.

Messenger: Death has already come to you, petty mortal. You have learnt nothing. What have you learnt old police culprit?

Gunanidhi: All things I hold dear are subject to change and decay and separation, and I cannot avoid it. I am the outcome of my own deed and whatever be my deeds, good or bad, I shall be heir to them.

Messenger: So? In one sentence what you have to do to get rid of this hell? You must have to raise your consciousness. It is a fundamental thing in existence; it is the energy, the motion, the movement of consciousness that creates the universe and all that is in it. There is no immortality except in truth. For truth alone abides forever. You can overcome anger by love, evil by good, greed by liberality and the lie by truth.

Kamananda: Stay like brothers, be like brothers: one in love, one in holiness, and one in your zeal for truth. Now begin the experiment now. Gunanidhi and Jayant! You killed each other; now hug each other with love.

(Gunanidhi and Jayant hug each other in love and friendship for each other)

Kamananda: Now Swati and Saubhagya: You have spoiled your marital life lacking trust for each other. Now embrace each other in love. God has given these hands only to embrace each other.

(Swati and Saubhagya embrac each other)

Kamananda: Now, Bhagirathi! South Pole Behera! You have estranged you son Sagar. He moves like an orphan. Accept him. And Sagar! He is your father. Touch his feet.

(Sagar touches Bhagirathi's feet. Bhagirathi embraces him)

Messenger: Holy Rascal! You have fought with me! Let us hug and work together!

Kamananda: *Sahaveeryam karavasvahai*

Trjaswvimaavadeetamastu

Mas vidvishaa vahai.

Messenger: Oh, you live-sufferers of the hell! You have experienced hell before your death because you did not know how to live. That was your folly. Now you have surpassed your follies and touched the tangents of civilised live. You are free now. Do whatever you like! Lights, go off from the stage and enkindle in their hearts. Amen!

25-2-2019

****

The Emperor with His Pot

(A pseudo-Epic farce)

The Stage

The stage for the play should be built in Vikrista Natyamandapa, a style having a Rangaseersha, Sada daruka, Patti, Apatti and Mattabareni. The ground plan and the set design are provided as model references. However, innovative directors are allowed to disregard them.

A platform measuring 20 'x3 'x3' is built upstage, which we may call Ranga seersha. On the right wing, there are three steps and on the Left Up, there is a ramp (a sloping way) to be used to wheel the Emperor up the stage, on a small wheeled wagon generally used by the municipal workers for carrying garbage. This is to be used for the entry and exit of the Emperor, Vajrabahu.

On each side of the ramp and the steps, two rectangular pillars (6'x1') are fixed. These four pillars on the two sides of the platform (called Patti and Apatti gates) should suggest a gothic palace.

A Sada daruka stands up stage center (Height: 6' and width 2 1/2'). On the two pillars (6') of the Sada daruka six battens or/thin bamboo strips are nailed. The two pillars on the two sides of the Sadadaruka are also rectangular in shape, the width of which would be 2 $^{1}/_{2}$', and classical palatial motifs would be fixed to it. Dazzling glass beads (even though they would distract the attention of the spectators) are preferable.

On the back of the Sada Daruka and at the front of the cyclorama, there would be three steps, though not visible to the spectators. At different phases of the play, the Emperor, the Minister of Philosophy, the Minister of Announcements, the Dream Merchant, Queen Ketakigandha and her two sakhis and the dead man from Mahakantara would use these steps to make their entries from behind the Sada daruka.

Eight small and square wooden blocks ($1^{1}/_{2}$'x 1') are placed on both sides of the platform, as well as on down right and down left stage. These blocks, obviously, would be used as sitting places for various characters.

ACT-1

In the dark, heavy lurking daskathia (percussion played with two sticks) sound starts low and builds. As the lights come up through the dimmer operation two daskathia players enter with their three-beat rhythm and foot work. (These folk singers play two small wooden sticks and beat it as percussion instruments for their songs.) They enter from the two wings of the down stage costumed in red silk dhoti and matching red kurtas with turbans wrapped in concentric circles and a long frill hanging from the back of the head. They have also decked themselves with breast – plates with appliqué work. The rhythm of their songs/ narrativizes change from time to time.

They enter with stylised walking gait and continue to perform with abhinaya (enacting) and Vachika with recitative sung-verse, occasionally intercepted by pure prose passages of south-Orissan (Telugu) modulation, with touches of Telugu intonation]

Performer-I — I'll sing my lines, and you follow!

Performer-II — No, No! I'll sing my lines and you follow as it comes.

The audience is full of Rasikas!

Performer-I — We'll sing you out this pseudo-epic. But before that: we do offer our *Pranam* to you, Ladies and Gentlemen!

Performer-II — *Namaskar!* To the *Rasikas* of Theatre, Namaskar!
To the cow-keepers
Of the world! To the cloud-colored Krishna
And to the blue-bodied Rama
Namaskar!
To Lord Ganapati
And to Goddess Saraswati! Namaskar!

[They stop playing the stick with tihai beats]

What's this epic about, Pal?

Performer-I — The epic of Emperor Vajra Bahu.

Performer-II What's that? I haven't heard of this epic since this face had a nose!

Performer-I Don't poke your nose into my *Purana.* Better fit a pair of electronic magic ears and listen!

Performer-II But what's the epic about, Gurudev?

Performer-I There lives an Emperor in the city of Hastina.
Great in his deeds, indeed.
People in his regime scale emotional heights
in the nights. Plenty of wine one gets.

Performer-II Let's go there, my dear:

But since how many years

Is he enjoying his high chair?

Performer-I Twenty five springs has he enjoyed
The fragrance of the flowers of paradise.
Twenty five years have passed
Since the King was coronated. Not so fat, not so lanky
This emperor of ours is always happy
But when he laughs
He sounds like an ass. [The daskathia stops]

Performer-II Why?

[*Sound of the emperor's stylised laughter (He-eh-He-eh-He-eh) It should imitate the braying of the ass. The sound reverberates with a bang and it is followed by the sound of the trumpet announcing the arrival of the king*]

Performer-I Look, the Emperor comes:

[*He points towards the audience. The middle gangway is lighted. The emperor enters from the back of the audience through the middle gang way.*

Performer-I (Almost awe – stricken) Ah! What a physique! What an anatomy of an Aryan King!

Performer-II Ah! What a brain! An Aryan brain after all. But the Aryans are outsiders here! They're from Caspian lake area. We are the original people here.

Performer-I Stupid! How can you see his brain? Look at him. Only look! Don't describe. (He describes) What an antique gait in his walk! Seems as if he is coming from the delta of the Indus River!

Performer-II Hey! Here's a chance to meet the king. *(He looks at the Emperor's Procession in which a tripod and the colored pot are carried)* But I just can't figure out what to do:

Performer-I we'll have to transform ourselves – transform from Performers to Characters.

Performer-II What characters? We're not characters from this pseudo-epical story! We should behave like absent presences only!

Performer-I Why? We can stay here as *Vidoosakas*. They can be fitted into everywhere!

Performer-II But how can we survive 'ere? I wonder!

Performer-I won't have to do anything, Pal! Only we've to flatter the king! He is in need of heavy exaggerated praise!

Performer-II You mean we will act as sycophants?

Performer-I Yeah, Just you need to polish him smooth!

Performer-II So, never call a spade a spade!

Performer-I (Angry at the other) what do you mean? Are you suffering from cynicism? That's outdated! Better keep shut, you stupid! *[A sudden bang of the historical trumpet music with band to announce the entry of the Emperor. The daskathia players freeze. The Emperor advances slowly with stylized steps from the back stage, through the central gangway. The daskathia players start showering praises as the marching rhythm starts and they come down from the dais to the down stage. Before the king climbs up the stage, two workers from the Ministry of Announcements would pass by and climb up the stage with a giant sized colored earthen pot and a tripod. The pot is painted with multi-colored stripes, preferably using white, green and orange. The characters bring the pot on to the stage with its decorated iron stand and place it at the down center of the platform. They announce in choral voice]*

Chorus: Victory to his Majesty, Mighty Emperor of Emperors, Invincible and Indomitable, owner of seven million square miles, Sri Sri, invested with one thousand and eight Srees, Emperor Vajrabahu completes his silver jubilee year of coronation.

Character-I Give it a big hand ladies and gentlemen! This POT is the emblem of our Emperor's Power.

Character-II Of our superiority!

Character-I Of our prosperity!

Character-II So, ladies and gentlemen! Give the pot a big hand.

[The audience would be requested to clap. The artists from the chorus group would be posted in the auditorium. They would initiate the clapping and climb on to the main stage. Members of the audience would be inspired to clap. As the clapping stops, the marching rhythm played for the Emperor continues. Two characters would leave the stage; bring a large, pompous looking black chair with silver studs and a very high back, something like a mythological Indra's Simhasana. The Emperor, now, makes a move toward the painted pot, puts pebbles into it and then laughs his stylised donkey-brand laughter.

The laughter sounds like the braying of an ass. Classical Rhythm in Tabla or any percussion instrument is played. The Emperor takes a small pebble (Keep some small pebbles in a container on the tripod), drops it into the water and looks at the shaking reflection of his face in the water of the pot. Again he brays his laughter.

Chorus: Victory to his Majesty, Mighty Emperor of Emperors, Invincible and Indomitable, owner of seven million square miles, Sri Sri Sri, invested with one thousand and eight Srees, Emperor Vajrabahu completes his silver jubilee year of coronation

Tabla continues in the back ground music. Now he moves in his stylised steps round the platform and his throne; laughing as if overwhelmed by his own power. The rhythm takes on a classical roll. This provides the emperor a cue for a stylised, choreographic circling. The percussion beat would, then, transform into the rhythm for a classical dance. The two performers of daskathia would freeze downstage.

The Emperor would occupy his throne and immediately with the classical roll in the percussion, one or two classical dancers would enter from right up wings and perform for two/ three minutes a dance with faster movements. The Emperor will close his eyes and doze off. As the classical rhythm starts to back off in volume, the dancers would freeze in tableaux. The two frozen daskathia players would de-freeze and start showering accolades.

They have transformed themselves into Vidoosakas and begin to pelt these words of sycophancy:]

Vidoosaka-I Aha! Oho! Eehi! What a dance!

Vidoosaka-II What a music! May be purely classical. Purely. No fusion.

Vidoosaka-I And what beats! Fully classical. It's Indian.

Vidoosaka-II What anklets! Purely pre-Vedic design.

Vidoosaka-I (Advises Vidoosaka-II) Aha! Pal! Tilt up your head a little and see. Steal a glance over the frozen dancers! Paragons of beauty!

Vidoosaka-II Ah! What breasts! Pure breasts. No extra padding!

Vidoosaka-I (Holding his chest as if injured) Ah, Ah... Ah.!

Vidoosaka-II (feels worried and goes near) What happened? Pal!

Vidoosaka-I Pricks! Pricks of Cupid's arrow my dear! It has struck here! (Points at his chest and falls down. The other helps him to get up and stabilize himself. Music. Rhythm continues for some time. With this, the dancers defreeze and find a space to exit behind the *sada daruka* bowing at the king.

The vidoosakas move down right. The emperor gets up with a jerk and shouts at the daskathia players. The actor should note that he behaves like Almighty as long as he is on his throne)

Vajra Bahu Who the hell are you there! Dance critics from South India, eh?

(The Vidoosakas freeze again with fear down stage. The emperor continues shouting)

Are you in a sleep-walking dream? Hey – you!! Critics of dancers' anatomy! (The king goes to the up left and asks) Hey you! (then to the audience) Who's hired this pair of meatballs here? Did you hire them my dear subjects? *(He goes to up right and asks)* Did you hire these punks? (*Coming back to vidoosakas*) Who're you by the by? What are you doing here?

Vidoshaka-l Your Majesty! No... *(He shakes)*

Vidoshaka-ll No one has hired us, your Majesty! *(He shakes too, and gesticulates in the style of a sycophant rubbing his palms)*

Vajra Bahu: Are you flattering me?

(He goes to the pot and sees his face after throwing a pebble in to it …)

Heh... Eh... Heh... Eh... Heh... Eh!! Buttering and flattering are prohibited in my empire. Flattering is a post-colonial epidemic, you must know! Where did you catch it from?

Vidoshaka-l From the beaurocratic colonies of Odisha sir!

Vajra Bahu Odisha! Where's that? Oh! That stupid place near Kolkata? The land of Mango-kernel Eaters!

(He looks around and shouts) Who's there?

(Two sentries from the Ministry of Defense appear from the back of the sada daruka. They are in mediaeval get up with headgears. They arrive and salute the Emperor. He ignores them. VajraBahu seems to have lost his head. He orders:)

Arrest these two strangers!

(The mediaeval – looking sentries march toward the performers. Music. The performers shake with fear and they fall prostrated at the feet of Vajra Bahu. He gestures them to go. They leave the stage.

The Emperor asks the prostrated performers.)

So? Where did you catch this postcolonial disease called flattery? From the beaurocrats, Eh?

(Vidoosaka-II gets up and nods)

Vidoosaka-II *(Pointing at Vidoosaka-I)* From this Odia biped, Your Majesty, from coastal Odisha! *(Trying to force a smile)*

I'm from South Odisha, Your Majesty. In Odisha they ignore me since my granny was a citizen of Madras Presidency!

Vajra Bahu That's okay! But why did you drive my dancers out? (To *Vidoosaka-I)* Why did you eave-tease them? (To Vidoosaka – 11) And you! Why did you murder my dreams?

Vidoosaka-II I'm no murderer Sir; but where were your precious dreams, Your Majesty? I never saw them!

Vajra Bahu I was dreaming on my throne when the dancers performed on the eve of the silver jubilee celebration of my rule! Do you understand? You dream killers?

(The Vidoosakas shake in trepidation, and to ward off the fear, they begin to play the sticks and generate a rolling beat.)

Blow it off, you stupid stick-players! What the hell are you doing here?

(They stop playing daskathia)

Vidoosaka-I We are not eave-teasers here, Your Majesty! We would love to be called Vidoosakas!

Vidoosaka-II Yes, Your Highness! We are fit to be vidoosakas in your court!

Vajra Bahu Vidusakas! Who are they?

Vidoosaka-II We're *Gandharvas* incarnated as stick players in *Kaliyuga!*

Vajra Bahu Who are these *Gandharbas* by the by?... Sounds esoteric!

Non-realistic *(The emperor thinks for a while and declares)!* He-eh, He-eh! Great!

Vidoosaka-I Hail his Majesty! *[They play the sticks]* Hail Ho!

Vidoosaka-II Hail him Ho! *[Plays the sticks]*

Vidoshaka-I Hail to his Majesty who is a profound scholar of Gandharba *Veda! [plays the sticks]*

Vidoshaka-II All the *Gandharba Vidyas* belong to his Majesty! *[Plays the sticks]*

Vidoshaka-I *[plays to the audience]* The warrior of the border wars, on the path of God, the great accomplished deployer of knowledge, and excelling everyone in handsomeness, the friend of the Red Indian Chieftain, the friend of the subalterns, the truthful and the Just, Sri Sri Sri and to be exact, invested with one hundred and eight "Srees", His Merciful Majesty Emperor Vajrabahu!

Vidoshaka-II *(Competing with him in flattery)* Victory to his Majesty, Mighty Emperor of Emperors, Invincible and Indomitable, owner of seven million square miles, Sri Sri Sri, invested with one thousand and eight Srees, Emperor Vajrabahu completes his silver jubilee year of coronation.

[As the Vidoosakas shower praises, Vajrabahu moves to the coloured pot, picks up a small pebble and endeavous to create a spectacular event like a ripple and after gazing at his own rippled image for a short while, offers his stylized donkey-brand laughter to the audience.]

Vajrabahu: Heh-eh-Heh-eh-Heh-eh... *(Silence. He mutters with a new confidence)* we are the most handsome human being of this Universe!

Vidoshaka-I & Vidoshaka-II Aha-! Aha-! Aha-!

Vajrabahu: We are the most powerful emperor of this Universe!

Vidoshaka-I & Vidoshaka-II Oho-ho! Oho-ho! Oho-ho!

Vajrabahu We are the Emperor "Human-Divine"! We are the Monarch of all that we survey!!

Vidoshaka-I & Vidoshaka-II Hi-hi-hi-hi-hi!

Vajrabahu: *(feels impressed by the flattery)* You are hereby appointed as the vidoosakas to the Emperor and his court! With immediate effect!

Vidoosaka-I & Vidoosaka-II Victory to the Emperor!

(the vidoosakas sit down like marionettes on two wooden blocks, on two sides of the stage)

Vajrabahu: And I command that my administration would henceforth run from this Garden of Entertainments. With immediate effect! And the emperor is, now, pleased to fixate at his own reflection in the ocean of his power! *(Sharpens his mustache and renders his stylized laughter)*

Vidoosaka-I Aha-ha! What a glowing countenance!

(Brahmadutta enters from the slope up-left. He is the Minister of Philosophy. Vajrabahu before noticing him, shouts):

Vajrabahu: But why is this pot so small, Minister Brahmadutta?

Brahamadutta That would be easy for your Majesty to see your own reflection.

Vajrabahu No, Brahamadutta! As the Minister of philosophy in my court, you should take extra care that this pot grows everyday! At least symbolically!

Brahamadutta: But how can this be possible Your Majesty? The pot is a common noun and common nouns do not have the grammatical power to grow!

Vajrabahu: Mr. Minister of Philosophy!

Brahamadutta: Yes, Your Majesty!

Vajrabahu: How much of common nouns do we have in our Royal Treasury?

Brahamadutta: I regret, I'm not able to follow what your Majesty exactly wants to know!

Vajra Bahu: Vidoosaka!

Vidoosaka-I: Your Majesty!

Vajra Bahu: What do you mean by a common Noun?

Vidoosaka-II (Stands up) exactly the same thing as Your Majesty means!

Vajra Bahu: What d' you mean? Won't this pot grow?

Vidoosaka: (Stands up) Never, Your Majesty!

Vajrabahu: We're the Emperor of Hastinapur! We're the Emperor *Nara-Vishnu,* the king-Divine! Now WE command this pot of power to grow everyday inch by inch till my powers encompass the seven seas! Ultimately this pot would contain the waters of the seven seas! So, it must grow!

Vidoosaka: That'd be a marvel! Never did such an event happen in this sub-continent!

Vajra Bahu: *(Shouts)* Why didn't it happen?... Minister of Philosophy!

Brahmadutta: Your Majesty! Only living things grow! Bipeds and quadrupeds; Birds and fish.

Vidoosaka-I: Only dogs and cats do grow Your Majesty! Pots don't!

Vajra Bahu: Find out an alternative! His Highness Emperor Vajrabahu desires this!... Commands this pot of power to grow regularly!

(Brahmadutta and the Vidoosakas clap. The characters from the chorus posted in the audience also clap)

And before we breathe our last, we'd like to see this pot grown so big... as big as to contain the water of the seven seas!

(Brahmadutta and the Vidoosakas clap. The chorus characters in the audience also clap)

Brahmadutta The order shall be carried out, Your Majesty!

Vajra Bahu But how? We, the Emperor of Hastinapur, put this question to the entire court! Please clarify this to the Emperor! We command you to clarify!

Vidoosaka-II Your Majesty would command all the potters of the state... ask them to make the biggest pot of the world!

Vidoosaka-I Yes! the biggest pot of power!

Vajra Bahu Let them bring the pots to me. What d' u say Minister of Philosophy?

Brahmadutta Yes Your Majesty! These new recruits have come from a brainy stock!

Vajra Bahu I have appointed them as the Vidoosakas of the court!

Brahmadutta — Hello! Congrats! You're welcome to the court of Hastina!

Vajra Bahu — (To the Vidoosakas) You should occasionally visit Brahmadutta to overhaul your brains! Our Minister of 'Philosophy takes care of all intellectual matters of Hastina! He is a brainy person!

Vidoosaka-II — So... we can be trained under his brainy head!

Vidoosaka-I — Three cheers for the brainy heads of this country! Four cheers for the Minister Brahmadutta!!

Vajra Bahu — Now Vidoosakas! It's time for administration. You go down and sit on those blocks down there.

Vidoosaka-II — Victory to His Majesty, Mighty Emperor of Emperors, Invincible and Indomitable, owner of seven million square miles, Sri Sri Sri, invested with one hundred and eight srees, Emperor Vajra Bahu for the celebration of His silver Jubilee year of his golden reign!

Vidoosaka-I — Victory to His Majesty, the warrior of the border wars, walking steadily on the path of God, the great deployer of knowledge, excelling everyone in handsome features, the hero of the heroes, friend of the Red Indian Chieftain and all subalterns!, Truthful and Just, Sri Sri Sri, invested with one hundred and eight srees, Emperor Vajrabahu.

(*The Vidoosakas go down and occupy their seats down stage on the blocks. The Emperor goes to the colored pot drops a pebble into the water and laughs his stylised laughter*)

Vajra Bahu — Heh-eh-Heh-eh-Heh-eh-Heh-eh-Yes, Minister of Philosophy! What are the news headlines for today?

Brahmadutta — No one is capable of thinking in Hastinapur. Software crisis, Your Majesty!

Vajra Bahu — That's no problem! I don't think! Why should my subjects think? Thinking leads to insomnia, hypertension and all sorts of psychic disorder! I have therefore decided —No one should hereafter think in my country! Vidoosaka-I *(To Vidoosaka-II)* Look! His Highness thinks on his shoulders!

Brahmadutta Victory to the Merciful Emperor!

(The Vidoosakas sitting downstage suddenly feel inspired by Brahmadutta's flattery. They get up. Vodoosaka-l recites eloquently:)

Vidoosaka-I Victory to the warrior of the border wars, walking steadily on the path of God, the great-accomplished deployer of knowledge And excelling everyone in handsomeness, the hero of the heroes, the friend of the Red Indian Chieftain, the Truthful and Just, Sri Sri Sri invested with one hundred and eight Srees, His Majesty, and Emperor Vajra Bahu won't think hereafter. We'll think for him!

Vidoosaka-II *(Competing with Vidoosaka-I in flattery)* Victory to his Majesty, Mighty, Emperor of Emperors, Invincible and indomitable, Conqueror of seven million square miles, Sri Sri Sri, to be exact, invested with one hundread and eight srees, His majesty takes care of all the brains of his empire! Yet, we'll think on his behalf!

Vajrabahu Well said! I've the most fertile "brain treasury" in Hastina. Why do you choose to be silent Brahmadutta? As the Minister of Philosophy you should give a message to our people.

Brahamadutta: Your Majesty is my Philosophy! Your Majesty is my message.

Vidoosaka-I: All messages are given to be flouted by people.

Vidoosaka-II: His majesty's presence itself is a message to the world!

Vajrabahu: Haven't I appointed the right kind of Vidoosakas?

Brahamadutta: They should be promoted to the ministry of Announcements!

Vajrabahu: Ask the Ministry to announce that the Emperor treats them as his own sons and daughters.

Vidoosaka-I What a touch of Humanitarianism in his Majesty's brain!

Vidoosaka-II The Patron and Promoter of all common men!

Vajrabahu: Heh-eh, Heh-eh, heh-eh Minister of Philosophy! These two bards from Odisha seem to be proficient in my propaganda. Now tell us, whether they'd be deputed to the Ministry of Announcements or to the Ministry of Entertainment? Ask them to stay for all the time to come.

(Brahamadutta moves to the downside of the platform and tells)

Brahamadutta: His Highness is pleased to appoint you in this court. So you've to stay glued to these entertainment blocks.

Vidoosaka-I Your Highness! The entire country is celebrating the silver jubilee festival of the Emperor. If his Majesty permits, we'd take a round!

Vajrabahu: Brahamadutta! Inform Seelabhadra, our Minister of Announcements to distribute *Soma Rasa* in all the villages of my Empire... They should arrange day and night services.

Vidoosaka-I Ah! *Soma Rasa...* Pure Indian *wine! (feels really intoxicated before the indigenous drinks are tasted) [The Vidoosakas enact the probable effect in the villages after the soma rasa is distributed.*

Vidosakas-I climbs upon a block and totters.

Vidoosakas-ll asks in an intoxicated modulation]

Vidoosakas-ll What are you doing Pal? (He totters)

Vidoosaka-I: Scaling new alcoholic heights! *(He is about to fall)*

Vidosaka-ll Hail to the silver jubilee *soma rasa* of the Emperor.

Vidoosaka-I Hail to his dreams original!

Brahamadutta They say your dreams are original, Your Majesty! Not plagiarised!

Vajrabahu: Original? What's that? There's nothing called original!

Brahamadutta: You have not copied your dreams from Hollywood! You don't produce simulacra and pastiches!

Vajrabahu: I am a turning point in the history of Hastinapur!

[Vidoosaka-I, who was tottering on the block, now falls down with a turn and Vidoosaka-II catches him. They freeze in falling posture. The lights fade out]

SCENE-II

As the lights come up we find Marigold and Zinia, the two sakhis of the queen enter from two sides of the wings-Zinia from the left wing and Marigold from the right. Both of them produce the "kooing" sound of the cuckoo in a playful manner. They imitate and feign the sound of the cuckoo and play the game of hide and seek with the queen.

Zinia *(Looking toward the sada daruka)* Queen Ketakigandha! Where have you hidden? See, we're here! *(They hide behind the different blocks and* go *on producing "Kooing" sounds till Ketakigandha enters from the sada daruka area, flabbergasted)*

Ketakigandha: Where are you Zinia, my *Sakhi!* Where are you hidden? *Sakhi* Marigold! Come we shall play. See, the spring has come, the cuckoo is kooing, come! It is time for play! *(While Ketaki searches for them, they koo and Ketaki catches Zinia and Marigold shows up with a burst of laughter). Oh,* I see, you were fooling me around! Look *Sakhi,* I've got enough of fooling from the king...

Marigold: Did the emperor fool you?... Cajoled you by deceit?

Ketaki: He's not interested in my body! He does not play the game of sex with me. Only titillates. What does he think? Don't I need the physical pleasures?

Marigold: These days he is only obsessed with his coloured pot. He wants the pot to grow every day. He sees his reflection in the water of the pot and laughs!

Ketaki: The pot is then my enemy! But how can I be a rival to a fragile earthen pot? One day I will break it if the king does not come to sleep with me in the night!

Zinia: What a torture it is! The king does not sleep with the queen of the state. But why? You are not sterile, or physically unfit!

Marigold: You should have been pregnant by this time. It is already seven years since you are married.

Zinia: That's why no child is born to her.

Marigold: That's why the land of Hastina is sterile. No crop is harvested there!

Zinia: And that's why there is continuous famine in the country for three years!

Marigold: Cursed is the country where the king is impotent.

Zinia: He holds the court during the night.

Ketaki: That is to avoid me! I have to bear. This solitude for ever writhing under this aloneness. This biting pain of not becoming a mother.

Zinia: Is then the emperor impotent? Is his virility lost? Let him check up with the palace physician! Marigold: Come, we will summon the palace physician.

Zinia: Call him to our secluded room for consultation. (They *exit through the side wings and Ketaki exits through Sadadaruka. Lights go off)*

SCENE-Ill

Vajrabahu enters with the Ministers in darkness and shouts a command at Brahmadutta

Vajrabahu: Brahmadutta! Ask the minister of Announcements to declare that our court shall be conducted hereafter in darkness only! Darkness is pleasant! Knowledge is light! – a curse, … poverty!

(*Lights come with a bang*)

Brahmadutta: How can the court run in darkness, your Majesty?

Vajrabahu: Not a streak of light should be allowed to enter into our empire!

Brahmadutta: Even to the fringes of the empire! But how?

(*Vidoosakas would enter now*)

Vajra Bahu: Command the Sun to shine in the east as usual, but ask him not to disturb the slumber of our subjects. They'd sleep during the day!

Brahmadutta: What'd happen to our work-culture? And to the agriculture of our empire, Your Majesty!

Vidoosaka-I We can till our lands in darkness!

Vidoosaka-II Our lands are so fertile, pal!

Vidoosaka-I Victory to the Emperor who has allowed us to cultivate in darkness!

Vidoosaka-II Our lands shall yield and breed

Vidoosaka-I Gold! Golden children! Golden crops!

Vidoosaka-II (enamoured) Where's gold?

Vidoosaka-I Where?

[*Vidoosaka-I and Vidoosaka-II are searching for imaginary gold down stage*]

Vajrabahu: May be I'm also going crazy for gold! My imagination is running wild!

Brahmadutta: We must search for gold your Majesty. There are treasures hidden in this land of the Aryans!

Vajrabahu: Brahmadutta! Inform the Minister of Announcements and the Treasury to make an appearance in the court! Seelabhadra! Minister Seelabhadra!

[*The Minister of Announcements enters from down stage right. He steps for a while to see the Vidoosakas and then says*]

Seelabhadra: (Enters) Hail to thee! Oh Emperor, Vajrabahu, KCIE, B.L., Padmabhusana, Parama Veera Chakra, M.B.B.S., Ph.D, Founder of Hanuman Temple, and the chief Architect of Hastinapur!

Vajrabahu: Welcome, Seelabhadra! As Minister of Announcements and finance you're to inform the public about the new law promulgated in the country!

Seelabhadra: What's that law, your Majesty?

Vajrabahu: Inform all the homosapiens and insects of this country that all discriminations between light and darkness shall be waived off. Equality is granted to all under darkness!

Seelabhadra: But the law itself is a flash of Enlightenment! [*Vajrabahu goes to the colored pot, puts a pebble into it and brays his ritual laughter. The vidoosakas, in their choreographic movement of gold – hunting freeze for a moment. Light spots on Vajrabahu and then fades into darkness*]

SCENE-IV

The scene opens in darkness and the Vidoosaka-I in the freeze position cries for light.

Vidoosaka-I Lights! We need new lights for continuing this search for gold! This is the silver jubilee year!

Vidoosaka-II We need a golden enlightenment!

(*The lights downstage suddenly bang with golden yellow. Music*).

Seelabhadra: (*Enters from Sada daruka*) The king of Karnata is waiting outside to meet your Majesty! Brahmadutta is talking with him.

Vajrabahu: Allow him to step into this court. But has he brought any gift for us?

[*Seelabhadra goes to the wings at right down stage and gestures with claps. The king of Karnata makes his entry empty handed, escorted by Brahmadutta. He bows down telling*]

King of Kamata: Hail to Emperor Vajrabahu!

Vajrabahu: (*shouts, annoyed*) Minister of Philosophy! *[Everyone freezes]* This King does not know royal etiquettes!

King of Karnata: Did I commit any blunder, your Majesty!

Brahmadutta; He's a long-distance King. Doesn't know the revised rules of greeting your Majesty!

Vajrabahu: The richest king of India should update his knowledge of addressing the Emperor of emperors! He has come empty handed!

King of Karnata: Abbah! What a corrupt practice!

Brahamadutta: Seelabhadra! Teach him the revised rules of Hastina headquarters!

Seelabhadra *(To King of Karnata)* you've to address His Majesty in a different way. Now, speak as I say!

King of Karnata: Okay!

Seelabhadra: Hail to his Highness, the great warrior and Emperor Vajrabahu!

King of Karnata: Hail to his Highness, the great warrior and emperor Vajrabahu.

[*The king of Karnata repeats. The Vidoosakas feel inspired and start training the king of Karnata*]

Vidoosaka-I Hail to the warrior of the border wars, walking steadily on the path of God, the great accomplished deployer of knowledge and excelling everyone in handsomeness, the friend of the Red Indians' chieftain in USA, the truthful and just.

Seelabhadra: KCIE, BL, Padmabhusan, Paramaveerchakra, MBBS, Ph.D, M,B.A. founder of Hanuman Temple and Chief Architect of Hastinapur!

King of Karnata: Abbah! What a long list of titles!

Seelabhadra: Speak as I say!

King of karnata: KCIE, BL. Padmabhusan, Param Veer Chakra'

Seelabhadra: MBBS, Ph.D, M.C.A,

King of karnata: Abbah! Too much!

Vajrabahu: Not now, later. Yes, King of Karnata! You are hereby commanded to report the psycho-political status of your state. How do our beloved wise folks spend their days in Karnata country?

King of Karnata: The population of the cyber freaks is rising in geometrical proportion in our state!

Vajrabahu: Who are these cyber freaks? Invisible virus?

King of karnata: No, they are visible! These cyber freaks are visibly devastating our inner space, your majesty! They create one more illusion to add to our confusion.

Vajrabahu: What confusion?

King of karnata: Great confusion! Everybody's walking asleep, eyes open! The cyber freaks work overnight! They don't come home and their wives in revolt divorce their cyber husbands!

Brahmadutta: Wonderful! Congratulate them for the divorce! Give them awards! Sleeping with wives will lead to gynecological accidents. There would be explosion of population. We need to check them. Award the divorcee cyber engineers for doing something in this regard! Anyway, your state's stinking with riches. Now tell us about your internal problems if you have any.

King of karnata: Cuvery is the only problem Your Majesty! The holy river flows in many states! Every state needs Cuvery water! How can we leave our waters to the outsiders? Kindly settle our water dispute. Problems crop up due to this river.

Vajrabahu: Your problem is geographical! Brahmadutta! Do we have solutions to such geographical problems? Can you solve?

Brahmadutta: I need the map of Karnata and other countries to trace the river's course.

Vajrabahu: Look, Brahmadutta! A river is creating troubles there! This will lead to a water-war later. Not a trifle! We have to solve it, anyhow.

Brahmadutta: If you give this prince the entire Cuvery water then another Prince from another state would come and claim for the same. It will lead to greater troubles. Your Highness will be in trouble.

Seelabhadra: Are they planning for a rebellion? Or something like a water war?

Vajrabahu: That will be a more serious affair! So, it's better to dump the river itself with sand. Kill the river, divert its course. Well Prince, we will sanction an amount of two thousand millions for dumping the river. Take the money and go.

King of Kamata: That'll be a childish solution, my Lord!

Vajrabahu: Childish or oldish, you have to obey our orders. We are nipping the problem at the bud. Tell me about other problems, if any? Tell me how do our dearest subjects carry on?

King of Kamata: They are keeping their heads cool in sandalwood forests! Others smear their foreheads with the wood paste! But still, there's crisis your majesty! The rate of suicide increases!

Vajrabahu: That's wonderful solution to all psycho-political problems! Minister of philosophy!

Brahmadutta: Yes, your majesty!

Vajrabahu: Ask the king of Karnata to pay us hundred million dollars toward sandal wood tax, every year!

Seelabhadra: Sandalwood tax? Never before was it imposed!

Vajrabahu: Yes, sandal wood tax! You reap huge profits out of those jungles, why? Why won't you pay the tax?

King of Karnata: I fall at your feet, your majesty; my folks are already squeezed dry under the pressure of heavy taxation!

Vajrabahu: No, they aren't! Minister of announcements and finance!

Seelabhadra: Yes, your majesty!

Vajrabahu: Explain the tax rates to this long distance king!

King of karnata: But we need forty thousand billions only to control the cyber freaks, Your majesty! And our agriculture has suffered for want of funds. There's a big setback this year because we couldn't concentrate on WCE, I mean, Water Conservation Effect!

Vajrabahu: That's the reason; you should pay sandal wood tax

King of Karnata: But we can't! We can't submit to such blackmailing from the centre! A funny emperor it seems!

Vajrabahu: (shouts) Seelabhadra!

Seelabhadra: Yes your majesty!

Vajrabahu: This king misbehaves the power pot on the stage! He must have to pay the tax: If he doesn't wish to go behind the bars. Sentries! Take this long distance king away!

(*Vajrabahu claps and the two sentries come. They take away the king of Karnata forcibly!*)

King of Karnata: Abbah!

(*Vajrabahu goes to the pot. Lights focus on him! He puts a pebble in the pot and he looks at his face and laughs*)

Vajrabahu: Heh-eh, Heh-eh, Heh-eh, Heh-eh, Heh-eh!

(*Lights focus and fade out on Vajrabahu*)

SCENE-V

(*General lights fade in dimly on the stage and then slowly a violet light fades in slowly at the front of the Sada daruka area. Background music builds up as the violet light intensifies. There is a suggestion of sunset. Then the light effect builds up the image of a moonlit night. Music should be soft and mellow. At the front part of the sada daruka, a cage with a toy parrot in it hangs under a spotlight. Queen Ketakigandha enters slowly climbing the steps behind sada daruka.*

A deep green spot light follows her till she reaches the parrot cage. Music grows in volume. It would fade slowly as she would stand in front of the parrot and say in an incantatory soft voice. The lines are in free verse modern poetry. This has to be recited in an incantatory recitative voice, but loaded with tender emotions of loneliness)

Ketakigandha: Toy parrot!
How long would you stay
frozen?
You have turned me into a marionette
Of pain,
In this palace and court!

[*Background music begins. A choral humming fades in from low to high volume*]

I am caged here as a piece of art
I am a toy parrot.
A drop of tear on the stone's heart!

[Two of her attendants, Marigold and Zinia, enter. Zinia from the right side of sada daruka and Marigold from the left. The background music should be melodious and on four beats, and Zinia and Marigold enter with dancing steps slowly in 2-beat stepping. Improvise music to provide the cue for the footwork of Marigold, and Zinia. Their movements should be choreographic.]

Zinia: What nostalgia bugs you?

And wriggles through your heart?

Marigold: What nostalgia, like a bee it

Stings you ever so smart?

Ketakigandha: Yes, Marigold and Zinia dear
The nostalgia of becoming a mother
of a son.
To provide a heir
To the throne,
To this country's unfortunate soil
Lying sterile, writhing under the Emperor's neglect.
He is infertile, and impotent.

Zinia: No, my queen, sweet!
The king's busy, his schedule is tight!
Happy to dictate, plans to administrate
finds no time to celebrate the gift
of life. He is in a fix
No time for the queen's sex.
That disturbs you in the cluster of flowers within you!
Thus, his seed couldn't negotiate your open crimson mouth
Forget, we will quench your thirst!
Come, dear queen.
This Zinia with Marigold would try to vibrate your mouth,
breaking your hunger into a song of lust.

Marigold: Yes Ketakigandha!
I care your cares
Hate your hates
Like your likes
And love your love.

Zinia: Unwillingly though, I too became your shadow
My splendid queen!
Am I not another persona of you?

Ketakigandha: How can't you know how I pine?
A virile king to oar into my tiny boat
And inseminate me with a dream
I could have shown him
How fertile is this country.

Marigold: Don't bother, come! Show me
Where to press my mouth hard.
Hold me hard against you!

[She embraces and kisses Ketakigandha]

Ketakigandha: Yet, I need the king, dear Marigold. He promised
To press me hard
And bless me with a child.
My skin's blazing
And my egging field
Now dry and arid
is waiting for a future breed.

Zinia: Forget the king;
the father of a failure unspoken.
Probably he swings himself on a spider's thread.

Marigold: Let us turn your libidinal embers into a fire
We'll show you a rainbow
At the south pole of your lonely sky!

Zinia: You'll only have to endure; wait,
A son would be born straight!

(*Music. After the embrace and the kiss, Ketakigandha gesticulates the fulfillment of a dream sex with a sigh of satisfaction*)

Marigold: Wow! Mother earth, Of Hastinapur,
Foliate; give this land a future green.
Come! Come to your bed
My darling queen
Let the twilight linger!
We'd always love the morning spread
abroad among the snow-capped mountains

blazing with new hopes, Come!

[*As Marigold speaks these lines, Zinia and Marigold configurate themselves as two male kandarpas (Cupid-like) positioning Ketakigandha as Rati The composition should be like a sculptural erotica of Konark or Ajanta caves. Front lights go off. The cyclorama turns orange and the configuration is silhouetted. Music intensifies with choral humming. The tableaux break with the humming backing off in volume. The beats change. Marigold and Zinia lead Ketakigandha through the steps behind the Sada daruka. Lights dim and the cyclorama transforms into an alphabetized night sky. Music changes. A moon appears in the sky. Hold the composition for some time till it fades out slowly*].

SCENE-VI

[*The lights bang on and the trumpet blows. The announcer enters upright stage with a rounded drum hanging from his neck. As he beats the drum with two sticks and announces, the chorus characters, sitting in the audience, would repeat the words in chorus. The audio/space between the two utterances would be filled in by the drumbeats]*

Announcer: *(after the drum beats)* Attention! Attention!!

Chorus in the audience]: Attention! Attention!! [Drum beats]

Announcer: His Majesty, the great warrior and Emperor Vajrabahu, KCIE, B.L, Padmabhusan, Parama Veera Chakra and Jnapeeth Award Winner MBBS, MCA and Ph.D, M.B.A and urban anthropologist declares that his silver jubilee beard shaving festival would be ceremonized on this centre stage. He would arrive on the stage after two minutes riding a small sledge wagon drawn by two human beings dressed as dogs.

[*The announcer would salute the colored pot and exit into the auditorium through the front steps to join the other eight choral characters. Blank stage. Trumpet blows to signify the arrival of the emperor. Two sentries drag a wheeled wagon through the slope upstage left. The wagon should be designed like the improvised mini-chariot of Arjuna in Mahabharata. But the size of the wheeled wagon is like a small sledge driven by two human-dogs in the Eskimo country. Otherwise, the wagon is an improvised filth-carrier used by the corporation scavengers A barber with an embellished large size kit (shaving bag) is following the wagon. When the chariot reaches the centre stage, the barber says:*]

Barber: Here, Your Majesty, right at this centre! This is the right place for your Majesty's beard shaving ceremony.

[*The emperor gets down, comes to the colored pot, puts a pebble into the water, gazes at his own reflection intently and brays his stylized laughter*]

Vajrabahu: Hey-eh! Hey-eh! Hey-eh! Hey-eh!

The light focuses on Vajrabahu and then fades.

SCENE-VII

The lights bang in.*The barber asks humbly while sharpening the knife.*

Barber: The auspicious *moohurtam* for your majesty's shaving ceremony is getting near, your honour! Kindly come to this sledge vehicle and get seated. We will begin the shaving ceremony.

Vajrabahu: Okay! Have you made all arrangements by the way?

Barber: Yes Your Majesty! This servant of yours is always at your service! This shaving cream is from foreign country. It's imported Your honor. The Knife is sharpened kindly get seated on the sledge!

Vajrabahu: Okay! (He comes. On the way)

Barber: Only one mistake I have committed.

Vajrabahu: How dare you! What mistake barber?

Barber: I could not arrange the golden container to keep the scented water. We have to manage it with this plastic mug!

Vajrabahu: Here after we will manage with plastic mugs only. We have started believing in democracy. Here after, the king shall behave like an ordinary democratic citizen.

Barber: Glory to his Majesty Vajrabahu! Hail to thee! But this poor barber could not understand one thing.

Vajrabahu: What's that? (*The Emperor sits. The barber starts shaving work*)

Barber: Your majesty has come to the shaving ceremony riding a dog driven vehicle? Why didn't you come in a horse driven chariot, my Lord?

Vajrabahu: We have started believing in democracy! Emperor Vajrabahu declares that here after her would board dog-driven vehicles only! Democratic vehicles!

Barber: Glory to the clean shaved, clean hearted Emperor! Let him live for three thousand and one years!

Vajrabahu: Barber!

Barber: Yes, Your Majesty!

Vajrabahu: On the occasion of this auspicious beard shaving ceremony we declare that our doors would be kept open during the day time and any visitor from any part of the country can enter into my palace premises to meet the emperor! Take one hundred gold coins and go.

Barber: Glory to the large hearted king! Glory to the clean shaved, clean-hearted Emperor for his free style governance of Hastinapur. We take leave of your majesty (*The barber leaves. A stranger in royal costume barges into the stage praising the emperor in baritone voice*)

New Comer: Hail to his highness, the great warrior of the Border wars, walking steadily on the path of God, KCIE, Padmabhusan, Paramaveera chakra, MBBS, Ph D, Founder of Ganesha Temple and chief architect of Hastinapur! Hail to the most intelligent emperor who is also most handsome; Hail to friend of the Red Indian Chieftain in USA and great believer in democracy! I salute you your majesty!

Vajrabahu: Wah! What polished manners! You seem to be a perfect gentle man. Where have you come from, king?

New Comer: This humble representative is from Gouda Desa, your Majesty, from what the new fangled people call the west Bengal, the land of the Bengalies!

Vajrabahu: We are celebrating the silver jubilee year of our administration. And we are pleased to keep our doors open to all the States of Hastinapur. Now tell us frankly which way we would help your Gowda Desa?

King of Gowda: The land of the Bengalies is lying low in crisis.

Vajrabahu: What has happened?

King of Gowda: Crisis, your majesty! There's acute fish crisis in the country!

Vajrabahu: What has happened to the sumptuous treasure of fish over there? There were lots of fish rearing tanks in your state. We have sanctioned 3000 crores to dig out tanks over there!

King of Gowda: The tanks are there your Majesty, but the water dries up.

Vajrabahu: Piscatorial trouble?

King of Gowda: Not much! But the trouble is with the vanishing of the fish, the women there vanish in taxies.

Vajrabahu: What do you mean? What connection can be there between fish and women?

King of Gowda: The fish transform into *Matsya-Kanyas (mermaids),* and travel around "garden-reach" area. The male folks are in deep trouble "*Kalankyari*" your Majesty! People in Bengal call it "*Darun 'Kyalankari*" ("*Darun*"in Bengali means "severe" and "Kalankyari"is a Bengali pop word meaning acute "trouble:")

Vajrabahu: Deep trouble you mean? But this does not sound realistic! Women turning into fish and fish becoming *Matsya Kanya* (mermaids). What is the real trouble?

King of Gowda: It is occult, your majesty! Pure witch-craft!

Vajrabahu: The women folk are witch craft practitioners there. What a dangerous country yourule? Must be troublesome.

King of Gowda: A woman is trying to dislodge me from my throne-insinuates rebellions against me your majesty. People revolt there for sundry reasons., even for "Sandesh Crisis"

(Sandesh is a favourite sweet in Bengal) No, there is fish crisis-to add to trouble the woman folk turn into dauntless damsels, turn into slippery fish and vanish in four wheelers.

Vajrabahu: And they practice occult! Dangerous!

King of Gowda: Cause the fish to disappear from the tanks. Generate artificial fish crisis! That's a fish revolt!

Vajrabahu: Drown the women in water. Drown all women.

King of Gowda: But how can that solve our problem? Feminists would hang me!

Vajrabahu: We order you to drown the women! They will turn into fish again-your problem is solved. Go back!

King of Gowda: That'll aggravate the situation!

Vajrabahu: Take resort of occult, you king of Gowda! Don't disturb the Emperor! I'm not a fish eater. However, we are pleased to grant you seven thousand crores for development of pisciculture – go. I will also go. It's time for my bath. Drive me to the bath room. *(The trumpets blow. The dog driven cart, is about to leave. Enters King of Kalinga with lots of gifts. The gift packets are held by the king of Kalinga and Seelabhadra, one of the ministers. Sheelabhadra has come with the king to introduce him.)*

King of Gowda: The King of Kalinga begs excuse for having entered into the palace of His Highness, greatest of the greatest of the greatest, the valiant and the kind!

Vajrabahu: (Stops his dog driven wagon, turns and gets down)

Yes, we have excused! Who's this young man Sheelabhadra? What are those packets?

Seela bhadra: He's the king of Kalinga. He has brought these gifts for you Your Majesty. His country has declared emergency.

Vajrabahu: What emergency? Keep those gifts inside. (He Keeps the gifts inside)

King of Gowda: Political instability. Fiscal bankruptcy!

Seela bhadra: Why? Two emergencies at a time?

King of Kalinga: Gang rapes of women-Social instablility.

Seela bhadra: They have sold their skies and mountains and rivers and the personal treasuries of the politicians are filled

Vajrabahu: Our minister knows about your problems. Tell me only about the urgent problem if any!

King of Kalinga: It is raining there without any cloud your majesty.

Vajrabahu: Rains without cloud? What do you mean?

King of Kalinga: Yes your Highness! We have seen sixty five floods and thirty cyclones during the 25 years of your reign! Floods are there everywhere!

Vajrabahu: How was it not known to us?

Seela bhadra: I know about it. But why should I report it to your majesty? "Floods in kalinga" is a cheap news.

King of Kalinga: Half of Kalinga is drowned under water

Vajrabahu: It's a grave affair. We should shed tears, but today is my beard shaving ceremony... I can't shed tears. However we express our deep regrets for that.

King of Kalinga:Floods occur there in tanks and wells, in water pipes and tube wells... everywhere there is flood.

Vajrabahu: Sheelabhadra! Call the painters of Hastina! Let them paint the scenes of devastation on my court wall! We'll look at them and mourn tomorrow!

Seela bhadra: The fame of your highness will spread as a great sympathiser of floods. The posterity would know that his highness has expressed his deep sorrow!

Vajrabahu: My mood is off now for the floods in Kalinga! Call the Vidoosakas!

Seela bhadra: Vidoosakas! "Vidoosakas!" where are you?

Vajrabahu: Come soon. My eyes are in tears.

(The vidoosakas appear with choked voices)

Vidoosaka-I: No your majesty! Don't Cry.

Vidoosaka-II: We will cry for you!

Vidoosaka-I: If you cry, there will be a flood of tears in Hastina city.

King Kalinga: Then only you shall realize the depth of the tragedy

Vidoosaka-I: Then imagine that the flood has entered Hastina.

Vajrabhu: (Frigtened) No!

Vidusaka-II: It has already entered. It has come to Hastina with the king of Kalinga. (*The Vidoosakas would pelt the following short dialogues and try to create a psychedelic delirium in Vajrababu's mind. They may play the stick or any other instrument with fast rhythm to enhance the effect*)

Vidusaka-I: The Rivers of Hastina have gone bersek

Vidusaka-II: Everywhere there's flood

Vidusaka-I: Floods, floods, floods

Vidusaka-II: Have blown our heads

Vidusaka-II: I' am terribly frightened.

Vidusaka-II: Hold me, tightened.

Vidusaka-I: Everywhere rains

Vidusaka-II: Houses are in ruins

Vidusaka-I: People are drowned

Vidusaka-II: Fields are inundated

Vidusaka-I: Schools are drowned

Vidusaka-II: Townships drowned!

(*The vidoosakas recreate a scene of war and emergency*)

Vidusaka-I: Our city of Hastina will be drowned.

The City faces a great devastation; save us from a ruin.

[Enters Brahmadutta]

Brahmadutta: What has happened? What has happened?

Silabhadra: Hastina is ruined

Vidusaka-II: Our city is flooded.

Brahmadutta: We are lovers of mankind.

Vajrabahu: I will tame these rivers.

Seelabhadra: How your majesty? How?

Vajrabahu: We will construct a roof over the state.

Brahmadutta: Roof over the State? Five hundred thousand *yojanas* of length! seven hundred thousand *yojanas* in breadth!

Vajrabahu: Not a drop of water should fall into the rivers. No flood's allowed.

Seelabhadra: Such a big roof we need. What is the budget needed?

Vajrabahu: Let the entire treasury be drained we don't care! We will control the flood.

Brahmadutta: Ask the ministry of Announcements. Let them beat the drums. We will build this giant umbrella roof over the state's sky. Close all the Gurukul Ashramas. All the Rishis and Acharyas will carry bricks and cement and stones.

Seelabhadra: We will announce it today.

Brahmadutta: His Majesty's brain is out of order. He is suffering from extreme hunger.

Seelabhadra: We will lead him to dinner.

Vajra bahu: You have rightly read my mind! we'll go to the dinner

Ask the prince of Kalinga. He will also have his dinner with me.

Seelabhadra: King of Kalinga: you follow Emperor! Have your hunger appeased.

Brahmadutta: Your Majesty!

Vajrabahu: Our court is adjourned we will go with the Prince of Kalinga (*Vajrabahu, King of Kalinga and The vidusakas go. Lights off.*

SCENE-VIII

Music

Lights come up slowly. We discover a new comer sitting on one of the blocks. He is fully fair looking, as white as snow. Bright costumes. A bag hangs from his shoulder. He is a merchant from a foreign country. He pronounces all "S" sounds as "cha"

Merchant: (*Looking at the audience*)

Hello! cha-cha-chu-chu-chi chi! I was waiting here in darkness. I want to meet the Emperor of Hastina. Well, I am not from Hastina – I am almost an Indian! I am a red-Indian! I am a merchant, I trade in art and culture and dreams. My country is rich in dream culture. But where is the king? Why does this country run in darkness? Are you saving electricity? The streets of Hastina are full of thieves (*Sound of thieves running*) Jackels howl (*Sound of Jackels*) A woman was gang raped (Shrill cry of the raped woman) I moved away from the scene and entered into the palace. But no one is here! Ah! here is one! Some one is coming here!

(Brahmadutta enters)

Brahmudutta: Hello! I am Brahmadutta! Minister of Education and culture.

Merchant: Cha-cha, Chu-chu-chichi-I am a merchant from Red Indian country. I trade in art and culture and dreams, I want to start global market relationship with your country! Can I meet the King, please?

Brahmadutta: You can meet him in the midnight in the garden of entertainment. It is not yet midnight!

Merchant: Okay! Two minutes more!

(Seelabhadra arrives)

Seelabhadra: Good midnight gentle man. Brahmadutta! Is he the visitor who wants to meet the king? Hello!

Merchant: Chacha...chu...chu...chi...chi!!

Brahmadutta: He is Seelabhadra! Our Minister of finance and constructions; and this is the visitor from the Red Indian country. He trades in art and culture and dreams.

Sheelabhadra: I got the news from the Emperor. He would be arriving now. Emperor Vajrbahu is the incarnation of divinity in a human being. He knows a great deal about art and culture!

Merchant: But why are the streets dark today?

Brahmadutta: Our people despise bright light; they prefer to do everything in darkness! Darkness is pure here. There is no adulteration.

Merchant: Selling dreams in darkness in convenient. Can I meet the queen, Minister of Finance and construction?

Seelabhadra: You can take her appointment...

Merchant: How can it be done?

Seelabhadra: The honorable queen has two sakhis (friends): Marigold and Zinia. They are like fragrant flowers blooming in darkness. I will introduce you to them!

The trumpets blow up. The emperor emerges through the Sada Daruka.

Seelabhadra: Victory to his majesty, mighty Emperor of Emperors, invincible and indomitable, owner of seven million square miles of land, Sri Sri Sri invested with one hundred eight srees Vajrabahu enters his court!

Brahmadutta: Victory to the warrior of frontier wars, Parama Vira Chakra, Friend of the Red Indian Chieftain, profound scholar of Gandharba Veda, Owner of all arts and culture and dreams arrives at his court. (Trumpets and Pipes)

Merchant: Cha cha-chuchu-chi chi

Vajrabahu: Who's this chi-chi-chi? What does he say?

Brahmadutta: That's the way he greets you your majesty. He is a merchant and he trades in art and culture.

Merchant: We have heard very high of Hastina's art and culture. We want to buy some of them.

Vajrabahu: Art and culture? What's that? We have lots of agriculture and pisciculture. But art...and...Culture, what would you do with that?

Merchant: We would make fusion art with them. We would mix your art with ours and prepare fusions and convergence art. Instead, we'll sell you dreams. Rich dreams; fertile dreams. You can buy some for your domestic use.

Seelabhadra: Yes your majesty 'Our country does not produce dreams. We are sterile that way.

Vajrabahu: Okay! Can you plant dreams in our palace?

Merchant: It'll be my pleasure your majesty! Here is a small gift from our country.

(Presents a bottle of wine) well, where do you want me to plant the dreams, my majesty?

Vajrabahu: Ministers, look to the administration of the court I'm taking this gentleman inside the place. Come with me!

(Vajrabahu exits through sada Daruka with the merchant)

Seelabhadra: Brahmadutta! Why did you allow this foreigner to go inside the palace? The king will be duped. May be betrayed.

Brahmadutta: How can I help it? I am not responsible for that.

Seelabhadra: Who entertained this foreigner inside the palace? You! you have.

Brahmadutta: Don't put the blame an me

Seelabhadra: These days we find all such weird characters around the palace! Why should they enter into the palace? They should not know our secrets. You should have prevented the king from committing blunders like this.

Brahmadutta: You should have prevented the king from the plan of constructing a roof over Kalinga's sky to prevent the rain water. Who permitted you to close the Gurukulas? Who permitted you to engage the Acharyas for carrying bricks and stones?

Seelabhadra: What are they doing in the Gurukulas? They don't bring any profit to the nation. They are not productive people, after all.

Brahmadutta: Minister of finance! You will be held responsible for the rain of Hastina.

Seelabhadra: I have to look to the interest of the Emperor. He wanted to build a roof over the sky.

Brahmadutta: Our duty is to guide him.

Seelabhadra: The emperor's orders are sacred for me!

Brahmadutta: The emperor of Hastina is not sacred. He is impotent! That's why this land is arid. The sky vomits fire and the city is barren.

Seelabhadra: Don't get upset. You are the minister of this country's culture. I will give you some imported drinks brought from foreign country. Come with me! Don't break your head for the king's follies! Let the country go to hell. What's that to you! After all we are employees here. Let the country of Hastina go to hell with the king. Come with me. Drink with me and forget these mundane worries.

Both of them booze*Seelabhadra takes Brahmadutta inside.*

SCENE – IX

Soft music, dreamy choral humming creating an eerie atmosphere. Light focuses on the cage in which there is a myna. Ketakigandha enters, reaches the cage where the toy myna hangs. She softy speaks in an incantatory, recitative voice.

Ketakigandha: Oh, my dearest myna!
What' d happen to this dynasty?
Would the lineage be blocked here
and the towers of plenitude burnt

into ashes with my hot breath of sex?
Would I have to wait for ages
Like a storm whirling in summer?
The sky is cruel,
There are thunders and lightening
No rains
What a curse befell this land?

[The king, Vajrabahu appears in the Sada Daruka like a phantom. His voice echoes: lights focus and defocus alternatively. It should appear as if the presence of the king is a figment of Ketakigandha's dream. Lighting should be done accordingly)

Vajrabahu: *(His voice reverberates)*

Don't be amazed, my queen
My voice is an echo; I am
a phantom without a body.
A mind I do have, without dreams
I am living in the fire house of power.
I am the harbinger of a golden era
And the dispenser of endless nights
of dreams stretching for thousand miles.
The emperor can't procreate, my dear queen
He is divine, beyond all creations

Ketaki: Why did you deprive me of the creation?
I need an iota of dream.
The dream of a green landscape and spring

(The maids appear: Zinia and Marigold, Music and rhythm for their choreographed stepping)

Zinia: Why is her majesty in paleness and gloom

Ketaki Void.
Despite all this affluence I burn
in the cauldron
Of an unpromising night.

Zinia: I know.

This naughty moon has warmed you up

Marigold: And her majesty's nerves are worked up
Ah! Anguish only
build up a sky
Do you grope for something already lost?

Ketaki: Yes my dear!
Every thing is empty
Like the hunger of famine-stricken land.

Zinia: Tell us frankly if you have lost
Anything of the past
We'll bring it to you

Ketaki: Can you fetch me a handful of cries
From a new born babe?
Can you curse me
With the pain of child birth?

Marigold: Why don't you sleep for a while
You'll feel better.

Ketaki: Sleep?
Where is that flower born?
What is the colour of its petals?
Sleep!
Where's that drowned?
In which forbidden Sea?

Zinia: Do you need dreams my dear?
Tell us frankly

Ketaki: Please! fetch me some dreams!

Marigold: There has come from abroad a merchant,
Seller of dreams
He has a flute that makes women mad
He has come with a body full of dreams
His body smells like a *champak* tree

Zinia: He is merchant of dreams
He vends it endless and limitless

Marigold: He gives as much as you need

Zinia: But he'd take his price

Ketaki: I can bargain my body
My whole entity
What more do I have?
I will give me heart, my love
My tears and warm sighs
Let him fill me with dreams

Marigold: Alright! Stand here,

Close your eyes

Ketaki: Then?

(A sound of flute)

Zinia: Can you hear him?

(Choral humming)

Ketaki: There's an earth quake within me.

Marigold: Close your eyes and visualize. River Yamuna flows with her gurgling sound. Krishna comes with the sound of *"ghungur"* on his feet.

(The dream merchant enters from the Sada daruka area. The sound of his choeographed steps)

Ketaki: Is it the dream? (Closing her eyes)

Zinia: The beginning of a dream! (Then she calls)
Dream! Hey you dream! Come closer.
Closer to this arid land

Merchant: The dream merchant pays his regard!

(The queen opens her eyes. She is struck by the handsomeness of the Dream merchant)

Kdtaki: Are you a fallen angel?
Or the material shape
of my sleeping desire?
Who are you, Oh sweetness!
I welcome you
Into me; again and again

Merchant: Neither an angel
Nor worthily of your praise, O, Queen!
I am a servant of your desires
Selling dreams is my profession
Barren lands turn green
When I touch

(*Music. The words should be choreographed with music*)

A lotus would bloom in you
And you'll be transformed
A heart I need as price

Ketaki: A heart?
Where do I get such a thing?
Where's that heart O, Prince
It is petrified in this place.

Merchant: I've wandered throughout the world
Rivers have I crossed, oceans and valleys.
To reach this garden of dreams.

Marigold: Enough of talks you had.

Zinia: So much poetry in the beginning
Take out now your dream and inject
it into the queen

Marigold: Dream merchant. The queen feels restless. Be quick.

Zinia: Do what ever you want to do to sell her the dreams!
But don't make the prelude bigger.

[Music with choreographic rhythm is louder. The dream selling coitus-pose compositions of choreography shall be enacted with freezing montages of sculptural composition. The choreographer may include Zinia and Marigold if he feels comfortable. (*The theme of the dance should be like "Rati and Kandarpa dance" of the temple erotic sculptures. The dance should enact the erotic art of dream selling for not more than three or four minutes. colourful lighting and lilting music, fused with classical beats. We don't need a purely classical dance. Our artists can't learn it. Make it a convergence of classical and modern musical and choreographic stepping. The artists freeze and light fades slowly.*

SCENE-X

Full lights come and the announcer enters with his hanging drum and sticks. Drum beats

Announcer: Hark! Hark! Hark!! His highness, holy king Vajrabahu commands that his beard and mustaches shall be preserved hereafter in the state museum. The women folk of Hastina shall, hereafter, worship his beard and mustaches instead of stone idols.

(*Drum beats*)

Announcement number Two. Listen! Listen! His highness, Param Veera chakra, the most bold and courageous king has got the information that the Rishis and the Acharyas of the Gurukul Ashramas of Hastina have gone on a strike. They are not carrying any bricks and stones for construction of the greatest roof of the world-for the five hundred thousand yojanas length and seven hundred thousand yojanas breadth roof over the state of Kalinga. The rishis and Acharyas must know that this is dire flouting of the Emperor's orders. If they don't carry the bricks by the coming Sunday all Gurukul of the state shall be closed. They will bedismissed from their service. (*Drum beats*)

Announcement number three. His highness, bold and valiant, large hearted king Vajrabahu is pleased with the service of the Vidoosakas. He is further pleased to promote Vidoosaka No.1. as the Chief Secretary of the State. (*Drum beats*)

The announcer leaves the stage and the Vidoosakas No.1. and 2 enter from alternative sides.

Vidoosaka-I: Dearest Pal! I feel a great pain at heart when I think of quitting this palace.

Vidoosaka-II: But you are going on a promotion. Secretary of the state! You'll move to a palatial quarters.

Vidoosaka-I: But I will miss your intimate company... You are more precious to me than the quarters! I will never forget the joyous days we've spent together in the palace!

Vidoosaka-II: Thank you!

Vidoosaka-I: Tears come up to my eyes when I think of taking leave from you.

Vidoosaka-II: You are a big officer now. That's a great consolation!

Vidoosaka-I: If I have done any wrong to you unwittingly kindly forgive me! Pal (*His voice chokes in melodramatic tragedy*) won't you forgive me for the wrongs, if I would have committed?

Vidoosaka-II: My tears are welling up like an ocean in the full moon night!

Vidoosaka-I: (*Weeps with sound! Loudly*)

Vidoosaka-II: *(Weeps loudly as a reaction)*

(They embrace each other and weep loudly.

Light fades out)

SCENE-XI

Lights fade in slowly on the two ministers. Brahmadutta and seelabhadra. Both are seen boozing an over – dose of wine.

Brahmadutta: (intoxicated) Ha...Ha...Ha...Ha...!

Seelabhadra: Do you feel tipsy?

Brahmadutta: Seelabhadra! Where have you got this wine from?

Seelabhadra: Shhh...! speak slowly!

Brahmadutta: Why should I? Don't I have the right to speak loud? Drink wine? Who'll forbid me?

Seela bhadra: You are little high! Why don't you rest for a while? After each peg you have increasingly become a saint. You behave like a philosopher and a wise man. Wisdom is not necessary these days to operate as a minister!

Brahmadutta: Unfortunately, I am one of the wisest persons of this country.

Seela bhadra: Why do you brag unnecessarily? Aren't you aware of Emperor Vajrabahu's power?

Brahmadutta: He is a foolish autocrat! But how long would he fool along as an All powerful Earthen Pot? People have started agitations.They are revolting against the Emperor. Who is he to close all the Gurukulas?

Seela bhadra: The Rishis shall be hanged if they go on strike.

Brahmadutta: I will quit this foolish country before that!

Seela bhadra: You are ungrateful! Selfish!

Brahmadutta: All of you are corrupted. The Emperor is a lunatic! This is unbearable!

Seela bhadra: Brahmadutta! You are crossing the limits. I will arrest you! You will be tried before the emperor!

Brahmadutta: I don't care for that lunatic bragger!

Seela bhadra: No! I can't tolerate this from you unfaithful betrayer! I shall arrest you! You will be tried in the court of the emperor!

Brahmadutta: Ha, ha, ha, ha, ha! Do you think I care? Do I care for the sycophant minister of a foolish King?

Seela bhadra: *(Takes out his sword and raises it*

Freeze. Music.

Lights go off)

SCENE – XII

In darkness people shout slogans like "Down Down Vajrabahu" "step down Vajrabahu" "Foolish king-down down" "Mad King-down down". "Give food to hungry" men!" "Or we'll kill you down" "Give food, give clothes" "Give food to hungry lots!"

Lights bang up all on a sudden as an effect to the abrupt banging music in the background. As the lights boom quickly we find Vajrabahu marching with quick steps from left to right an right to left repeating it for ten times and seelabhadra on the "Sada Daruka" area is found to make feeble attempts to pacify the agitation and protest rally outside with touches of aggression and violence. Vajrabhu is in tension.

Vajrabahu Suddenly stops on the mid centre and shouts at Seelabhadra in an agitated voice:

Vajrabahu: (*Shouts*) Seelabhadra!

What is this? What's going on at the palace gate?

Seela bhadra: That's a protest really against your Majesty! Do you care for that? Send the army to kill them.

Vajrabahu: How dare they? How did they dare to protest against Emperor Vajrabahu? And why do they protest?

(*Brahmadutta comes from sada daruka area (from the back). He holds a stick.*) Who' is there? Brahmadutta!! What news you have brought from outside?

Brahmadutta: There's a big protest against you, your Highness. Around one thousand people shout slogans against you!

Vajrabahu: But I ask you, why?

Brahmadutta: Because they are hungry, These hungry men are in need of food. They ask for food from the Emperor.

Vajrabahu: But why are they hungry?

Brahmadutta: Hungry because there is a severe famine in the country. The land of Hastina has become sterile. There are lightning and thunders in the sky, but it doesn't rain. There have been no rains in Hastina far three continuous years!

Seela bhadra: They have not paid the revenue taxes this year. We have sent the tax collectors for three times.

Brahmadutta: Hell with your tax collectors! How would they pay you the tax when they are hungry? They could not harvest any crop this year.

Seela bhadra: The royal treasury is empty. That's why we could not sanction any grant for your education and culture heads.

Brahmadutta: Let the culture be blown with the wind!

Vajrabahu: We are not worried about your culture Brahmadutta, we are more concerned about agriculture!

Brahmadutta: Your Majesty's simple concern won't yield crops in the land, Emperor! Ten thousand people in Hastina have died of hunger. It is a disgrace to you!

Vajrabahu's reactions! Slogans are louder. "Give food for the hungry lot—you fool emperor!" "Down down Emperor! Shame Shame Emperor!" Vajrabahu is perturbed. All on a sudden the ghost of a hungry and dead man barges into the stage and asks in an agitated voice)

Dead man: Who's emperor Vajrabahu here?

Vajrabahu: (*Shouted*) Who are you? With whose permission you entered the court?

Seelabhadra: He is the emperor! Who are you?

Dead man: I am a dead man. I don't care for the living kings.

Vajrabahu: Strange! You talk and walk like a living man! How did you die? Why did you die? Tell me

Seela bhadra: Dying in our country is a serious offence.

Vajrabahu: Why did you die without my permission?

Seela bhadra: That's an offence!

Dead man: You could not provide me any food you misfit of a king! And a rascal of a Minister or whoever you are!

Vajrabahu: Strange! Ghosts and dead men have started a revolution against me! How could it happen in Vajrabahu's country!!

Brahmadutta: There's an inner force still retained in this dead man. The inner force stirs up his heart. That's how he appears here! It is the heart!

Vajrabahu: Heart! What's that commodity? How much of hearts we have in our royal treasury. Seelabhadra?

Brahmadutta: The heart is not a commodity your honour! The Westerners have commodified it.

Vajrabahu: The Westerners have done it! Then it must be a fine thing! The Heart! Seeelabhadra! Give an order and announce it. Ask the people to deposit their hearts in the royal treasury! We need hearts to destroy them.

Brahmadutta: That's the only thing the people of this hunger-ridden country do possess.

Dead man: Stop this nuisance! Stop this nonsensical talk minister! You are fools! Your Emperor is a greater fool.

Vajrabahu: Seelabhadra! Hang this man! Finish him! Guillotine him thrice!

Dead man: Ha, ha! Ha! (*Mythological laughter of hatred in Indian style*) you can punish me as much as you like. I do not bother! Once I am dead, I am beyond fear, I am beyond all sorts of regal tyranny you fool of an Emperor! You have to provide these hungry men food! Not punishment!

Brahmadutta: There are thousands of such hungry and dead men outside, Emperor! They'll break open the iron gate of the palace. They will enter into your court and rip you off. They will break this pot of power.

Vajrabahu: Brahmadutta "You seem to have excited them. You have insinuated this agitation!.

Brahmadutta: If no one takes the lead, I have to do that!

Vajrabahu: I will hang you first!

Brahmadutta: And before you do that I will break your power pot! Come here dead man! I have empowered you. Take this stick and break this power pot! Dead people don't care the power! Break the pot! Let me see what he can do!

(Brahmadutta gives his stick to the dead man. Music. The dead man goes and breaks the earthen pot into pieces!)

Brahmadutta: Emperor! Your power pot is broken. You are to step down now. You can't stick to your throne anymore! Step down now! Step down!

Dead man: Step down Emperor! Or, I will call all the hungry men of the country. They will chop you off. Cut your flesh and mince you into bits. They'll eat you up! Before this ugly thing happens, step down. We, the subjects of Hastina don't need you as our king!

Vajrabahu: Seelabhadra! You have misguided me all these years as my minister of finance you're dismissed now. Brahmadutta! (*Music. The king moves toward him*)

: I will give you 3 thousand Elephants, a million horses, two million golden coins! Save my throne!

Brahmadutta: King! I'm not selfish like you! I don't need golden coins! I don't need awards and honors. Look! Now my eyes are open. The only thing I need-is the death of this arbitrary rule I wish the victory of these hungry people…

They must be free from your tyranny!

Vajrabahu: Almighty! I'm ready to die.

Brahmodutta: Die quick. After the brains and hearts are sold, there's nothing left in this country. There's not a single human being left in this land! Every one is a beast, a savage! They will tear you up! Rip you off!! your body will be the fittest dinner for the hungry animals

Vajrabahu: Brahmo dutta!

Brahmodutta: Leave the throne. Pass an order that-you are dead! Get down! your power pot is broken now!

Vajrabahu: Yes! I will pass that order!

Music. Funeral band.

We, Vajrabahu, the king of Hastina, announce that today, in the last hour of this night, we appear to be the greatest sinner of this country. We shall bathe in the Viswesvar tank at the earliest hour of the dawn, and tour over the streets of Hastina; and then hang

Ourself at the busiest cross of the capital! Make arrangements for our death!

(Funeral trumpet sound.
Vajrabahu steps down one rung and freezes.
Brahmadutta rises one rung up and freezes.
Seelabhadra and the dead man are in their respective positions.
Back lights are up and the front lights fade out to create a Silhouette. Music continues)

****

WAITING FOR THE BUS

The play was performed for the first time on 14-10-1968 at Ganjam Kala Parishad, Berhampur, Odisha and was directed by late Prof.Narayana Satpathy and Dr.Surendra Prasad Das. Then it was staged at Annapurna Theatre, Buxibazaar, Cuttack in December, 1968 with the following cast:

Bichitrananda: Dr. Surendra Prasad Das

Gobinda Sahu: Dr. Sailendra Prasad Sahu

Gurubaria: Balakrishna Dash

Makundi: Achyutananda Praharaj

Chakradhara: Dr. Abhoy Mishra

Biswamohan: Dr. Madhab Chandra Miishra.

Atanu: Dr. Chhabindra Prasad Mohanty/Purna Chandra Rath

Surajit: Pramod kumar Dash

Dolagobinda: Shyama sundar Satpathy

Banya: Alpana Bose

Set and Lighting: Kedar Apte

: Gagan Pattanayak

Pradip Padhi

Ashok K. Padhi

Music: Prasanta chitta Sahu(kunu)

Singer: Dr. Bibekananda Mishra

Preface

The play was captioned *Mu, Ambhe –O-Ambhemane* (I, we, and All of Us) in Odia and was staged by the artists of Ganjam Kala Parishad, Berhampur on 14th October, 1968. Manoranjan Das's *Banahamsi* was staged in April, 1968 and Bijoy Mishra's *Saba bahaka Mane* was staged in June, 1968. These three plays stood against the clichéd, story-based melodramas of the six commercial repertoires that mostly toured over the length and breadth of Odisha for their survival. Manoranjan wrote about the devaluation of love and Vijay Mishra's play was a reconstruction of Ben Johnson's *Volpone.* Our motto was to produce naturalistic plays. I would prefer to classify them as a kind of soft-centered Naturalism. I did not accept naturalism as a mere attempt to create photographic reproduction of external reality. It is superficial. My aim was to present an existential, value-free, scientific and experimental exploration of reality in its widest possible sense including the subjective reality of the artists' temperament through which he perceives external reality.

This approach logically led to the rejection of already made formal conventions and implied the acceptance of organic form dictated by the nature of subject matter. Thus our naturalism opened the floodgates for a new stream of poetic possibilities in the theatre. Further, I have never sought to write plays that primarily tell a story; nor have I sought deliberately to create new forms. I have been most concerned with dramatizing something of the dynamism I myself find in human motivations and behavior.

I regard *Waiting for the bus* as a composition rather than a story; as a distillation of life rather than a narration of it. The characters of this play verge on the stereotype and gain their meaning from their total context of performance, but even thus they seem to resemble theirs is a world deprived of transcendence, with no spiritual dimension, no purpose to serve beyond a sexual impulse which is only momentarily liberating. They have dreams they unimposingly reach out toward something vaguely perceived, but never realize those dreams or embrace anything but human flesh which turns out to be the springing of a biological trap.

In the 1960s, then, the Odia theatre seemed to stir. It ceased to concern itself quite so much with the dramatization of the liberal conscience or the plight of the poetic sensibility forced back against the reality of an experience which was hinted at, but rarely presented.

We had two wars, one against China in 1962 and another against Pakistan in 1965. We lost two prime Ministers during the 1960s- Jawaharlal Nehru and Lalbahadur Sastri. The Nuxalbari leftist revolution on one hand and the rise of feminism on the other caused a topsy-turvy in the socio-economic-political sector and people clung to science laboratories for finding out authenticity and truth. But they, in India knew it pretty well that science fails to wipe out a drop of tear from the eyes of the suffering beings in times of calamity. Theatre bifurcated into two distinct streams: one that believed in capitalism and technocracy and highlighted individual psychology and explored the subconscious and unconscious terrains of the characters; the other that believed in socialist progressivism and aimed at portraying the dramatic conflicts concerning the individual and the society.

However, 1968 offered us a melting pot of diverse contradictory phenomenon, generating paradoxes. In a period of extraordinary and rapid change, with its attendant surprises and sufferings, it is no less true that in such a day all serious dramatic thought must try to find in it a pattern of sense. I have focused upon the concept of the real, suggesting a course of action in performance that is related to what is likely to be our experience in 1968, as distinct from what are our habits from the past multi-scene dramas of the commercial theatre houses. We chose to write one set plays with symbolic import based on different geographical locations.

In Ganjam Kala Parishad, Berhampur we involved non-professional actors and directors. They were mostly painters, musicians, dancers and sculptors. In one of our productions poets and left wing activists joined as actors in the theater workshop conducted by Dolagobind Rath, a gold medalist from the National School of Drama, New Delhi. One of the virtues of our amateur group was that it allowed us our own pace. We did not have to please the audience. As a playwright I no longer felt compelled to seek the endorsement of reputed commercial theatre companies. Berhampur provided us with a more receptive environment. However, the emergence of this *alternative theater* was of critical importance and its rapid expansion a sign of crucial changes in the economics and politics of culture. *Waiting for the bus* has been performed for about 1000 shows and its Hindi version was staged in the *Canmass* National Theatre Festival by an Amateur Team from Delhi, designed by Delhi based director Shri Raj Narayan Dixit. An actress from Malayasia was in the leading female role.

Ramesh P. Panigrahi

SCENE-1

Morning in a suburban bus stop: It is a small bus stop and is less crowded. On the "right-up" there is a small tea joint. Gobind Sahu, the owner of the shop has gone to the pond behind his shop for morning ablutions. A crow continuously caws from the branch of a banyan tree under which Gobind Sahu's tea stall is built. In the absence of the owner, his adolescent son Gurubaria (but he behaves like a ten years old kid) is looking after the shop. There are no customers and Gurubaria is playing a kind of hop step-and-jump solo game of rural Odisha. A minute after the stage is lit, Makundi, a middle aged rural barber arrives and asks for a small glass of tea. He spreads a tattered gunny bag on the floor and sharpens his knife on a whetstone. Gurubaria comes to Makundi with a small glass of tea; keeps it nearby and requests:

Gurubaria: Graze your knife a little on my cheek, Maku Dada! Do it quickly. Otherwise papa will come and lash his tongue! I'll give another glass of tea free.

Makundi: Hmm; but there is no beard on your cheek.

Gurubaria: There is some, Dada. Once you start shaving you will know it; apply that cream and work out a rich lather first. The razor would run smooth. Then dress up my cheek with that sweet smelling after-shave lotion. You may exclude my mustaches

Makundi: Why should I work that long procedure on your adolescent face where there is no sign of hair?

Gurubaria: Because I will go to Nehru Palli today to attend to that great convention.

Makundi: What will you gain from that convention? That is for the political folks.

Gurabaria: No. That is our Eden of bliss, a customer said. Everybody from our nearby villages goes to Nehrupalli today. Your fate will metamorphose if you go there! You will get whatever you wish!

Makundi: What magic is spelled in Nehrupalli? Is Mr. Nehru Coming there?

Gurabaria: The professor was telling that if you attend to this mighty convention people will live in simple contentment, free from ambitions and strife. So, I will also go to Nehrupalli by the next bus. Graze your razor fast. I must look smart.

Makundi: We in our times, when the struggle for freedom was going on, knew Jawaharlal Nehru. He was a great *desi* sahib who inserted Gandhi in one pocket of his coat and Jinnah in another. Tell me now what is your ambition in life?

Garubaria: To catch two large fishes every day from this pond. If I will go to Nehrupalli and listen to the inspiring speech of the leader all my dreams shall be fulfilled. Why don't you go and try your luck?

Makundi: I have no trust in politics. Politicians and apparently sycophantic bureaucrats run this nation. I am a barber with no ambitions in my quest. Why should I go?

Gurubaraia: You are true to some extent, Dadi. You shave the cheeks of the people and help them look gentlemen. But how many of them become real gentlemen of free India?

(Enter Gobind Sahu, Gurubari's father. He has taken bath in the nearby tank and enters with wet towel and lungi. He feels irritated looking at Gurubari shaving his cheeks)

Gobind: Rascal! I told you to keep an eye over the shop, not to shave and apply face creams! Why should you allow running a shaving razor on your adolescent cheeks? Not only unnecessary; it is an illicit luxury… spoiling the smoothness of the skin of your face.

(Gurubaria runs away, wipes his face and sits on the stool like a sincere shop keeper. Gobind hangs the wet clothes on a line behind his thatched tea shop shadowed by the big banyan tree on the banks of the huge pond.)

Makundi: There is nothing to be serious at cropping and trimming our growing beard. Your son is growing up into a fresh young man.

Gobind: Hmm! This is called a "barber's" mind set. A boy of twenty is not supposed to use a barber's knife. Don't you know that? This rascal is having the itch of the city-based-fashion of the day.

Makundi: You are unnecessarily getting indignant about his facial, Gobind Bhai. Today he is going to Nehrupalli convention.

Gobind: Nonsense! Why should you go and attend that political meeting?

Gurubaria: I will have a *darshan* of the great political leader.

Gobind: Have you gone ever to the Jagannath Temple nearby to have a *darshan* of the God? Have you ever?

Gurubaria: Lord Jagannath never fulfills all our wishes. The political leader, on the other hand, would show us the short cut to Paradise! Do you know that Bapa?

Gobind: I don't believe in political superstitions. Empty assurances are conventional in political speeches. But why do you need a short cut to the political paradise? It is a utopia.

Gurubaria: Utopias are necessary Bapa! Dreams, however foggy they are, necessary in our times.

Gobind: But you must be ready to pay the price for following your dreams.

Gurubaria: But I am also thinking: to what extent our dreams can be manipulated?

Makundi: Would you give me a glass of tea or shall I come after some time?

Gobind: Why don't you give him his due Gurubaria? Wait a minute Makundi, Let me change first. I asked this rascal to keep the oven live. He went to graze his beard instead.

Gurubaria: No, I was just scraping my cheeks.

Gobind: Hell with you. Your oven is put off. Flare the flame first. *(Looking at somebody at a distance, speaks loudly)*

Mohanty Babu! Where are you going? To Cuttack or Nehrupalli?

Mohanty: *(from behind the wings)* Nehrupalli:

(Chakradhar Parida, a famous pettit politician of the area enters, looks behind at Mohanty and responds:)

Chakradhar: I am also going to Nehrupalli Mohanty; we will meet there again. What did you say? *(Chakradhar runs back to Mr. Mohanty, an invisible villager)*

Makundi: Pour your glass of tea in the kettle, Gobinda Bhai, I am going.

Gobind: Wait a moment. It's prepared.

Makundi: Chaki Parida has come. I won't look at his face, inauspicious fellow.

(Makundi exits quickly and dashes inadvertently with Chakradhar Parida who was coming from outside. Makundi runs away with his shaving kit).

Chakradhara: Sahu! This suburban bus stand is infested with barbers and tea-sellers.

Gobind: Namaskar Sir! Kindly be seated.

Chakradhar: Prepare a special glass of tea for me. What about the special bus plying toward Nehrupalli?

Gobind: No Sir! The special bus has not yet come.

Chakradhar: Thank God, I am not in power. Had it been 1952, when I was the minister of Transports, things would have been different. I feel like lodging a complaint to the commissioner of Transportation about delays in rural bus service. Leave it! How is it that you are alone in the shop? Where has the boy gone?

Gobind: Went astray Parida Sir! Does not care for my advice

Chakradhar: That is the new generation; It's the new fangled mindset, to disregard elders and to flout civil norms.

Gobind: He has gone to Nehrupalli today.

Chakradhar: What for? He can't understand that the policy of the new government is to promise paradises, to sell lofty dreams. This is all talk and no work. It ruins this nation. I have been studying this phenomenon of cheating and blasphemy since 1952, when I was the transport minister…..

Gobinda: (*Cutting him short*) Here's your tea sir!

Chakradhar: (*Sips a little and blows it off*) Tschhi…. Tschhi…. Tschhi…. What is this tea? Have you boiled banyan leaves instead of tea? Besides the tea is too hot to burn the tip of my tongue.

Gobind: Everybody likes hot tea Sir! This is pure Assam Tea, not banyan leaf. Tea should be served hot.

Chakradhara: That does not mean that I will gulp fire! Ah! Gobinda! Your tea smells.

Gobind: Smells of what sir?

Chakradhara: Smells of bed bugs.

Gobind: How can it be possible sir? This brand of Lipton tea smells like crushed bed bug? I can't blame the tea company.

(*Chakradhara gets up displeased, puts the half drunk glass on the bench and says*:

Chakradhar: Tschhi, Tschhi! What a rotten stuff you have given me as tea!! Write my name in the credit account. I don't have changes with me. (*He hollers some unseen traveler roaming in the bus stand vicinity*) Hello there! Behera Babu! Hold on for a moment……!

(*He runs toward the invisible Behera Babu. Instead of Behera Babu enters an old man of fifty eight. He is recently superannuated from his job as a school teacher. He Is Biswamohan*)

Biswamohan: Would you please give me a glass of water?

Gobind: Only water Sir? Nothing else? If you order I will fry some vadas for you.

Biswamohan: No, No, I have not yet brushed my teeth. Travelled the entire night…. from Bhubaneswar to this place. I need to reach my home first. My wife was sick.

Gobind: Shall I make a glass of tea for you Sir? Aren't you the Headmaster of Nuapada M.E.School, Sir?

Biswamohan: Yes I am retired now. But the pension papers are not ready. I'm running through financial hardship without any pension and salary. That's why I had been to Bhubaneswar! Okay, give me some tea!

Gobind: Here is your glass of tea Sir. (*He hands over the glass*) Taste it sir. Is it bad?

Biswamohan: No, it is alright. What's the matter?

Gobind: There's a tout called Chakradhar Parida roaming around this bus stand. He tells my tea smells of bed bugs.

Biswamohan: No, no. Your tea is good (*He drinks the tea and keeps the glass on the tea table*).

Gobind: These touts and once-upon-time Ministers are blatant liars Sir! They adulterate all eatables, mix pebbles in rice and oil in ghee; nobody questions them since they are political folks. They'd put flies and cockroaches into your food and induce food poisoning.

(*As Gobind Sahu delivers this speech enters a middle aged lunatic with a tattered dress and unkempt beard on his checks. Somebody has given him a five gallon cow boy hat and he puts it on. He holds a pet cat on one hand and a cheap glass on the other. He goes to Gobind Sahoo marching, stands in front of him and salutes; while the passengers waiting for the bus are staring at this new comer intently. The person, who appears like a lunatic is Vichitrananda, aged about sixty five with black and white beard.*)

Vichitrananda: Good morning boss! Your speech on post colonial corruption was good. You are right. The *Netas* are insensitive to the deeper and more complex areas of human emotion and belief.

Gobind: Take your quota of tea, professor! Would you like to eat some hot *pakodas?* Take some (*He gives some tea and a leaf-made plate of pakodas. Vichitrananda exits from the stage for a while. This time he goes toward the large tank behind Gobind sahu's tea joint. Biswamohan advances few steps following Vichitrananda and comes back*)

Gobind: Do you know this man Sir?

Biswamohan: I've seen him several times on this bus stop.

Gobind: He is very wise and a learned man Sir! Speaks Latin and French

Biswamohan: I didn't know. But how has he gone insane?

Gobinda: That's a long story Sir, People say that this man was a professor in Utkal University. He was married and used to live a cozy and comfortable life. All on a sudden his wife eloped with somebody to Mumbai. Since that day he was disheartened and despondent and gradually his cognitive faculties were impaired. He distributes his pension money to the poor and the needy and lives with this pet pussy, that little soft furry thing!

Biswamohan: Oh! How sad! What's he doing here on this bus stand? How does he live by?

Gobind: He lives on his wits. People help him and he helps people. Our villagers still call him 'professor' and he moves here freely.

(*Vichitrananda returns from the tank side and asks Gobinda Sahu*)

Vichitrananda: Your tea joint is the nicest territory I've had yet. I'd kind a like to settle here for a while. Any objection, Gobind?

Gobinda: No, Professor, Kindly be seated.

(*Vichitrananda sits on the bench, eats pakodas and feeds to the pussy. This time he gets up and moves across the stage.*)

Bichitra: Eat hot *pakodas* pussy cat and wag your tail. Remember! We live in a different society. We live in a time when obedience counts, not the ability. Those who are able can lead a civilization; those who live without any spine – they obey.

(*Biswamohan listens to what Vichitra says, gets interested, goes little closer and watches him. As Bichitra looks at him, Biswamohan feels flustered and nervy.*)

Biswamohan: Namaskar!

Bichitra: Namaskar!

Biswamohan: I am highly impressed by your erudition. I have never found as knowledgeable a person as you in this rural bus stop.

Bichitra: Direct flattery. All direct approaches are prohibited in our society. You should be sneaky and back-biting…….. If you want to butter me, do it sneakily. Subterfuge your advances and poison me slowly. Otherwise you can't succeed. Ha, ha.

Biswamohan: I was a poor teacher sir. Not been able to get my pension money after retirement. I went to Bhubaneswar to meet the Minister. They didn't allow me to see him. I came back spending all my money. Still I have kept my mouth shut Sir! The government officers may kill my family. That also I would tolerate, but I can't revolt.

Bichitra: That's right. You have to keep your mouth shut if you are after success. Success comes only to the mute and the reticent.

Biswamohan: I stand up to the depths of despair and bitterness with stubborn hope. I feel strongly that it is also a kind a tyranny; tyranny of the political dictators. They perpetrate a reign of terror like they do in totalitarian states.

Bichitrananada:That is inevitable in a milieu inflicted with loss of religious faith and the depletion of inherited cultural values; encroaching industrialization and the growth of the "expendable" society.

Biswamohan: That's right Sir. They think that nothing will happen if a poor teacher named Biswamohan Pradhan would die without getting his pension money. This is the destination of the expendable society. The society does not care for deaths in our families. They treat us like rats and vermin. Where does this society move?

Bichitrananda: It moves through tunnels and alley ways leading through the rubbish to dark and filthy homes of sickness.

(*Drum beats signifying the procession carrying a dead body to the funeral ground is heard. Gobind pays heed to it and goes to rear stage.*)

Gobinda: Somebody is dead in the village, Sir?

Biswamohan: (*He is shocked*) who's it? Who's dead Gobinda?

Gobinda: Might be somebody Sir. They are carrying the corpse to the graveyard and they'd burn it there. We'll ask them to which funeral ground they are taking it.

Biswamohan: My wife Kanak was very feeble and indisposed when I started for Bhubaneswar. God knows what has happened to her!

Gobinda: Nothing unlucky and vile would happen to her Sir. God always helps the ill-fated folks.

Biswamohan: Does He? (*He sighs helplessly. The drum beats come closer and a procession follows.*)

Makundi: (*The barber comes running out of the procession and says to Gobinda, while the drummer stops playing it*)

Makundi: They were carrying the lady to the hospital. She died on the way.

Gobinda: Who is that lady?

Makundi: Wife of some school teacher of Nuapada village.

Biswamohan: (*Shocked*) which Nuapada?

Makundi: Bishnupur Nuapada Sir! It was a pathetic death. Her husband was not at home; had gone to Bhubaneswar to expedite his pending pension case. The eldest son was at home. He is only twenty years old. The other four are kids. They were confounded and weeping helplessly.

(*Among the two front corpse-bearers was Biswamohan's twenty years old son. The corpse was carried on a stretcher by four people. A mourner holds a thick rope made of rolled up hay. Fire is enkindled at one end, but it emits smoke and the stage is shrouded with smoke. Biswamohan stands in front of the procession. The twenty year old son discovers Biswamohan and wails:*)

Son: Bapa! (*He weeps loudly. Biswamohan goes to him, lends his shoulder to hold the stretcher-like carrier of the corpse. There is a choral humming with the refrain "Ram Naam Satya hai" The procession passes by. Bichitrananda stands up and salutes Biswamohan who now joins as a corpse-bearer. The procession again proceeds toward the tank behind the tea stall*)

Bichitrananda: Pussy Cat! Can you see this great hero of our expendable society? He is a real solider in war-field of life; one of the best soldiers of our country. I bow down to you soldier! I salute you.

(*Choral humming continues. Enters Chakradhar Parida from outside and feels annoyed of the smoke*)

Chakradhar: Oh, Gobinda Sahu! Hell with your oven! Why has this smog settled here? Is it from your oven? The smoke suffocates me. What happened to the bus that would take us to our utopia? Hello! Gobind! What happened to the bus destined for utopia?

Gobinda: Gone to hell! (Pause)It hasn't come yet! You've to wait, may be, till when I don't know.

Chakradhar: The hope is receding farther and farther. The seventh heaven can never be reached. Everything in our country is vestigial since 1952, when I was the transport minister!

(*He discovers Bichitrananda standing frozen in saluting position looking toward the grave yard located behind the tank in up – right stage. The choral humming is repeated once.*)

Chakradhar: Hello! May I help you Sir?

Bichitrananda: (*Casts a sharp look at Chakradhar and comes closer to him after turning back*) Help? What kind of help? Fiscal? Spiritual? Social? What kind of help you can render? Who are you by the by?

Chakradhar: I'm Chakradhar Parida, former Minister of Transportation Department in 1952 and now a Socio-political worker. You may call me a politician.

Bichitrananda: Oh my! More than half a century in politics, that means a long life of hypocrisy and guilt?

Chakradhar: Yes, Since 1952. I have not seen Mahatma Gandhi and Nehru. But I garland their photos and worship them burning incense sticks in front of them

Bichitrananda: G.B.S. once said politics is the last resort of a scoundrel. You don't seem to be one though. Any way, how many parties you've changed in your life time?

Chakradhar: I believe in monogamy, I believe in a single party membership and in a single ideologue.

Bichitrananda: What is that ideologue?

Chakradhar: I live by scavenging and exploiting the weakness and folly of others. There is only one moral principle- SURVIVE.

Bichitrananda: Any way! It is either by killing others or by encroaching others' territories; gunning school children and polluting river beds. You SURVIVE, okay! But why don't you let others to survive?

Chakradhar: I didn't commit any of the crimes you mentioned. I have never eked out any precarious existence for any one in my village woods and meadows. Yet these trustless people found no usefulness in me, in my social service; they have rejected me in the last election. What a dangerous society we inhabit!

Bichitrananda: This society is like a retarded child with a machine gun in its hand. We are managing to survive in a world full of predators by cunning and smooth tongue.

Chakradhar: Arrest those sweet tongued hypocrites. But how can you? People know you on this cross as the "pussy-cat man". They think you've taken leave of your senses. *(Background Music)*

Bichitrananda: I have not taken leave of my senses-friends! My memory is still very strong. Fifteen years back, I had a handsome physique and a fairly acceptable visage. I was not in such rags. I was well clad and I served as an assistant professor in Ravenshaw College*(pause)* I had a wife whom I loved ardently *(pause)* but suddenly one day, when I returned from the college I found a letter or my table (*He takes out a tattered letter from a bundle of papers tucked into his pocket. He reads the letter holding it in his trembling hands and the voice of his wife is posted.)*

Female Voice: I was honest with you so long. But I am feeling now I am reaching the limit. I had enough of shopping and the tea parties and the ghastly television programs that I watched while waiting for you to come home from work. Today, when you come back from college, "you will not find me at home. I am going away from you, running away from your dreamless days to a distant sky forever". Good-bye!

Chakradhar: Did your wife come back ever?

Bichitrananda: Never after that, I never tried to find her address.

Chakradhar: Are you normal? Is your conscience troubling you? Have you done, something you shouldn't have?

Bichitrananda: Nothing I have done to search for her. I have no regrets now. It is too late to begin again. So, with this beard and this pussy cat I am trying to stay cool, to stay normal.

Chakradhar: What's normal in you?

Bichitrananda: Normal is anything that makes you forget who you are and what you want, that way we can work in order to produce, reproduce and make money. I don't need money. I need to live by my lost dreams.

Chakradhar: Since 1952 Sir, People say you have one thing in your mind, your ex-wife Shakuntala. You are handsome, rich and effortlessly personable---but she left you for a fashionable poet and it is a sting you never recovered from.

Bichitrananda: Yes, I've recovered. I may be a man of rare intensity and cold intelligence but I trust this pussy cat. She possesses nine lives and symbolizes a fresh start. My pussy cat is a symbol of good luck. My white cat is resilient and will enable me to get my Shakuntala back.

Then I shall do some research on her dreams. Ah! I'm tired. Gobinda Sahu!

Gobinda: Yes Professor!

Bichitrananda: Can I sleep here on your bench for some time?

Gobinda: You may get disturbed here! There is another bench on the backside…There! You may go there!

Chakradhara: It seems you didn't have a sleep last night.

Bichitrananda: And yet I planned to catch the bus for Nehrupalli.

Chakradhara: But the bus won't come. We are waiting in vain. You can go and sleep there professor! But what will happen to your pussy cat?

Bichitrananada: Nothing, It's an obedient creature, it sleeps all the time or at least it seems to sleep.

(*He goes out of sight to sleep on the hidden bench*)

Gobinda: Yes Professor, you may take rest here. I am closing the shop I must go home. (*He prepares to pack his essential gadgets*)

Chakradhar: Buses are most unreliable in our state. This special bus was scheduled to arrive at 7.30 in the morning. This is 7.30 in the "evening"! Still we hope that the bus'll come!

Gobinda: Do you need another cup of tea?

Chakaradhar: No I will go home. There is a Panchayat meeting.

(*He exits, Gobinda also exits annoyed*)

Gobinda: This rascal Gurubaria's fishing expedition is not yet over. God knows what fish he is catching. (*calls at him loudly*) Gurabaria! Hey you perennial fool! Get drowned in the pond, I'm going.

(*Gobinda Sahu exits. Evening smoke shrouds the stage. A pale moon gets up the horizon. Background music is eerie. The entire atmosphere is also spectral and spooky. A choral humming constituted of male and female voices is heard. In the pale moonlight, Shakuntala emerges from amidst the smoke and walks as if in dream searching for her divorced husband Bichitrananda.*

Bichitrananda takes out his wig and beard and transforms himself into a young man of thirty five. Shakuntala advances toward sleeping Bichitrananda, wakes him up into a flash back of young days. They walk shoulder to shoulder and more toward down stage. Lights change.)

Bichitra: Listen! I've seen a dream today. We' have grown fabulously rich. We're moving from mall to mall for shopping in a big car; the costliest one.

Shakuntala: Ha! A dream is a dream, not a reality. How can you buy a car that costs fifty lakhs? Don't I know how insolvent a vagabond you are!

Bichitra: You are ridiculing me. This is a disrespectful banter.

Shakuntala: No. Most of the rich persons of today were once riding green model Hercules bicycles. But now Junk food sellers have become five star hoteliers. You are the only person who shows apathy toward money.

Bichitra: Today's millionaires were once-upon-a-time burglars; some of them were selling boiled peanuts in master canteen cross. Fate favored them…. A special providence preserved them from catastrophe……. Don't worry! When fortune's keys will open the box of our good luck we'll overtake them in the race.

Shakuntala: Why should the goddess of fortune show you a favor? What prayers do you recite? Which god you pray? You've never uttered a mantra in your life time.

Bichitra: What wrong did I commit? I don't touch chicken or fish on Mondays and Thrusdays; reciting *Hanuman Chalisa* every Tuesday and Saturday. What more shall I do? Perhaps the Goddess knows that I am an under-sized employee…, hence she is niggardly with me!

Shakuntala: Don't blame the goddess. Don't blame your teaching profession. Teachers become assistant professors and Professors….. But you are good for nothing; only publishing poems in non-paying magazines and getting accolades, no money.

Bichitra: What about the love and recognition I get from my connoisseurs? How many money-minded men get that kind of love and respect?

Shakuntala: What do you get from that abstract word called "love"? You are now a half old hack. Why are you pursuing after love and recognition and a barren philosophy of life?

Bichitra: But my dream was broken half way.

Shakuntala: Let it break. We don't need brittle dreams.

Bichitra: You're right. What shall I gain out of a dream? I'm after all an insolvent haggard.

Shakuntala: Why should you be a bankrupt and a vagrant for all times to come? I was just joking. A poem of your diary costs me a million rupees. I am proud of my poet husband. (*She imprints a kiss*)

Bichitra: Why, Should you be proud of your ridiculous husband? He's just a down-and-out character.

Shakuntala: Who says? I made a friendly joke about you. Everybody runs after money while you don't care for it. This is unique about you. You are the only one in a million; my priceless poet!

Bichitra: I am damn tired Shakuntala. Let us go and sleep.

Shakuntala: Okay, you sleep. But, don't dream. Your dreams are like fire in Hanuman's tail. Come!

(*She carries Bichitrananda in a sleep walking state and disappears behind the back wall of Gobinda Sahu's tea stall. Silence. Lights and music change. It's dawn. The sun rises in the cyclorama. A crow caws on the tree. Gobind Sahu enters and shouts*)

Gobind: Gurubaria! It is already seven in the morning. The first bus will come in ten minutes. Why haven't you enkindled the oven so far? Where has he gone? (Shouts aiming at the pond behind his stall) Garubari!; I'll break your fishing rod; wasting time in cogitating on a small fish! Useless!! (angrily) Why don't you understand that you have other fish to fry here? (*He puts on the fire in the coal-oven and it starts burning. He puts the kettle over the oven and discovers the professor sleeping on the bench backside. He goes to him, shakes him and calls:)*

Gobinda: Professor! Professor! Get up! It's already morning. Customers would start coming

(*In the meanwhile Bichitranananda puts on his black-and-white beard and wig; Then he goes forward in time to his present state. He gets up.*)

Gobinda: It's alright professor! Go and wash your face. I have prepared hot tea for you.

(*The sound of a small bus stopping at a little distance is heard. It blows its horn*) Madanpur bus has come. It's seven thirty professor. Hurry up!

Bichitra: Let me go to the pond side and finish my morning chores. (*He exits toward the pond. Gobinda Sahu finds some people getting down from the bus and he hollers at them in his usual vending voice.*)

Gobinda: Hot home-made tea Sir! *Chai*! Hot Lipton tea..... Crunchy *Pakodas* and *Vadas* Sir! Step into our shop! Get into an agile morning.... Supple and Sweet! Hot Lipton tea!

(*A handsome young man with French-cut beard holding a thin attaché full of documents and poems enters. He is Atanu, about 35, a branded poet of his state*)

Gobinda: Come 'ere Sir! Have a glass/Cup of Hot Lipton Tea!

Atanu: (*Holds the small glass and takes a Sip.*) Give me a little sugar please

Gobinda: (*While giving a spoon of sugar*) where have you come from Sir?

Atanu: From a long distance, from Rourkela.

Gobinda: Whose house you will go to? To Mr. Parida's house?

Atanu: Who's Mr. Parida?

Gobinda: Former Minister of Transportations! He is from our village. People from Cuttack and Bhubaneswar come and meet him. They buy some eatables from our shop. (*Pause*) How was the journey sir? Must not have been comforting. The dwarf bus and the muddy roads with poodles in the middle of the road make your journey hurly-burly.

Atanu: That's Odisha. The roads are like this everywhere. Why don't they repair the roads? People must complain about this to the government. Well, shop owner, which road leads to Nehrupalli?

Gobinda: This is the road Sir; four kilometers from this cross, but it will take half an hour.

Atanu: Why?

Gobinda: The road Sir; made of concrete and mud with large and small poodles throughout. The contractor repairs it every year and every year the condition worsens. But why shall you go to Nehrupalli Sir? It's a dingy, drab village. The government has planned to inaugurate a coal mine there, somebody said.

Atanu: Yes, On the occasion of that political convention they are holding a poetry recital session. I am invited to recite a poem there; when will that connecting bus come?

Gobinda: We are not sure Sir! It should have come yesterday. Didn't come. We've been waiting here for long three hours now, It hasn't come. You can pretty well take a walk to Nehrupalli, Sir, only four kilometers. It will take maximum one hour.

Atanu: No, I'm not interested to take a four kilometer walk to the poetry station now. Can I get an auto rickshaw or taxi? I made a mistake; I should have brought my car.

Gobinda: This is a rural bus stop Sir. These modern facilities are not available here.

(*Bichitrananda returns from the pond side pathway, and discovers Atanu standing there. His face is brightened up. He comes and tells*)

Bichitra: Hi, Atanu-Babu? (*Arrives and stands in front*)

Atanu: I'm Sorry I couldn't get you. I mean….

Bichitra: I'm Bichitrananda Das. Once upon a time you were my colleague at S.C.S. College, Puri.

Atanu: What's wrong with you Sir? Since when have you kept this beard?

Bichitra: Since the day my wife Shakuntala ran away with you deserting me. How is she Atanu? Tell me about her wellbeing.

Atanau: Your Shakuntala has absconded with a film director. She is acting in a couple of mega soaps now and has probably signed for a new film last week. She is a feminist leader now; and she changes husbands like blouses. Why should you feel nostalgic about her, Sir? She will drag you to a lunatic asylum. She is a new fangled feminist – cares very little for patriarchy, rather revolts against husband figures.

Bichitra: I never knew about her new fangled dualities. When I married her she was like a tiny squirrel. She was like a caged parrot. Later, as you say, she more or less forcefully inscribed her masculinity. Did she ditch you too?

Atanu: Yes, I reported about that. Perhaps it is true. Reality really is stranger than fiction.

Bichitra: You are right poet! She is a dangerous woman. She can turn my tragedy into an interesting play. But one thing I want to know. Is she in the top line cast in the film industry?

Atanu: No, but then life for her is like that: she is in the glamour market. Don't complain Sir! I never complain. I don't expect too much either from life.

Bichitra: Why did you entice her to leave me and go with you?

Atanu: I went one day with the manuscript of my second anthology and you were not at home. She seduced me; called me "a handsome stranger" and invaded my southern frontier.

Bichitra: I understand. She's capable of doing that. How did she behave with you?

Atanu: Sucked up all my energy and finally, got rid of me.

Atanu: Then she dreamt of becoming a celebrity, started to attend parties. Gradually she was asked to appear in advertisements promoting various products. And finally she ended up mating with powerful men in the industry and the sexist actors of Cuttack. Then I heard one day that she has earned a large amount of money, because she was young, pretty and her agent constantly fed her vanity and got her loads of contracts.

Bichitra: That's good news poet. Instead of becoming a woman, she turned herself into a consumer item. She sells her body in the flesh market, successfully. Why should she live with poets? Good. Allow her to cross all borders of the sky and scale the blue horizons. Don't be jealous of that pretty woman.

Atanu: No point being generous either of that-sex-doll Sir, She is very critical about patriarchal domination and oppressive phallocentrism. Come we will talk for some more time sitting in a lonely place. This is not the place for such talks. (*Both of them exit towards the tank side. Gobind Sahu comes out and looks at both bearded men going toward the tank*)

Gobinda: All these people who come to attend the Nehrupalli convention are loony. And I am just a tea shop owner. How can I read their minds? This bearded baboon ordered for a glass of tea and vanished when I have prepared a fresh glass of tea for him. (*Gobinda comes out of his stall and hollers*). Hey Babus! Your tea is ready! Where are you going?

(*Atanu returns and takes the glass of tea*)

Gobinda: He is a loony professor, all the time talks to his pet cat, what will you discuss with him there? He'll make you mad. Come, take the hot tea here and wait for the bus with a cool head.

Atanu: That ok shopkeeper. I know him since last twenty years. Somebody said a film star is coming to the convention. Is it true? Is it a he or she?

Gobinda: True Sir! Lots of people attend the Nehrupali convention only for that heroine. You are correct. She's the centre of attraction (*Whispers*) There's somebody Sir! May be the film star!

(*Chakradhar enters first and invites the two new comers. They are Surajit, a film director and Banya, a film actress*)

Chakradhar: Come here madam! Here's the hotel.

Banya: Hotel? Sura bhai! Can we call it a hotel? It's smaller than a motel.

Chakradhar: This a rural hotel Madam! You can get *Vada* and *pakoda*, *Kachodi* and *Singada* also.

Gobinda: Please come here Sir, Be seated on this bench. We don't have chairs here. But if you order for a meal in advance, I can cook rice, dal, curry and fish. For you A meal will cost you fifty rupees Madam. Mine is the only hotel in this panchayat selling food in such cheap rate!

Chakradhar: They are rich people living in cities; film stars. They are not Panchayat villagers like us. Why should they dine here?

Gobinda: Will they exhibit a cinema today? We'll go.

Surajit: Not here; at Nehrupalli. We'll have to go there. I thought of coming by my car. But somebody said the car would be damaged if I go by this rough road. So, we came by public transport. Our outdoor van is coming shortly.

Chakradhar: The Road is not repaired since 1952. It was constructed when I was the transport minister. Buses used to ply in time during my tenure.

(*Chakradhar exits with a self-praise telling*)

Chakradhara: No one pays me any respect in this blind generation. They don't reckon my abilities as a politician.

Ungrateful bipeds! They are rootless. How is it possible that they don't know me? Ok Sir, I'm hanging around here. If you need my help, give me a call; I'll be here within a minute. (*Chakradhara Parida exits.Atanu sitting on the bench sips his glass of tea and does not pay any heed to Surajit and Banya who are standing near the tea stall.*)

Banya: Shall we order for a cup of tea?

Surajit: No, I don't feel like.

Banya: Is there a hotel nearby that can give us a pot of tea, shopkeeper?

Gobinda: You mean a big pot of tea with extra sugar cubes? No Sir, this is a remote countryside

(*Atanu looks at Banya and intends to tell something. But he does not speak*)

Surajit: Anyway, make some tiffin and tea ready. Our outdoor van with artists and the crew will arrive here within ten minutes. We will shoot a scene for our film in this location.

Gobinda: What film Sir?

Surajit: "Waiting for the bus"

Atanu: (*Advances toward Banya*) Excuse me, are you Shakuntala?

Surajit: No! She's Banya, not Shakuntala.

Atanu: I am not asking you; asking her. (*To Banya*) Aren't you Shakuntala?

Banya: Shakuntala is dead since long. I'm Banya.

Atanu: You look exactly like Shakuntala.

Banya: Are you Mr. Atanu Das, the great lyricist and poet?

Atanu: Exactly. What are you doing here with this dandy here? Come, we'll go round our golden home. You don't know Shakuntala what a whirlwind I weathered in your absence. (*Pause*) What happened to our child Shakuntala? What happened to our dreams? You were pregnant when you left me and eloped with this dandy!

Surajit: Aye, you French-cut! You are crossing the threshold of my patience. It will be better for you if you leave us alone and go your way.

Atanu: No. I have found her after a long gap of desperation. I' will take her home. She is my wife. Come Shakuntala! (*He drags her hand and requests her to come with him and Surajit obstructs him*)

Surajit: Hey! Who are you to take away the heroine of my film? She is the perfect model for my film I can't part with her in the middle of our shooting schedule.

Atanu: Bloody, She's my wife, my own property.

Surajit: What? Property? Ha, ha! Now listen! She is a fairytale existence for me. Don't touch her.

Atanu: I can't leave her with a loafer, with this vagrant film director; once I have found her, I can't leave her insecure with you. Come, Banya, we'll go.

(*Again Atanu drags Banya and Surajit registers a slap on Atanu's face and Atanu retaliates upon him. Banya intervenes and separates the two fighting males*).

Banya: Surabhai, don't lose your temper! He was my husband once upon a time; long back though.

Atanu: So, what? The past is buried in the cemetery of time. And Mr. Director? Why are you after my wife? Give her back to me. I won't do her any harm. I am incapable of harming any one. (*Banya goes to Atanu, pats at his hair and tells her*)

Banya: Don't upset yourself. You have written a couple of lyrics for films. That does not mean you know much about films. I am busy now for an outdoor shooting. After this they will pick me up for Nehrupalli. I will inaugurate a textile shop there in the village. Then only I can be free to think about you.

Banya: Tell me why have you come to my area? This is my village.

Atanu: That does not mean this cross is given to you for shooting!

Surajit: Aye! You get out from my shooting spot. Otherwise I'll go to the police and take their help. Shop Keeper! Where is the police station here?

Gobinda: There's no police station in this area Sir! You have to walk down three or four miles alone to Nehrupalli to find a constable. Otherwise, there is no possibility.

(*The sound of a Outdoor Van stopping is heard The camera man, his two Assistants, three/four crew boys arrive with a tripod, a camera and two reflectors. Surajit is engaged in conversation with them*).

Surajit: (*To the camera man, Ajoy*) Ajoy! You fix the tripod here. It's a wide angle, full frame shot. Hold the tea stall and its back drop. And before that ask your spot boys to guard over this anti-social.

Ajoy: Who's he?

Surajit: He claims to be the husband of our heroine and wants to kidnap her.... Before that you lift him from the location and throw out somewhere till we finish the shooting.

Crew boy-1: Aye! Who are you here to trouble us?

Atanu: Shakuntala is my wife. Your director Surajit has eloped with her. I want to rescue my wife from his clutches.

Crew Boy2: Look gentleman! Our heroine is not your Shakuntala. She is Banya. There may be some physical resemblance, but she is not your wife. If you disturb our shooting we will force you to get out of here. Come, clear out from here like a good guy!

Atanu: She has changed her name, but she cannot change her visage, you know! Can't I recognize my wife with whom I lived for more than two years?

Crew boy 1: She was your wife, may be true, but "once upon a time". Now she's our heroine. Don't disturb her. Yes.... Do you have kids from her?

Atanu: Yes. She was pregnant when she left me. What happened to my child, Shakuntala?

Banya: I didn't want to be a mother, Honey! I'm a market oriented woman.

Atanu: So you aborted it!

Banya: Obviously. This is an expendable society we live in. You were a liability to me since you didn't have a monthly salary. I couldn't have taken the burden of a child with fiscal constraints. Besides, to be a mother in the market is a sign of deprecation.

Atanu: Oh, it's embarrassing, what are you talking about it for? Who says motherhood drains down your market value? It endows you with a new kind of charm and grace, endows you with the milk of kindness…. You acquire a dignity for becoming a creator.

Banya: That is the nineteenth century concept of an ideal mother…..I have to live quite a different life in the twenty first century, honey! I attend parties way often at the home of my producer, which by the time I come becomes full of guests strolling around, kissing and embracing, giving little yelps of recognition, clutching cocktails of every possible hue just to have something to do something with their hands and to keep a check on their anxiety, as they wait the buffet to open. I have to eat in moderation of course, because these diets and plastic surgery are to be considered for the suppers at the end where I have to eat even though I am not hungry because that was what etiquette required.

Atanu: So, you are a great heroine now with parties and free caressing, free sex and free joy. Great! Be a free commodity and stay happy. I'll say good bye to you forever. Stay happy. Keep smiling. When you will lose everything in your life, when you'll become extremely lonely and helpless, don't forget to knock at my door.

Surajit: Rubbish Banya! Snap off that gibberish! We are wasting time in this risky location. Look! (*He points at the sky*) there's a patch of cloud there we have to finish the scene before it gets dark or it rains.

Banya: Brief me the scene, Surabhai. Give me some cue to the sequence. This nuisance has quit the location and now we are free.

Surjit: In this part of the screenplay you have left your home and divorced your husband. The memories of the bucolic village have faded away; and with that the landscape of the paddy fields and the coconut trees. The Eastern mountain range filled with mango orchards turning the hills azure have faded away from your mind. Suppose, after a long, long time you were going on a picnic trip to the distance hills and your vehicle was broken down on a rural bus stop. You have come down the bus to sip a cup of tea on a bus stop like this, just for time pass.

Banya: Surabhai, who has written this script? The story seems to be a slice of my life.

Surajit: Forget your life story; I am giving a cue to your sequence. Listen to this first.

Banya: This is my life story. May be it's a chance resemblance.

Surajit: That's good; you've already migrated into the story of the film.... You are no more a girl named Banya. You are the heroine of our story. What shall you do now? Listen! You've sipped a cup of coffee from a rural tea joint and as you've turned your face little right you discover a loony old man. Do you know who he is?

Banya: Who? (*She has closed her eyes for better concentration*)

Surajit: Your husband; your first love.

(*Heavy back ground music is played, Banya opens her eyes and turns right. Bichitrananda returns from the pond side path and stands there with his pussy cat. He recognizes his Shakuntala, points the finger at her and laughs because he could identify his teen aged wife Shakuntala now*).

Bichitra: (*gazing at her intently*) Eureka! Ha, ha, ha, ha! (*A melodramatic laugh suited to the role of a mad man*).

Banya: No! I don't believe my eyes! Surabhai!! Who's he? (*She hides herself behind Surajit*) That man?

Surajit: (*Does not listen to Banya and continues with the narration*) A long time has passed in the meanwhile. You have weathered storms and tempests...... you have attempted your best to climb the top ladder of your career but you've faltered half way. You could only assuage your physical hunger..... but you could not escape the reality, the life itself. Life chases you through ins and outs. Reality becomes more dramatic than drama.

Banya: Look! He's coming toward me. I'm frightened Surabhai! Save me! (*She hides herself behind Surajit*)

(*Bichitrananda slowly advances in pantomimic steps in which he moves his legs, but does not advance. He is standing on the same spot moving his legs. Banya's fretful behavior continues. Back ground music*).

Bichitra: Shakuntala! You're Shakuntala! I've identified you at last! Yes! You're Shakuntala (*He moves his legs in walking fashion*) I married you when the mother earth was young and juvenile.... But now, you've broken the golden cage and flown away. Tell me how do I love you? Let me count the ways. I love you to the depth and breadth and height my soul can reach. Come back to my arms Shakuntala, Come back!

Shakuntala: Shakuntala is dead since long!

Bichitra: How can she be dead? Her love was fire. I can't visualize her as a handful of ash. The fire is spent, but the holy essence of experience remains.

Shakuntala: Nothing remains now. Shakuntala's wedding ring is lost in the river of time. How can king Dushyanta recognize me?

Bichitra: I carry your heart with me. I carry it in my heart. Any where I go, you go my dear! And whatever is done by me is your doing. Know this my Shakuntala. We're inseparable!

Shakuntala: I am Banya Das, Female Actor Banya Das….. I know my acting in the role of a wife. But Shakuntala is dead since long. Her innocence is lost.

Bichitra: Doesn't matter whether you are Banya or Shakuntala. I seemed to have loved you in numberless forms; in life after life, in space after space, forever, my dear! For ever!

Surajit: Don't advance old man! This is not your bed room. This is my film's location and we are shooting a film here.

Bichitra: We were born together in love; and together we shall be forever. You will be no more here. We shall be together when the white wings of death scatter your days. Come to me dear, till that death will wait!

(*Bichitra goes and holds Banya in tight embrace. Banya screams, and escapes from Bichitra's clutches and runs away*)

Surajit: Camera! Roll. (*He runs after Banya. Bichitra stands alone. A recorded song in male voice is played in stereo.)*

Song

I've gone on exile for you
For fourteen years,
I've submitted my self
To a nameless oaf.
        How could you fly over to another bush?
        How could you relinquish?
        My warm homely space?
Oh my pigeon of love
I bought for you a golden cage,
Fed you with emeralds;
How could you depart?
From my cozy resort
How could you rip my dream apart?
Aye the pigeon of my cage
How could you turn a bird savage….?

(A spot light holds Bichitra to register his solo acting. He moves to the electric light post standing on one corner of the down stage. After the song is over, Bichitrananda's heart continues to be heavy. His notions of ideal love are bombarded. He holds on to the light post. There is no light from the top of the post. The bulb is fused. He utters in a quivering voice.)

Bichitra: I do not like being moved to your destination: but my desire and will are excited; and action, here, is a dangerous thing. I tremble for something factitious. I crave for some malpractice of heart and illegitimate process. We are prone to these things my absent presence. I will wait; wait for the bus, I will wait; wait for the light to come on this post. I must also gather courage to wait for darkness.

(Background music is heavy on the keyboard. Bichitra holds on to the light post and looks upward to see whether light has come on the post. Then his hands slip and he slides down slowly till he rests on his knees. Light brightens up for a moment on the post, stays for some time and goes out.)

Curtain

****

FROG STORY

SCENE-1

There is an opening like an entrance at the up stage. There are steps behind to climb up and enter from the upstage. The upstage area denotes Prof. Krishnamohan 's house. The bed room is set to the right-up with a bed. There's another bed to the left, demarcated for the guests of Krishna Mohan's family. The lane between the two bedrooms is used like a foyer. To the down-left in the Professor's Laboratory there's a chair and a table; and over it a microscope. A big card board basket is placed on the floor. Live frogs are kept in the basket for Krishna Mohan's use. A ladder like bamboo structure stands to right down stage. It is used mostly as a window and as a dividing device between the 'inside' and the 'outside', the inner space and the outer space.

These suggestions are given to intimate that a constructivist stage is preferred to a realistic one. As the play opens Madhabi, (aged 35 years) wife of Prof. Krishna Mohan is found in the laboratory talking to the frogs. She's married for eight years. She accepts the frogs as her imaginary children: she calls two of the frogs as Phulia and Tikili. There is a pattering sound of continuous downpour of rain outside.

Madhabi: (*Talks to the frogs*) Listen, to me children! I'll tell you a story… the story of a loony monarch. (*sound of croaking of a group of frogs. Madhabi is irked*)

Beware! Don't croak or hop while I speak! Listen!

(*Background Music*)

The King has gone in a hunting spree. And the queen is alone in the palace. (*Music*) Such a colossal building… replete with precious jewellery, but the queen was sad. She didn't feel like doing the daily chores! (*Phulia croaks, the croaking sound*) Phulia! Stop croaking! It's bad manners; don't croak when the elders speak! Didn't I tell earlier? Why do you flout? Our Tikili is the best among children, a golden frog:

(*Tiliki jumps up very high*) Aye! Why so high? You, too, have gone astray, off the track, huh? Rascal! No. It's getting more and more cumbersome, day by day! Let your father come! I'll report against you! Dad is too irritable a guy! Don't you know how itchy and restless he is! He'll take out his little knife and dissect you! Finally he'll mince you up to explore a jewel. (*Background music mixed with the sound of rain and a chorus of croaking frogs*) But where's your dad? Left the home since two days hazarding this torrential rain. God knows where he is searching for the frogs! That too he needs live frogs! Ah! Who'll tell him not to go mad for live frogs? There's life risk! You'll have to put on a long rain coat and move in swampy and shrubby fields in the dark nights; holding a long hunting torch light and a net to catch the frogs. Who knows you may encounter snakes?

(*Suddenly there's a knocking sound on the door*)

Madhabi: See! He has come back! Now what you'll do little croakies? Guard yourself! Hide somewhere! Otherwise he'll dissect you! Come, let me hide you somewhere! But where shall I hide you? (*croacking sound increases*) Oh! Don't cry Tikili! I'll knit a warm woolen bag for you. That'll be better. (*The knocking on the external door grows louder)* Oh! Going! Wait a minute! (*Madhabi opens the door. Enters Birabhadra, a young man in his early thirties. This handsome dandy has covered himself in a rainy coat and carries a folded bed and a touring suitcase.*)

Madhabi: (*unable to identify*) Excuse me!

Stranger: I'm Bira Bhadra!

Madhabi: (feels relaxed) Oh! Birabhadra! (*she smiles*) It's such a pleasure! Get in, get in!!

Bira: Why were you taken aback? Couldn't identify me? Eh?

Madhabi: It's incredible Bira Bhai! You, on this rainy day, after such a long time… Knocking at my door… what a pleasant surprise!

(Birabhadra comes in, keeps his folded bed and suitcase on the floor and takes out his rain coat. Madhabi takes the coat)

Birabhadra: I wetted your house! *(looks inside)* Your husband?

Madhabi: He has gone out for collection of frogs.

Birabhadra: He's a professor of Zoology, am I right?

Madhabi: Yes, but he doesn't have classes on the rainy day. He is on his research tour. *(Birabhadra looks at Madhabi intently)* What are you looking at me so intently for? As if you see me for a first time?

Birabhadra: A rounded mark of vermillion on your forehead, glass bangles on your wrists, putting on a sari and drawing a veil on your face… It is amazing Madhabi you look so transfigured and cute! You're right! I see you in this get up for the first time!

Madhabi: Eight years have already passed since I am married, Birabhai! You very well know that! *(Pause: Background Music denotes nostalgia)* But you're ageing very fast. There's a black shadow beneath your eyes… *(smiles)* How fast the time flows!

(Birabhadra comes closer to Madhabi, raised her face up by lifting on the chin and then talks in whispers)

Birabhadra: Are you the same Madhabi whom I explored eight years ago? It's unbelievable!

Madhabi: *(She feels the current of love passing through her body, feels quaked and then suddenly changes the topic)* come in: we'll sit and have a mug of coffee first. Then we will graze through our bygone memories.

Birabhadra: Why? Can't we stand and embrace each other? Can't we kiss each other?

Madhabi: But your hands are so naughty – they'll navigate my body beneath the clothes.

Birabhadra: *(Laughs mischievously and loudly; then Birabhadra surveys the room.)*

Birabhadra: So..? This is your drawing room?

Madhabi: You may call it a multipurpose room: a drawing –cum-guest room-cum laboratory-cum… etcetera – our little world!

Birabhadra: A zoo! Your husband, you said, is a zoologist!

Madhabi: A luminous scholar, Bira Bhai; his research papers are published in international magazines. The professors count him as one of the notable scientists of the country. (*she moves away*)

Birabhadra: Why are you distancing yourself from me?

Have I put you in an awkward situation by landing myself here? I mean, in a time when your scientist husband is absent? When shall Mr. Krishna Mohan return home? How can I predict it?

Madhabi: Our professor is not predictable. He went on tour when it started raining; said he'd come back before evening. And now it is the second day!

Birabhadra: Oh! The scientist seems to be a moody fellow! He is fully engrossed in his field study. Where has he gone?

Madhabi: To the pond side where there are frogs. He has gone to collect frogs, his specimen for research. It depends… I don't know… he may return after the rain stops.

Birabhadra: I thought he'd be at home because it is a Sunday. But if he returns home and discover me here, what'd he think? That'll be Improper. Well, Madhabi let me go to a lodging house. My company shall pay the charges. I will be calling tomorrow morning. Till then! (*He lifts his luggage bag and moves. Madhabi spreads her hand and refuses him to go*)

Madhabi: How can it be? Won't you meet my husband? Better you stay here till he returns.

Birabhadra: (*feels guilty*) No, I'll go to a hotel. They will reimburse my expenses… But.. What I notice, you feel kind of flustered in my presence, bit of discomfiture…

Madhabi: What discomfiture? Nothing! Rather, you are feeling uneasy.

Birabhadra: No, Madhabi! I remember how you moved like a squirrel eight years ago when I came to meet you alone. Where's that gusto now? You seem to be in two minds now: You're not able to decide whether to entertain me or to evade!

Madhabi: Look Birabhai! The world whirls very fast! Values change. Eight years is an adequate span to seek alternatives in life. Isn't it so? Besides, we are ageing now!

Birabhadra: (*nostalgically*) your mother would be busy with her betel box and you'd come to me like a flash of lightning to enjoy a tight hug or a warm kiss! We took advantage of the lonely rooms to actualize our fantasies. I miss that zest. I've got you here alone after long years. Won't I touch you? Should I become cold and freeze like an abstinent saint from the Himalayas?

Madhabi: No! No' Bira bhai! It'd be indecent!

Birabhadra: You're in two minds, Madhabi! You are afraid of your husband. That's alright. He may suspect you. But why are you looking for decency and indecency?

Madhabi: Why can't you comprehend the compulsions of this middle class married women, Birabhai? I'm the wife of an Indian Scientist!

Birabhadra: That I can guess. But to be frank with you, Madhabi! Meeting you after eight long years, that too, in an empty house, a house which shall lie empty in the night… the whole thing may make me vulnerable. My sensual feelings may get flared up. It's irresistible.

Madhabi: Don't worry. Take off your cloths and go to the bath; take a shower and drench yourself for five minutes. The fire inside will be put off.

Birabhadra: But if the fire does not extinguish?

Madhabi: I'll dial immediately to the fire station. Don't worry. I've the number with me!

(Both of them laugh. Birabhadra intended to go towards the bathroom, but by mistake he moved towards the exit door)

No! Not that way! (*She points at the toilet which is attached to the room)* Here! (*Birabhadra changes the direction and moves to the interior. Madhabi laughs and comments*)

Madhabi: Hats off to your orgy Birabhai! You act like lover No.1 for the starved girls; They 'd gobble you up! I'll keep you here for a week. I feel like grabbing you till I am satisfied, But I won't admit that before you. What do you think of me? Do I not feel excited when I see you in this lonely house? There's no guarantee that the scientist would return tonight. So, let us enjoy this rainy night in the absence of my sexless husband. Let's go inside

(They go and the lights go off)

SCENE-2

(The pattering sound of rain increases in volume. The lights dim and the stage lights go off. The croaking sound of the frogs fills in the darkness. A faint light increases in intensity to show that it is a torch light with weak batteries.

Prof. Krishna Mohan takes an entry holding an open umbrella to protect him from rain. His trouser and shirt are mud stained. Two garlands of live frogs are hanging from his neck. The rays of the street light show his unsteady movement. He knocks at his door and shouts)

Krishnamohan: Madhabi! Madhabi! Open the door! Yes, I've come back; yes, Krishna Mohan! Your humble husband! Open the door.

(Nobody responds. He tries to break open the door. Nobody responds. Krishna Mohan tries to enter into the house through the window, presses himself through the wide railings and jumps into the room like a frog. The sound awakes Madhabi. She is startled out of her sleep. The interior of the house is lighted.)

Madhabi: (*Shrieks*) Who's there? Who're you? Hey!!

Krishnamohan: Madhabi! What's wrong with you? I'm Krishna Mohan, your husband!

Madhabi: (annoyed) So what? What is the reason behind your howling? That too in the middle of a rainy night? Won't you allow you wife to sleep? I don't like howling husbands.

Krishnamohan: (*very serious*) What? Who was howling here? Why didn't you open the door? Are you able to realize in what a bad shape I am? Hold these frogs first. Take them off my neck. (*She tries to take off the garland of frogs*) Take care! My frogs are fragile!

Madhabi: They're alright! You look fragile!

Krishna: Fragile? How? Why should I look fragile? I am as strong as a scout leader! (*He parades like a scout leader, back ground music*)

Madhabi: Huh! You've forgotten how to walk. You're jumping and hopping instead.

Krishna: (*Hops and jumps*)

Madhabi: You look like a frog! (*Krishna Mohan continues to jump. She observes Krishna Mohan with awe and shrieks*) you have transformed yourself into a frog!! (*She cowers and her face cringes with distaste*) You smell of slime!

Krishna: What else should I smell of? I can't spray deodorant while drenching in the rains and hunting for frogs! I'm searching for these live frogs on the muddy banks of the village ponds, in marshy lands and under the shrubs. It's a herculean task; do you womenfolk know that?

Madhabi: Why are you doing the job yourself? Why don't you hire a man who'd supply you twenty / thirty frogs a day.

Krishna: I'm a Gandhian by temperament, I'm self dependent! I collect my own specimen for research. And I care a fig for your derisive behavior!

Madhabi: So, Mr. Self dependent! Go to the bath and cleanse yourself before you come to the bed.

Krishna: What did you say? I'll take a bath? In this cool weather? In the middle of the night?

Madhabi: Better you shave your face. You've not shaved since last two days.

Krishna: (*annoyed*) what sort of a woman are you? Torturing your scholar husband in the dead cold night?

Madhabi: What else shall you do? Sleep on the bed with a body smeared with mud and slime? You'll infect my entire house and make me sick!

(Sound of croaking frogs. Madhabi puts the frogs in a cardboard basket.)

Krishnamohan: Why are you croaking like frogs?

Madhabi: I'm not croaking. You're creating a scene here in the middle of the night. First, why did you jump into the house through the window? Are you planning to break the railings of the window some day? Second! Why are you fidgeting to take a bath? What shall you do now?

Krishnamohan: Anything! Anything I'd feel like! What's that to you?

Madhabi: Why are you shouting? Can't you speak in a gentle voice?

Krishnamohan: I'll shout here after. Like an actor. Like an actor in Grotowski's 'Poor Theatre'. I'll bring a microphone and shout. After all this is my house, I have hired it. I'm paying the rent every month to the house owner! And listen' If you force me now to take a bath, I will go back to the bank of the pond, again!

Madhabi: What shall you do there? Catch frogs in this rainy night?

Krishnamohan: (*Revolts*) No! I will smear slime all over my body, put on nothing except a groin-cloth and become a mendicant: may be a fakir… I'll call myself "Frog-Fakir" and renounce the family. (*He hops like a frog and laughs with anger*) Frog-Fakir! Ha, ha! What a postmodern dream!

Madhabi: (*Little nervous*) No! Don't do that! I'll switch on the geyser! Take a hot bath if you feel cold, Okay? Go, take a hot bath and feel fresh! What have you eaten for the dinner?

Krishnamohan: Nothing! Where'd I have a dinner in the marsh? There is no hotel in that low lying swamp!

Madhabi: Look at the wall clock. It's One A.M. I kept some bread and curry in the hot case. You can have something, but go and wash yourself first.

(*Krishna Mohan goes to the room in the left side. Lights follow and reveal Birabhadra sleeping. Krishna Mohan screams in amazement and jumps back to the middle corridor*)

Madhabi: What happened?

Krishnamohan: Somebody is sleeping there in my bed room? Who's he?

Madhabi: Shh! Bira bhai. Don't howl!

Krishnamohan: Bira bhai?

Madhabi: Yes, brother Bira bhadra!

Krishnamohan: Which Birabhai? I don't remember any one of that name having stepped into our cottage at any time before!

Madhabi: He is my uncle's brother-in-law's son – Birabhadra, not a college student.

Krishnamohan: (*feels harassed while calculating the relationship*) But how's he your brother?

Madhabi: My maternal uncle's brother-in-laws! You've seen him in a family gathering. Do you remember?

Krishnamohan: Which Birabhadra? What's he doing 'ere? Why has he pitched his tent here? Why should he sleep in our private bed? The entire thing appears to me like a quiz! Et cetera! Et cetera!

Madhabi: I told you who's Bira bhai!

Krishnamohan: Did he attend our marriage ceremony? I mean, was he the young man who smeared lacquer dye on my body and spoiled my new t-shirt while playing jokes during the marriage?

Madhabi: No, no, no!

Krishnamohan: The young man who took you to Bali Yatra festival of Cuttack and bought you beautiful glass bangles?

Madhabi: No! He's in Delhi these days!

Krishnamohan: The boy with whom you played husband-and-wife games when you were young?

Madhabi: How can he be my uncle's brother-in-law's son? It is my maternal uncle's wife's cousin!

Krishnamohan: (*He calculated the relationship mentally and fails*) It'd be better Madhabi... write it down on a small slip... No, better I'll note it on my diary. (*He collects his diary and writes*) Your maternal uncle's wife's cousin! Difficult equation... Uncle's son's wife's cousin, something grating!

Madhabi: Remember one thing. When he'd get up in the morning negotiate him like a gentleman. I mean...not like a frog man! He's very sensitive and bad tempered, may retort you oddly, may give you a slap!

Krishnamohan: On my face? Why?

Madhabi: If you behave like nuts.

Krishnamohan: In that case, instruct me what to talk with him when he gets up. I'll note that in my diary.

Madhabi: (*annoyed*) Oh! How many times shall I tell you about these formal talks? The other day you noted everything in your diary. Did you forget?

Krishnamohan: Not only noted; I've mugged up the entire set. I've made a chart of what to do when I meet a stranger. If I forget I'll refer to my diary! Okay!

Madhabi: Let me find out what happened to your water heater! (*She exits in a hurry. Krishna Mohan searches for the diary and finds it to his good luck*)

Krishnamohan: (*Reads out from the diary*) Guidelines for behaving like a gentleman. One! (*He rehearses something with an imaginary stranger, but silently moving throughout the stage. Birabhadra gets up and comes to Krishna Mohan's laboratory area. He feels frozen in amazement observing Krishna Mohan miming something holding a diary. At one point Krishna Mohan discovers Birabhadra.*)

Birabhadra: Hello! Good morning! Nice to meet you Sir!

(*Krishna Mohan stands pleased*)

Krishnamohan: Very good Morning! Just a minute! (*Then he refers to the diary and tells*)

Krishnamohan: Ah! What a fine weather! What about your family? Well, how many children do you have? (*Refers to the diary*) I'm sorry I left two more formal lines! Yes… I'm glad to meet you! (*refers again and then extends his hands for a shake*)

Birabhadra: (*Understands nothing from what Krishna Mohan does*) I'm sorry… I.. I…

Krishnamohan: (*checks his diary*) don't worry! I know you are Madhabi's uncle's brother-in-law's son… that means everything is 'difficult' to understand. But don't worry! I've noted everything in this diary. (*He turns the pages of the diary*)

Birabhadra: I'm sorry… I can't follow you.

Krishnamohan: Never mind! I've noted everything! Later I'll calculate and say what you'll call me! Ok?

Birabhadra: That's alright. I've heard about you.

Krishnamohan: (Tensed up) What?... What have you heard about me?

Birabhadra: That you're a genius!

Krishnamohan: Wow!

Birabhadra: That your research articles are published in European reearch journals. It's my good luck that I got a chance to meet you: a genius!

Krishnamohan: (complacently) Ha, ha, ha, ha, ha! Now I understand who you are! You're the person I was searching for all my life. I mean I was searching for a person like you; waiting all my life for you. Ah! You are also a genius. (*Music*) A genius recognizes a genius. Well… well. Where were you hibernating all these days? Now I should embrace you! Come, O I'll hug you great man! (*Birabhadra tries to escape and Krishna Mohan chases him in the hugging spree. Finally he catches and hugs him tightly. Birabhadra is about to fall. Krishna Mohan does not leave him. Madhabi appears suddenly on the scene*)

Madhabi: Aye, What are you doing to Bira bhai?

Krishnamohan: I'm glad, I'm happy, I'm ecstatic!!

Madhabi: What's the occasion?

Krishnamohan: I'm overwhelmed! (He gasps)

Madhabi: So what? Why are you panting for breath? Leave him and to to take a bath first. Actually Bira bhai, he has just returned from a study tours from a slimy zone! He's happy about his research. Let him be fresh first, okay?.

Krishnamohan: We can talk even now! We can keep the bathroom program a little away. (*He refers to the diary and picks up tips about niceties of gentle behavior*) We can talk like gentlemen: What a nice weather! How many children do you have? When did you come from? How was the journey? It's a pleasure to meet you dear!

(*Madhabi was trying to stop her husband, but Krishna Mohan went on delivering his newly learnt words of etiquette*)

How was my conversation style, Madhabi?

Madhabi: (*she does not respond to her husband; rather speaks to Birabhadra*) May be, you've boosted him up quite a lot. (*to Bira Bhai*) He's over – reacting now. Nobody in our locality praises him. He is not accepted by people as a researcher. They address him as Frog Man. Who has the leisure to stand and stare? Who has the time to applaud his research? We live amid shallow people you know! That's why my husband is bitter about them!

Birabhai: Oh! EvenI didn't know anything until recently! I mean about Professor's credibility in the society.

Madhabi: You lauded him in praiseworthy language and that made him happy! Thank you very much!

Krishnamohan: Oh, yeah! I'm overwhelmed!

Birabhadra: We, too, are happy in your happiness, Professor.

Krishnamohan: (*He hops like a frog in ecstasy*) Thank you, thank you very much!

Madhabi: (*sarcastically*) But that does not mean you'd hop like frogs to express your joy! (*She exits with the curt remark. Krishna Mohan goes behind her to observe what she is doing. Birabhadra gets his suitcase and sleeping bag, keeps them on the floor and extends his hand to shake with K.M.*)

Birabhadra: Well, I'm going. Thank you very much for giving me shelter for the night. It was a pleasure meeting with you Scientist. Best of luck for your frogs Let me go!

Krishnamohan: No! How can you go Sir? You've to stay with us for a week! I've lots of research findings to share with you.

Birabhadra: But I can't stay at one place. I'm little footloose and transient. I should go now.

Krishnamohan: Why? Do you feel uncomfortable 'ere?

Birabhadra: I'm a perennial mover, fond of the blue sky, the lush green forests and the blue-ocean. I mean, I love to move under the blue sky, to negotiate green forests and on Sundays I prefer to jump into the waves of the ocean. I'd feel suffocated if you imprison me within your four walls, professor!. So, I try to merge myself into the vast and limitless, into the boundless and the infinite.

Krishnamohan: Ah! Great! It's poetry:"He who binds to himself a joy / Does the winged life destroy?"

Birabhadra: Ah! "He who kisses the joy as it flies / Lives in eternity's sunrise! I hug eternity and kiss eternity Prof. K.M.! Keep yourself busy with your frogs, and allow me to disappear from your landscape of frogs. Allow me to listen to the whispers of immortality.

Krishnamohan: Why are you chasing immortality, genius? We live in a small, limited world of transience and death. My frogs are symbols of my dreams that die with time. I lead my life to join the living with the dead. No more I see the grove and the stream and every common sight appareled in celestial light. The frogs are mundane, but the jewel in their head is immortal.

Birabhadra: I couldn't follow. What jewels you are talking about Scientist?

Krishnamohan: I'm a constant dreamer, genius! I dream about strange things. Look, for example, at my hypothesis: In the beginning of the creation the primordial frogs didn't have jewels imbedded in their heads. But later, in a moment of magic realism, when the first drop of monsoon fell on them, the droplets transformed into jewels. When the snake devours a frog in the swamp, the jewel drifts into the snake's hood.

Birabhadra: How could you navigate such a hidden truth?

Krishnamohan: It's a dream, kind a' epiphany.

Birabhadra: Dream? May be you're the first scientist to believe in dreams! I'm afraid of esoteric people!

Krishnamohan: Don't get scared. I didn't choose to be a dreamer. In fact I'd rather choose to be anything other than this present because sometimes dreams block the realities.

Birabhadra: This is a dangerous terrain scientist! How do you inhabit such a shadowy zone?

Krishnamohan: It feels like when I'm dreaming I get to be or experience different things. But thanks to my wife Madhabi – she helps tame my wandering head. I know I don't always pay attention. I can't keep my dreams green. I also dream genius, but not like you. I dream monsoon skies, dark nights, swamps and slimy frogs.

Birabhadra: That's alright Professor! What you should have is an uncaged mind! Try to liberate yourself.

Krishnamohan: See, Mr. Birabhadra! You appear to me a chunk of blue sky and a patch of green forest... May be you are a figment of the ocean, deep in the soul that reflects the gale, the calm and the loneliness. Be in constant touch with your dreams. But you are depriving me of the good luck to share your multi colored dreams.

Birabhadra: I'll come again. Don't worry. Let me finish my tour program. (*Birabhadra moves towards the exit point and returns*).

Birabhandra: Where's Madhabi? (*calls*) Madhabi! I'm going.

(*Madhabi enters with a napkin wiping her hands*)

Madhabi: (*To her husband*) what are you doing here? Won't you take a bath? Your hot water would get cold. Go (*He pulls his arm and sends him into the bath. Krishna Mohan forcibly drags himself to Birabhadra*)

Krishnamohan: So, Mr …………. Er…….. I forget your name! What's his name Madhabi?

Madhabi: Won't you go to the bath and wash yourself?

(*Krishna Mohan hurries into the bath*)

Birabhadra: Since how long you've lived with this creature, Madhabi?

Madhabi: Eight years. Why? You know it. I've been living with this great man since last eight years.

Birabhadra: If I stay here for eight more minutes I'll go mad.

Madhabi: Then I won't press you to stay!

Birabhadra: Won't you feel sorry? Don't worry! I'll come again to your house. Professor is not willing to leave me. When I'll come next, I'll stay for two / three days. Bye! (*He leaves, Madhabi stops him and gives him a hug. Music*)

Birabhadra: Madhabi! I'm really sorry for you!

Madhabi: Why? Why should you feel sorry for me? My husband is a Professor, got his Ph.D. from Minesotta University. He's an eminent scholar! Can't I be happy with him?

(*While speaking the last two lines, Madhabi's voice cracks and tears fill in her eyes. Back ground music-somber*)

Birabhadra: Madhabi! Look at me straight!

(*Madhabi again holds Bira and represses the tears*)

(*Sighs*) Uncle has flung you into a pool of misfortunes.

Madhabi: What misfortune? Because I have not given birth to half a dozen children? I don't bother! The frogs are there! They are... All the time hopping and croaking in the basket! Can't I nurture them Birabhai? Can't they be my children?

(She attempts to laugh, but the laughter automatically gets transformed into a cry; back ground music. The lights dim and the stage is dark)

SCENE-3

(Full lights bang on the stage. Krishna Mohan has taken a bath and he hurriedly enters the stage tucking a shirt into the trouser. He buttons the pant and searches for the comb in the back pocket of the trouser)

Krishnamohan: Madhabi! Madhabi! Comb? Where's the comb? Madhabi! Where've you kept?

Madhabi: *(Enters)* It's in your trouser pocket! Why're you shouting? It's in your trouser pocket.

Krishnamohan: Where's the trouser pocket? *(He searches and finds out the comb. He combs .... Hair. Madhabi goes inside in hurried steps, brings the deo and talcum powder. She sprays deo and applies talcum powder on KM's body. Madhabi takes them back.)*

Madhabi: *(brings the tie and asks her husband)*.... Put it on!

Krishnamohan: Should I put on one? Won't I get stifled?

Madhabi: There a guest in the house. Maintain your status!

Krishnamohan: What's the guest doing inside?

Madhabi: He's taking his breakfast.

Krishnamohan: Go and feed him well. He's a genius. He must be fed sumptuously. Let me go to my microscope and examine the frogs. You may bring a cup of coffee for me!

(Madhabi goes inside. Krishna Mohan putting on his suit and tie goes to the card board basket where the live frogs are kept for dissection. He keeps the instruments: the scissors, knife and fork on the tray, and sits. The stage lights dim

and background music intensifies. Several frogs jump out from his interior space and hop around his head. In the faint light that streamed through his head, Krishna Mohan visualizes those frogs as big as teen aged girls. They devour him. The frog girls encroach upon his interior space. Back ground music and the strobe lights supplement the effect. As the effect continues on the stage, Krishna Mohan's voice reverberates through microphone)

Voice: When the first droplet of the monsoon water falls on the head of the frog, it metamorphoses into a jewel. When the snake devours the bejewelled frog, the jewel sticks on to the hood of the snake and the frog slips to the stomach of the snake.

(*Background music attempts to narrate this incident in bizarre sound effects. The frog girls disappear and light floods the stage with a bang. Krishna Mohan shouts*)

Krishnamohan: Eureka!! (*The frog girls run helter-skelter and Krishna Mohan frantically attempts to catch them. The frog girls hop and escape. K.M. addresses them like an Army Commander*) No! No, my comrades! Emancipation is a big word. Costlier than the jewels in your head! It can't be delivered to you so easily. You've been trying to hop away from the box for the last five years… Ha, ha, ha! You should know your limitations! (*Pause)* Yes! You can revolt! (*Catches one frog girl by her neck*) Against me! Against this laboratory! But what can you do? This is a cruel world; a world that rotates without any logic. You can't ask me why! You can't question why I'm so cruel! Because all 'whys' are not responded to with answers. I represent such an illogical universe! So, I'll administer chloroform to you all, till you sink into sleep so that I can lacerate you!

(*He administers chloroform to the frog girl; she collapses and falls fainted.*)

Krishnamohan: You can't hop now, dear puppet… you're finished. You can't dance like a puppet! Puppet dance! (*He hops and dances like a puppet. Madhabi enters with a cup of tea placed on a tray, is shocked to find her husband dancing and laughing. Then she is annoyed*)

Madhabi: What's this? What's happening to you?

Krishnamohan: I'm beatified! I'm blessed! I'm … I'm… I'm… (*He discovers Madhabi and recoils*)

Madhabi: Why were you dancing like a lunatic in frenzy? This is a professor's residence, not a loony's! Mind it! Oh! What a nuisance! Thank God! Bira Bhai has left, If he'd come to know this, what would he think? (*Krishna Mohan goes to his chair like a good boy and starts to look at a frog through the microscope. Madhabi goes on reprimanding*)

Madhabi: What impression would the neighbors take? Why're you shouting always like an opera artist? Did you find the jewel after all?

Krishnamohan: (*He was counting the questions Madhabi asked*) You've asked five question in total. Which answer do you need first? (*Madhabi is silent in deep annoyance*) None of your questions shall be answered. None of the questions raised by the prophets could be answered! (*He donned a pleasant smile*) I got the jewel, dear, I got it!

Madhabi: Where's it?

Krishnamohan: The jewel stands in front of me! Ah! You are my jewel!

Madhabi: Stop that balderdash!

Krishnamohan: The entire world is balderdash; all kinds of researches are balderdash. Your reprehensions are balderdash Madhabi. Our living, our home-sweet-home, our quest for children – everything! Everything is balderdash! (*smiles*) Okay? Now hand over the cup of tea to me and go and call your Bira bhai! I've summoned him for a philosophical discourse on frogs!

(*Madhabi gives the tea cup and exists. Birabhadra enters with a cup of tea in his hand and sipping from the cup!)*

Birabhadra: Hello Scientist! How's life?

Krishnamohan: (He's ecstatic) Hello! What a nice weather! What are your children doing?

Birabhadra: Children?

Krishnamohan: Yes children! How many children have you produced? Have we met earlier? I am sorry, I'm glad to meet you… yes! And then (*he recollects what he regurgitates from the diary long ago*) 'then hand shake' (*He extends his hand to Birabhadra who responds hesitatingly. Krishna Mohan holds his hand, shakes vehemently for a minute or two ostensibly*)

Birabhadra: (*draws his hand forcibly back*) Do you remember you telephoned me to come for an urgent work!

Krishnamohan: That's right!

Birabhadra: What's that urgent work?

Krishnamohan: I wanted to tell you about my recent discovery!

Birabhadra: I know! You're a genius! Did you find the jewel?

Krishnamohan: Yes, your guess is hundred percent true. You said you love the sky and the jungle and the ocean! I accept you as the sky… jungle is within the sky and the ocean is within the jungle and the bejeweled frog is within the ocean.

Birabhadra: Are you talking metaphysics?

Krishnamohan: (shrugs) May be, I don't know! My frogs have made me a Saint! I apprehend the frogs in the sky… sometimes in the jungles, in an island of the jungle in the ocean… (*He takes out a garland of frogs*) Here it is! What do you find here genius? These frogs jumped down from the sky! From my head! Hold it and see (*He hands over the garland of frogs to Birabhadra. The croaking sound of the frogs in chorus increases in volume. Birabhadra holds the garland of frogs with odium and contempt; he attempts to throw it. Krishna Mohan resists*)

Krishnamohan: No! You can't throw those frogs away. They are precious! Don't throw them!

Birabhadra: They are so dirty. How do you relish holding them with care?

Krishnamohan: I've to wade through dirt and shit to collect these frogs, you know! One of them does possess a jewel.

Birabhadra: Which one of these dirty frogs?

Krishnamohan: I'm exploring that only. For the last eleven years. I've slept under this table to dream about that frog, to see the jewel in dream. May be the jewel is with you!

Birabhadra: With me?

Krishnamohan: Yes! With you! Your face reflects radiance! Who knows? This glow emanates from the jewel you imbed in your body!

Birabhadra: But you said the jewel is in the head of a frog?

Krishnamohan: Yes! You're that frog, sure! You're the frogman with a jewel in your head! I'll dissect you! (*He searches for the knife, but finds a pair of scissors. He holds it and chases Birabhadra to dissect his head. Birabhadra runs scarified uttering:*)

Birabhadra: Hey! You scare monger! What are you doing? Do I look like a frog?

Krishnamohan: I'm going to dissect you! I'll administer a dose of chloroform and operate the jewel. Yes... you are the bejeweled frog!

Birabhadra: (*shouts*) No!!

Krishnamohan: (*shouts*) Frog! Yes my frog!

(*He seizes Birabhadra and Birabhadra retracts with a loud groan*)

You are croaking like a frog. Let me examine your head! I' want to be sure whether you contain a jewel! (*He forcibly holds Bira Bhai and strokes his head twice by the scissor. Birabhai, pitiably mishandled by Krishna Mohan falls like a half conscious patient, Madhabi barges in)*

Madhabi: Aye, Aye, Aye!! Who're you? Are you a human being or a monster? Strange behavior! Why are you obsessed with Birabhai? Birabhai! I'm sorry for what has been done to you!

Krishnamohan: You can't understand Madhabi! I'm not doing anything. I'm just experimenting with this frog man! I want to see whether the jewel is in this frogman's head or not! Do you understand?

Madhabi: There's nothing to understand! I'll telephone Dr. Kanungo to come and examine your head. Why are you attacking Bira bhai whenever your see him? Why are you trying to murder him? Bira bhai! Change your shirt! I'll put it in the washing machine. Now! Give it to me.

(*She takes the shirt and spits out the words of contempt*)

Madhabi: Chhi! What a brute you are! It's difficult to put up with you! How can I tame a wild monster?

Krishnamohan: (*thinks seriously*) May be, there's a grammatical mistake I've committed!

Madhabi: What grammatical mistake? You yourself are a blunder made by God and epitome of a botch! I'm put into shame by the neighbors for your eccentric behavior.

Krishnamohan: Neighbors? Damn them! Dr. Krishna Mohan's wife is afflicted by 'neighbors': it's news to me! Ha! Phase them out! Behave like the wife of a modern scientist. You are talking like an old woman of eighteenth century. You should have been born in century Odisha! eighteenth

Madhabi: I shouldn't have been born at all. I shouldn't have married you. That's oaky! But do you know what the time now is?

Krishnamohan: Yes! It's twelve twenty five!

Madhabi: Today is Wednesday! You've to attend a class at One O' clock! Do you remember that? (*in a commanding voice*) Go! Get ready!

(*Birabhadra dusts off his clothes and comes gradually to normal position*)

Krishnamohan: Mr. Sky and Jungle! I too love you. I am not going to part with you now. The jewel is definitely within you!

Madhabi: Oh! Why are you muddling here? Go to attend your class.

Krishnamohan: I love him! I must express my love! Why don't you allow me to act as a normal human being?

Madhabi: You are getting late! Hurry up to your class!

Krishnamohan: Bira bhai should stay here for some days! Ask him not to go after I go to college.

Madhabi: Why should he stay here; to get beaten by you?

Krishnamohan: He should stay here because he's a genius. He's the sky and the jungle and the ocean!! Three-in-one! He embodies infinity.

Madhabi: Don't go to the jungle! Go to the classroom. Otherwise, you will be fired!

Krishnamohan: No! I won't lose my job! These frogs would bring good luck.

(*He moves to the basket of frogs and tells*) You too must stay! Never try to hop out of the basket! Don't attempt to emancipate yourself. That's an illusion. So, my dear friends! Try to tune yourself to the environment! (*He shuts the lid of the basket*) Bye! I'm going to the college! (*He goes out. Madhabi holds Bira Bhai and apologizes*)

Madhabi: I'm so sorry for you Bira Bhai! He is not a normal man! Please bear with him!

Bira Bhai: It's difficult to live with a lunatic, Madhabi! Your husband is a lunatic. Is he normal with you in your bed room? (*Music intensified*) Emotional or grumpy?

Madhabi: He doesn't sleep in the bed room Bira Bhai! He sleeps on the floor of the laboratory uncovered and unprotected, (*Music*) some nights, when I need his presence I go to call him and … and I discover him curled up under his dissection table, like a street urchin! I cover his body with a bed sheet and go.

(Background music is raised high to a pathetic mood. Madhabi turns her head and lowers and she appears to be weeping. Birabhai goes near from the back and holds her from the back. Lights dim and fade out)

SCENE-4

(Before the lights fade in muffled whispering sounds are heard; as if ten/ twelve people conspire against Krishna Mohan outside his residence. The intensity of the light increases. Prof. Krishna Mohan is seen meditating on the jewel of the frog

through the microscope. The frog-girls surround him hopping slowly. The muffled sound of whisper increases in volume and the words they speak outside are audible:)

Outsider-1:This fellow is a rascal; is doing nothing except taming hopping frogs.

(the lights change. The frog girls hop and jump encircling Krishna Mohan)

Outsider-2: People keep dogs and cats, parrots and mynas as pets. But this fellow runs a froggery here: breeds frogs at home.

(*Krishna Mohan gets up, moves towards the entrance door, pays heed to what is spoken outside*)

Outsider-3: Fie on him! Dirty fellow; moves in swampy yards in the middle of the night.

Outsider-1: They croak all through the night.

(*Croaking sound of frogs in chorus increases in volume*)

Outsider-2 These frogs disturb the sleep of midnights.

Outsider-3: Unsocial fool! Calls himself a professor.

5/6 people laugh in loud voice. (3 times)

(*Krishna Mohan is disturbed. He moves again to the entrance door and tries to figure who the laughing men are, fails to know what it was for. He comes back and sits near the microscope.*)

Outsider-2: Tell whatever you may, but when I listen to these sex calls of the frogs, I feel a tremor in my south pole (*croaking sound*)

Outsider-3: Might be! Are you sure these are sex calls of the frogs?

Outsider-1: I've left my family and children in my village and staying alone… when these frogs croak I remember my wife sleeping beside me.

Outsider-2: That's a nuisance; nuisance caused by this froggery owner's! He should be driven out from this locality. After all this is a residential area. Listen Chandra Sekhar Babu! This crack head should be driven out. How much rent he's paying Mr. Chandrasekhar?

Chadrasekhar: Fifteen thousand.

Outsider-2: I'll find you a better tenant who would pay you sixteen. Okay? Drive this fellow out.

Chandrasekhar: (*laughs*) It's not that easy Dhiraj Babu. These days the tenants have started threatening the house owners!

Outsider-1: Does he pay the house rent in time?

Chandrasekhar: Don't remind me of the house rent, Sir! He has qforgotten to pay the rent for the last two months.

Outsider-1 How do you tolerate such laxity?

Chandrasekhar: What can I do Sir? His wife says the professor turns into a swamp-trotter during the monsoon, remains absent at home and goes out for collecting specimen!

Outsider-2: This is too bad Sir! Too irregular! Drive him out and we will help you finding out a more regular rent payer for your house!

Chandrasekhar: How shall I collect the pending rent?

Outsider-3: We will collect it now!

Outsider-2 :Yes, let's go now!

(*By this time Madhabi has arrived and she's listening to what the house owner and the neighbors say. Madhabi takes different positions and her gestures change. She leans on the walls, tries to peep through the key hole of the door, opens the window a little, takes a tool and stands on it and sometimes crawls on the floor. Krishna Mohan communicates with Madhabi silently through gestures. After this three minutes long pantomime scene the professor laughs audibly*)

Madhabi: Hey! Why do you laugh? Listen to what they say?

Krishnamohan: What's there to listen?

Madhabi: They are gossiping about us!

Krishnamohan: How do you know?

Madhabi: Listen!

(*Krishna Mohan crawls on the ground adjacent to the front wall and talks while crawling*)

Krishnamohan: Sure! They might talk about us! In fact they should talk about us!

Madhabi: Why should they?

Krishnamohan: Since a great scientist inhabits here! Since the pipsqueaks should chant hymns in praise of Great Men. Am I not a Great Man?

(*Krishna Mohan draws a wooden stool and climbs on it*)

Am I not? Am I not a Great man?

(*Madhabi examines Krishna Mohan's body as if it is a piece of sculpture. She moves round him like visiting an antique in the museum*)

What are you exploring in my body? Explore! Go on exploring… Explore with a microscope, explore with a telescope! Explore me standing on the table explore me sleeping under the table, explore from all possible angles. Ultimately you'll be forced to call me a Great Man, if not a prophet.

(*Chandrasekhar calls from outside*)

Chandrasekhar: Mister! Oye Mister!

Krishnamohan: Who is this fellow calling to?

Madhabi: They are calling you. The colony dwellers have come. They've come to drag and push you out of this house.

Krishnamohan: Why? Can't scientists and frog researchers stay in this locality? Shall only the fiscal giants and the whole-sellers stay in these houses? Who the hell are they? Why should those philistines dominate our society? (*Shouts*) Why? What will happen to the geniuses who search for jewels in the frog's head?

Chandrasekhar: Mister, shall you please open the door?

Krishnamohan: Why should I open the door? Who do they think they are? None of the doors are kept open in this universe. All doors are kept shut! If they have the power, let them open by force! Why should I open?

Madhabi: Shhh! Lower you voice! Go… open the door!

Krishnamohan: I can't open the door! You open! Who are they to command me to open the door? Don't they know who dwells inside?

Madhabi: Shhh! Lower your voice! They're able to hear you.

Chandrasekhar: Why don't you open the door sir?

(a): We have come from the colony to meet you Sir!

Chandrasekhar: Will you open the door or not?

Madhabi: Go, open the door! You are a gentleman.

Krishnamohan: There are more than one people, Madhabi. I can't face so many petulants at a time! You go and open!

Madhabi: You're the husband of the house! Why should I go and face strangers? I don't know anyone in this colony!

Krishnamohan: They won't harm you! Go!

Madhabi: Why are you insisting me on? You are a professor and everyday you face ninety eight students in the general class! Why can't you face four / five people? Go-

Krishnamohan: Oh! You're so cruel, Madhabi! I'm now in a critical condition mentally; and you are insulting me? Calling me a coward? What do you think of me? Am I a coward? I'll open the door. See!

(*He rushes to the door and opens it. Chandrasekhar, the house owner enters. He is a middle aged person with a fragile body; he is very sensitive and a single touch or stroke makes him tingle and he is prone to laugh abnormally*)

Chandrasekhar: What sort of a man you are, Sir? I've been knocking at your door for the last ten minutes, and you are not responding? What were you doing inside? I know you creatures! You are not sleeping before twelve in the night!

Krishnamohan: Creatures? Do I look like a creature to you? Creatures may sleep at twelve in the night. What's that to you? Who are you?

Chandrasekhar: Don't you know who am I? Don't you know this Chandrasekhar, your house owner?

Krishnamohan: Owner? What do you own? You own a thick head! What else?

Chandrasekhar: What are you trying at? Aye? Trying to irritate me? Provoke me? What are you trying to do?

Madhabi: I'm sorry for him, Sir! He's too much engrossed in his research work… he is… I mean, he's totally workaholic.

Chandrasekhar: How shall your research help me Madam? We are small people. We've given our house to you on rent! If you'll forget to pay us the rent, how can we sustain in such hard times? When shall you pay my rent?

Krishnamohan: Are you telling it to me?

Chandrasekhar: You have not paid my house rent for last two months.

Krishnamohan: (laughs) Have you lost your head Sir? Madhabi? What does he say?

Madhabi: I had given you the money to pay the house rent!

Krishnamohan: What house? What rent? The purpose of my living here is not confined only to paying house rents. There are other serious things in the world to think about; do you understand that?

Madhabi: (Sighs) Ok Sir! Please sit for a while. Give me a chance to serve you a cup of coffee. It takes some time for the professor to come down from the mental height of research!

Chandrasekhar: What will happen to my house rent for two months, to my thirty thousand rupees?

Madhabi: I understand! You are too much annoyed with us!

Chandrasekhar: (*Assertively*) Yes! I'll be angry, I'll be outraged, I'll be infuriated… I'll be (*his volume increases*), furious and enraged! What do you think of me and my fragile body? How long will it endure your indifference to my house rent? (*He is not able to stand straight. He raises both of his legs and to Krishna Mohan's exploring eyes Chandrasekhar appears like a hopping frog. He strokes below his stomach and Chandrasekhar gets tingling sensation and bounces like a frog)*

Chandrasekhar: What are you doing? Compelling me to get angry? Why?

(*A sudden burst of the croaking sound of the frogs*)

What this sound, the sound of your research? Come out of your froggery and listen to what people say about you! What do they comment about you? You only recognize frogs, not human beings. You have not paid house rent for two consecutive months, and when I ask for it, you start tingling me at my lower stomach? What kind of behavior it is? You've turned my house into a village pond. Give me the house rent now and vacate the house by the end of this month! You deserve such rough behavior. (*Pause, Chandrasekhar takes quick steps and he seems excited. But his behavior looks funny*) I was a perfect gentle man. But you turned me a brash and cockeyed person.

Krishnamohan: Why are you behaving like a lord? Are you the lord of this house? I'm in possession of it now. I'm a scientist, a senior scientist of the country! How much your house rent comes to? Thirty thousand? (*Searches for his pockets and finds bundles of currency notes*) Yes! Here's the money! I've kept it for you. But I've forgotten to give it. I mean, I didn't find time to go to your house and press the calling bell. Then you'd come and I'd pay you. This is an arduous process. So, I did not care to pay. I am sorry for that. (*He pays the money*) Now Mr.... whatever you are! I am paying you hundred rupees extra (*gives the note and Chandrasekhar accepts*)

Chandrasekhar: (*He's no more angry and he smiles*) Thank you!

Krishnamohan: Happy? Are you happy now Mrs. House Lord? Why did you calm down? Get angry and hop like a frog. That's something! (*He threatens him to tingle again, Chandrasekhar hops and laughs*)

Chandrasekhar: (*Laughs*) Ha, ha, ha, ha, ha! There was no other way for an untamed tenant like you! Ha, ha, ha, Don't mind! You are the pride of our nation…of our state….of our locality!

(*Krishna Mohan also laughs and given him a tingling stroke on the stomach and Chandrasekhar feels ticklish and hops laughing simultaneously. The lights dim and it is dark*)

SCENE-5

(*Pattering sound of torrential rain outside. Light fades in on a spot that holds Krishna Mohan sitting and peeping through the microscope. It's midnight. The wall clock strikes twelve. Back ground music. Madhabi appears in a sexy looking nighty and exudes erotic feeling.)*

Madhabi: it's already twelve. Come in, It's time for sleep. You've worked for the entire day. Enough.

Krishnamohan: (*He does not seem to listen to anything. He keeps himself busy*)

Madhabi: Are you paying me a heed?

Krishnamohan: Yes! Tell me what exactly you want?

Madhabi: Keep your research aside. It's enough for today! Come, you need sleep.

Krishnamohan: (*irked*) Oh! (*Madhabi comes near! Krishna Mohan stands behind him. She holds K.M.'s face from behind, caresses and coaxes.*)

Madhabi: Don't get irritated! Come! We'll sleep together. I feel sleepy.

Krishnamohan: You know I'm busy, Madhabi! Why do you suffer for me? Go and sleep.

Madhabi: We haven't slept together since a year! Come! You'll feel better during this rainy night. (*Pattering sound of rain increases in the background effect*)

Krishnamohan: Wait for one more night Madhabi! May be tonight I'll get the jewel. Go and rest yourself alone. Don't torture yourself for this workaholic person.

(*Music feeds the emptiness of Madhabi who sighs*)

Madhabi: It's the eighth year since I married you. Whenever I called you, you evaded me with this or that pretext. Have you ever thought for a moment how I've lived all these eight years?

Krishnamohan: Eight years! (*He counts with his finger*) Eight… Eight… years! Okay!!

(*Madhabi moves to the window which is perennially open. The croaking sound of Phulia and Tikili is heard. Madhabi monologuizes*)

Madhabi: Phulia and Tikili are calling each other for erotic union. They are happy within the card board house. In moonlit nights, when I become lonely and feel abandoned… I call him to share the calm and cool air, but he avoids me with some pretext or the other. It has been repeated all through these eight years and I could never taste the forbidden fruit of conjugal life. He has never kissed me during their eight long years. When the heat in my blood increases, when I feel animated, when fire of passion flows up I hug the pillow and weep amorously.

Krishnamohan: Amorously! Amorously enamoured and falling on bed love sick! Don't you know your husband who's an abstinent saint of frogs? Sex is a "vulgar act" my dear! Allow your husband to live a saintly life engaged in his research. Isn't it a kind of yoga?

Madhabi: But why should you forbid sex?

Krishnamohan: I'm scared of such vulgarity!

Madhabi: There's nothing to feel scared of; come! I'm with you. I'll teach you the modus operandi.

(*She takes hold of Krishna Mohan's arm and drags him to the bed) I'll cure your sickness.*

Krishnamohan: Why are you ragging me at this odd hour of the night? A single bout of sexual exercise would blow my project off. So, Madam! I can't accept your erotic invitation. Leave me!

Madhabi: Let it go to dust. Come with me to the bed. Come and eject into me your creative force... Fill in my fertile and fevered blank space with your stony phallus!

Krishnamohan: You are turning the society savage… Honesty speaking, you are distracting my research.

Madhabi: Honesty demands nakedness. Honesty generates thunder storms and lightening flash…

(Sound of rain increases in volume, lightning flashes and thunder sounds accompany)

Burn my depths. A divine universe lies there dormant, waiting for your exploding strokes!

(Madhabi drags Krishna Mohan and he protests. There is a free style tussle between them.)

Madhabi: Why are you fidgeting, Aye? Come to my bed … like a rod of thunder. Don't feel scared to eject the juice of life. Come to me as Rudra, the fire incarnate; come to me as a fulfiller of the erotic sacrifice. Ignite the fire lying asleep under the ashes of my blood.

Krishnamohan: Rudra is not *Pasu* Madhabi. You are invoking the beast within me.

Madhabi: There's nothing wrong Professor! The fire in you and me would encounter each other and become complete in simultaneous male female duality. In that wholeness, the sexual fire would burn us together into perfection. It would be an indefinable state of integrity.

Krishnamohan: Don't you know Madhabi, I am the bull and I am the cow, too, Don't you know my frogs are the thereomorphic symbols of the tantra of creation. I am trying to imbibe into me the essence of Rig Vedic Agni. The fire that lies within the frogs manifests as the jewel in their heads.

Madhabi: Invoke that Agni from the frogs. Inseminate into me the possibility of a new life. Why do you refuse to see your wife as a fertile mother? Act like an able father and inject your seeds into me. The frogs are like buffaloes bathing in slime and water.

Let us reenact the primordial union between Prajapati Brahma and the beautiful Ushas. Let us recreate in the wilderness of the first dawn of creation. Our coitus shall actualize for the well-being of the universe.

Krishnamohan: How can I celebrate the act of this coitus? I am an abstinent saint of frogs. I can't infringe the plenum of this Uncreate condition. Injecting semen into you will be a violation of the status – quo.

Madhabi: So? What'd you do now?

Krishnamohan: I'm sorry. I am reluctant to be yoked with you in any erotic performance. Accept me as the lord of frogs. You may also accept me as the lord of Yoga. I'm *Urdhwalingam* and *Udrhwa retas*... the phallus pointing upward. I represent the ascent of the semen, not its downward flow.

Madhabi: What do you mean by that? Won't you allow a drop of semen to flow from your body?

Krishnamohan: Yes, I'm controlling my sexual power. It's a kind of Yoga.

Madhabi: (*Flares up*) Why did you marry me, then? Why shall you control your sexual power? Why should you check the downward flow of semen?

Krishnamohan: To, achieve the state of desirelessness.

Madhabi: That's hoax. Prove yourself by becoming a father.

Krishnamohan: No. I am not going to be a father before the fire jewel is discovered on the head of a frog. (*Exasperated*) Didn't your Engineer father teach you how to behave with a scientist?

Madhabi: Hell with your science! My father didn't have time to explore that his son-in-law is an imbecile and a bungler of all joy. I fuck your research! You dunderhead!

(She pushes Krishna Mohan violently and Krishna Mohan falls down. Light changes. A choral humming bursts out. Seven/ eight frog – girls come hopping and surround the scientist. Strobe effect lighting makes the scene blurred. Light fades out. Madhabi is seen throwing herself on the bed. She throws one or two pillows at her husband, hugs a pillow and buries her head behind a pillow. The choral humming continues. Back ground music supplements Madhabi's action. Lights dim and fade out.)

SCENE-6

(Light fades in to discover Krishna Mohan sleeping on the floor, under his dissection table. A ray of light streaming through the skylight falls on him. He gets up like a guilty person, hiding himself from the view of his wife. But Madhabi is found sleeping on her bed. Light focuses on her. Then the spot holds Krishnamohan. Music.

Krishna Mohan dresses up quietly and puts on the rain coat. He takes out the net for catching frogs. Then he puts on his long joker cap, puts on his shoes and frisks away without looking back at his sleeping wife.

Background music. Madhabi gets up and moves towards the toilet, there's no knock on the door and Birabhandra enters with his folding bed and suitcase; keeps it on the floor, peeps inside and calls)

Birabhadra: Madhabi! Madhabi!

Madhabi: (*Enters wiping her hand in a towel*) How come, you're here so early, Bira Bhai?

Birabhadra: I'm here on my way to Koraput. I came by the first bus. Where's your lunatic husband?

Madhabi: He was in his laboratory working through the night! Where has he gone?

(*She ransacks the room and the entire house, does not find him*)

I don't know! Where has he gone? (*She goes to the shoe stand and tells from there) He has hopped away furtively*!

Birabhadra: How do you know?

Madhabi: His rain shoes are not here.

Birabhadra: Why does the scientist go out without informing you?

Madhabi: He avoids me. (*smiles*) Anyway, that's good for us Birabhai. There'd be no body in the house to disturb us.

Birabhadra: What does that mean?

Madhabi: He won't return tonight.

Birabhadra: How do you know that? The Scientist is not a predictable character.

Madhabi: It's raining throughout. There's a depression in the Bay of Bengal. The Scientist loves rainy days. He loves to catch frogs when they usually come out during the rain. We'll take an early dinner and sleep easily. Okay? What do you want to eat? I've some boiled chicken in the fridge.

Birabhadra: That'll do. I don't want to go out in this rain. It's very heavy.

Madhabi: Come in, I'll serve you a hot cup of tea.

(Both of them go inside. The sound of rain increases in volume. Light dims. There are lightning and subdued thunder sounds, music. Light fades in and it denotes night. Bira is seen sleeping on the temporary bed put down stage left. Madhabi is found sleeping on the right side bed. Music intensifies the effect of the rainy night. Madhabi gets up. She doesn't have proper sleep. She comes near the bed room of Bira, but does not dare to get in. Bira is seen tossing on the bed. He gets up and finds Madhabi standing on the veranda that separates both the rooms.)

Birabhadra: Did you call me?

Madhabi: No!

(Birabhadra tries to sleep turning his head back to Madhabi. Madhabi runs to her bed and feigns to sleep. Bira gets up and lights a cigarette. Then he goes to the veranda and peeps at Madhabi's bedroom. Standing there he speaks a monologue:)

Birabhadra: Madhabi! This is after a long time. After eight long years we got a change to stay overnight in a closed house. How can I sleep peacefully? The only distance between you and me is a wall. But it feels as if we are miles away. I don't know whether you remember or not? But I see it closely… which day and which time I met you where…. (*He goes back to bed*)

(*Madhabi tosses on the bed. She could not sleep. She comes and asks*)

Madhabi: Are you still awake, Birabhai?

Birabhadra: No sleep.

Madhabi: Better you sleep. Try again. You are tired after this long distance tour.

Birabhadra: What about you?

Madhabi: All nights are one and the same for me.

Birabhadra: Isn't there a difference between all other nights and this night?

Madhabi: Yes, there is. Tonight I feel like…

Birabhadra: Like?

Madhabi: I feel, I mean… if the first dark cloud of this monsoon whipped its rain on me… I mean, if I get a chance to drink a drop of it…(*Music*) it would have transformed into a jewel in my womb…

Birabhadra: Madhabi!

(*They come closer and embrace each other. Background music: A taraana of Raag Behag begins in "Madhya laya" (middle pace) and moves towards "drit laya" (fast rhythm)*)

Na dir dir deem tanan
Deem tana dere na.

(*Lights dim, fade out and fade in again. Birabhadra and Madhabi stand frozen on the same composition*)

Deem deem tananana
Na dir dir dir dir dir deem
Taad taad taa titikat gadi gan
Dha gadi gan dha gadi gan.

(*Lighting changes to show passage of time. Silence. The sound of rain continues. It is midnight with sound of cricket. There is a knocking sound on the door. But Bira and Madhabi do not respond. Light holds Krishna Mohan entering from the audience side and climbing the window that stands on the apron stage. He pushes himself inside and falls on to the floor inside. Krishna Mohan discovers Madhabi and Birabhadra standing still in embracing position.*)

Krishnamohan: (*Jumps in astonishment and cries*)

Eureka!

(*Then he goes to Birabhadra, snatches him and lifts him, finally places him on the floor near the dissection table for dissection. There he takes out knife and attempts to dissect him. Madhabi is frightened and she holds her husband hand.*)

Madhabi: What are you doing? Are you in senses? Stop this nuisance you brute!

Krishnamohan: I got it Madhabi, finally I got my jewel. Thank you for trapping this specimen! What did he say he was? He was the sky and the jungle and the ocean! I've dissected them.

Madhabi: Shut up!

Krishnamohan: It's not a pipe-dream anymore! Come! I'll fill in your empty sky with the glint of this jewel... There's nothing to be scared of now. I've lacerated the sky, deforested the jungle and mangled the ocean!

Madhabi: Mangled?

Krishnamohan: The esoteric limitless shrinks and lies now like a frozen slab of ice!

(*Madhabi leans on Birabhadra and freezes. Krishna Mohan raises his hand as a gesture of victory. Light fades out. Music*)

*****

A PLAY ABOUT A PLAY

The playwright's study is open. There is a large desk with stacks of unfinished play scripts, under which the playwright's face is buried. The playwright reposes on the papers of an ongoing script and has lapsed into deep intuitive thinking. Dim light. A saxophone is played from a distance. The music evokes nostalgia. Gradually, the intensity of light increases and the sound of music heard nearer. Now the sax player emerges from the left playing the horn. He moves around the stage playing as if he was inspiring the playwright, helping him dig from the deep unconscious a rare idea. But the playwright does not get up. The sax player disappears through the wings. Saxophone stops. Silence.

A knocking sound is heard from the outside door. There is no response from the playwright. The sound of knocking increases in volume. Some stray dogs bark in chorus. A male voice calls:

Voice over: Playwright! Playwright! Why don't you fix a calling bell here? Hello! Mr. Playwright!

(*The playwright gets up. The knocking sound is heard again. Barking of dogs.*)

Playwright: (*sleepy voice*) who's there? Give me a minute! Why are you battering my door so heavily? (he goes and opens the door. A stranger of about 50 years enters. He has put on a long jokers cap and has donned a wide laughter on his face. The playwright is intrigued to find this strange looking man bumping into his room.)

Playwright: Excuse me! Who're you sir, at this odd hour?

C C: I'm a CC, full form-"cultural contractor". Couldn't follow? Well, I smell of culture. I'm fed with culture and I breathe culture…(He goes to the playwright's desk and peeps in to a manuscript, takes out some and smells them. It feels good to meet a playwright at this odd hour of the night! Anyway…Don't you have an extra chair to get your guest seated? Okay, I will manage. Have you finished the play?

Playwright: Yeah! It's almost finished.

C C: Let me browse through it, give it for a moment.

Playwright: Well, ugh! I'd like to give a final touch to the play. But why should I handover the script to you?

C C: Who are you to denounce me like this? How long have you been writing plays? Eh! What do you know about our present cultural crisis?

Playwright: There's no crisis in our culture. You are inventing crisis to frighten the intelligentsia.

C C: Aye! You Banka bazaar hack! My job is to censor what you write.

Playwright: Ha! What do you think of yourself? You talk as if you are the Tsar of Russia!

C C: What's that to you? We want to censor if there's any acrimonious political matter in your play. You can't give it directly to the producer for staging the performance.

Playwright: If I give?

CC: You'll be arrested, holed up in the asylum until you are recovered from this frenzy?

Playwright: What? Recovered? What'd you mean by that? I'm not a patient!

C C: You are frenzied. You'll have to stay in the asylum until you publicly recanted your political views. Well, What's the title of the play?

Playwright: It's a play about a play; partly autobiographical.

C C: Whose? Yours? Autobiography?

Playwright: Not necessarily mine, because the Director says it's his autobiography and the heroine says it's her story and finally a bureaucrat…An I.A.S. officer claims that I am mis-portraying his character in the play.

C C: Have you vilified him?

Playwright: No! He's a supporting character only, doesn't like my physical presence in the story.

C C: why?

Playwright: May be jealousy, may be he's afraid of my popularity, my outspoken behavior.

C C: Jealousy? For your popularity? Ha ha ha ha! So you claim you are an outspoken guy (*He moves*) to impress me? Okay! Let's think I am impressed. Now I feel I should browse through your script at least. Give it to me for a while. (*He turns the pages*) It seems you haven't completed it.

Playwright: It'll take about an hour to give the finishing touch.

C C: I understand. *(He ponders)*They haven't paid you for the script. It was difficult for you to make both ends meet while writing. The problems that faced you were insoluble…

Playwright: But I managed to solve them, and yet that wasn't the end of my troubles. Believe me, there are no such things as miracles. I'm sure you realize that.

C C: Yes I do. You are working hard over the script, till it becomes a super hit and the producer pays you something-even though a measly sum. Don't misunderstand me you have to work hard; that's going to be your miracle.

Playwright: Miracle or not, I've to write plays to sustain myself in this city, just to carve a niche.

C C: Take me as your agent. Now write another play and give it to me. I'll pay you sumptuously.

Playwright.: But that doesn't mean you'll force me to write. The play will be performed virtually in my vision. The characters will stand before me and dictate their dialogues. I'll just take notes.

C C: You're dodging the real work, making pretexts. That won't do. Give me a play script. Now!

Playwright: The play script is not toothpaste so that it would eject when you press the tube!

C C: What sort of a playwright you are?

Playwright: Delete my name from the list of playwrights.

CC: But you must have to write this play. Why have I come to you at this hour of the night then? I expected you to be a spontaneous writer.

Playwright: Get out!

C C: *(he laughs)* I am not going so easily. If you can't write, give me dictation. If you don't dictate, I'll throttle you to regurgitate a play.

Playwright: Will you use physical force on me? I'll call the police.

C C: I have a henchman standing outside your quarters. Should I call him? *(Calls)* Hey you boxer! Will you come inside for a moment?

(A heavily built man of about 30 comes and salutes)

Henchman: Present Please Boss!

Playwright: Why did you call him inside? This is a playwright's house and it is twelve past fifteen in the night!

C C: Boxer! This playwright refuses to write plays, doesn't care for my orders.

Henchman: *(takes out a spring knife)* this knife was specially manufactured for this playwright, boss! It'll take just a minute to thrust it into his body.

C C: Bear with him for five minutes.

Henchman: Yes Boss! I'll wait because it's your order.

Playwright: You're forcing me to write a play; is that right?

C C: If you don't succumb to my straight finger orders, I have to bend it a little, right?

Playwright: Who's this goon with a knife?

C C: Kind a' chopper; he chops off all that is trash in our culture, all those good-for-nothings of our precious civilization.

(He takes away a bunch of papers and looks at them)

Playwright: What do you understand from that? It's neither poetry nor fiction…What you see in those papers is not narrative. Do you understand plays?

C C: Damn it! I read your papers with a goddamn casual attitude. Plays don't belong to sophisticated category of literature.

Playwright: You can't say like that. I've a special theory about its creation! Plays provide visual literature.

C C: Nobody bothers about theories these days. But there could be big stakes involved in this for us; if you had eye balls to see into the possibilities, if you thought for one second about the implications (laughs). But I wonder how you have chosen to become a character in your own play?

Playwright: I said I have a theory!

C C: What theory? Where do you cull the stories and the characters from?

(The sax player provides music and it is supported by keyboard. The music denotes the creative process narrated by the playwright in the following aria)

Playwright: I don't know how the story emerges for the play. I listened to stories since I was a child: fairy tales with monsters, jackals and wolves talk…I heard different sounds, before I recognized my own name....then sounds of gurgling, pounding under water….sounds of mother's heartbeat….sounds of the flow of blood. I heard ocean of blood swimming around me. Through other's veins. I heard it streaming down through ancient times, like it belongs to another body….then I understood the language of the jackals and the wolves. My organs were expanding. The sound of cells booming through wind through my nose-holes, toe nails rubbing blankets in the

	dark…Then one day, sound becomes what they call "music" and I recognize melody. The melody surges up…then calms down, drips down my soul as dialogues. The dialogues transform in to visual images and images in to characters. I see faces. Faces call me. Call me into those characters, and I discover myself in a dense forest, a forest of unknown faces. Then the faces become known. I'm dragged into a never-seen-before continent. I feel exhilarated. That's my play, the inexpressible; thrill of creation.
C C:	So, the act of creating a play is a thrill to you. Does this thrill continue after you are through with the play? I mean do you feel the thrill now?
Playwright:	This time it's a play about a play… Some others say it's a play within a play…may be, it's a new outlook about a play.
C C:	You mean I've to buy new spectacles to view your play from a different angle? Is that it?
Playwright:	No!
C C:	There's more?
Playwright:	Yes
C C:	What is it? Have you fooled your spectators?
Playwright:	What do you mean?
C C:	What was that mumbo jumbo you were talking about your plays? That doesn't make any sense at all!
Playwright:	What sort of a cultural contractor you are?
C C:	In every age playwrights and artists came to the cultural contractors. When they were especially in need of a platform, when they needed a dais or a stage to perform, they would definitely come to contractors. We contractors provide you suitable stages, with makeup and costume, with media and advertising entrepreneurs….So, it's your duty to fall at our feet and gather our blessings. *(He catches hold of the manuscript and browses through the papers and goes on speaking)*

C C: You seem to write well. Come to us occasionally and borrow ideas from us. You'll do it better. Okay! Let me take leave of you. It's already Four A.M. I'll have to contact two more playwrights and inspire them to write plays….Ha, Ha…..that's my routine job: to inspire playwrights to write good plays and to invigorate our naïve spectators. So long:

(*As the cultural contractor takes leave of the playwright and goes toward the exit door, someone knocks and hollers*)

Voice Over: Playwright! Hello! Are you awake?

Playwright: This is Roby Das, our friend, director of the play! Just a minute CC! (*he opens the door, Roby Das enters*)

Roby: How come, you are awake so early? What's wrong with you? You never leave the bed before eight o'clock! Who's this man? (*he fumbles*)I mean, I'm sorry, we haven't met before, have we?

Playwright: No, you've never before. He says he is a special class cultural contractor…He inspires playwrights to break new grounds in the field of drama.

C C: Every year I visit Mahakantar to spread our cultural messages, to enunciate the national cultural manifesto. Besides, I have shaped the political culture of India after a long time. The Tsar seeks my political intervention during the periods of cultural crisis.

Roby: That's something great. But I have never met you earlier!

C C: That's why your name is not there in the list of chartered theatre directors of India.

Playwright: We're sorry; we couldn't meet this cultural contractor earlier. Our play and the team's honor would have been escalated.*(The playwright takes out a comb from the back pocket of the trouser and dresses his hair)*

C C: *(to Roby Das)* You may come to me anytime you like. Now, keep this card with you. My telephone number is there! I'm coming. (He gives a card)I'm sorry I've to meet two more playwrights now. (*The CC exits)*

Roby: Hey hey! Looks like a cultural ghost. By the by have you finished the script, Playwright?

Playwright: Yes almost!

Robi: Read the beginning. The starting of the play is important. Now tell me how it starts.

Playwright: *(Reads and enacts)* The playwrights study; there is a large desk with stacks of unfinished manuscripts, under which the playwright's face is buried. The playwright reposes on the papers of an ongoing script and has just lapsed in to slumber. There's a type writer sitting at one corner of the script. A table light illuminates the playwright's reposing posture. It is past midnight. Somebody kicks on the door from outside. *(knocking sound is heard)*There is no response from the sleeping playwright. The knocking sound increases in volume. Following that some stray dogs bark on the street. The playwright is disturbed. *(Now the playwright start enacting)*

Playwright: Just a minute; I'm going. *(Then he reads and gets irritated)* Ugh! Who's there? Can't you wait for a little? *(He goes and opens the door)*A queer looking middle aged man of about 50 years enters. *(The cultural contractor appears, enters in and stands still)*. This is the cultural contractor!

Roby Das: I know this man! You may get out of this place. Vacate the stage.

C C: *(He exits silently)*

Roby Das: What next?

Playwright: Then enters Roby Das, the director. He deals with the cultural contractor and exits.

Roby Das: And then?

Playwright: The director asks the playwright to read the script. *(street dogs bark)*

Roby Das: And the street dogs bark.

Playwright: And the producer of the play hollered:

(The voice of producer from off stage)

Voiceover of producer: Playwright! Playwright!

Playwright: *(acts as if irritated)* What shall the playwright do at this hour of the night? Eh? Why do you knock at the door of my heart? You will reduce me to a heart patient, will you? What wrong have I done to you?

(He goes to the door and opens it. The producer bumps in)

Producer: Good morning, good morning, good morning everybody!

Roby Das: Hi Producer! How come you are here at this earliest moment of the day? OK, That's alright. What kind of booster you have bought to the playwright?

Producer: Is he through with the play? Mr. Playwright! Have you finished?

Roby Das: Have you given him any booster dose?

Producer: What booster? What do you mean Roby Das? And Mr. Playwright! Are you in need of booster doses to finish the play?

Roby Das: The cultural contractor supervises whether the playwright has been given any booster. Whether there's anyone for inspiring him to write the new play. You may bear the cost of his boozing expenses…You may provide him with a new X, I mean, provide him with a beautiful woman, woman to inspire the playwright! You may…

Producer: Where'll I search for a woman? At best I'll ask Shelly Das to inject him with fresh inspiration. That's the only solution at hand.

Playwright: She thinks she is smarter than I am. You know it. She can smell my thoughts before I even think 'em.

Roby Das: She should try to take care of you! Alright?

Playwright: No, You are not. You need Shelly more than I do.

Roby Das: What does that mean?

Playwright: You are after Shelly. If she comes to my room you will forcefully fondle her, cuddle her and dandle her…finally you'll end up fornicating…ha, ha…! Downloading your emotional liquid!

Producer: Roby Das should pull the reins of his instincts here after!

Roby Das: So, you want me not to enter Shelly's house, Is that so? You don't like Shelly offer me a cup of tea. Is that all you wish?

Producer: Shelly Das is famous for her high temperature. Put the kettle of tea on her body and prepare a cup of tea within five minutes. She is a little oven, viscerally.

Playwright: Right now, I am not interested in ovens. Fetch me little whisky…..three/four pegs will do.

Roby Das: Add four more pegs. Bring some ice if possible!

Producer: A carton of whisky bottles might be lying in my car. Go and bring a quart or two quarters.

Playwright: I've some bread and boiled eggs.

Roby Das: That'll do. Now, Playwright, read out some pages.

Playwright: *(reads)* "The playwright reclines on his desk burying his head on piles of papers n' manuscripts. Someone knocks on the door. *(Knocking sound)*

Roby Das: Stray dogs started barking. *(barking sound)*

*(Recites)*Stray dogs started barking *(barking sound)* See! I know what you think, even before what you think!

Playwright: Certain sounds are perennially repeated in my life. It's a part of my living process. A mysterious knocker pounds on my inner doors. Unseen dogs start barking on the dark desolate bypaths of my inner self.

Producer: Ha! That's interesting. Does it happen everyday? Or, are you sizzled before the whisky arrives? What's the matter Roby Das? How could you listen to the barking sound before the playwright heard it?

Roby Das: Playwrights have certain experiences in their repertoire which get repeated like leitmotifs. I know these blind spots since the playwright is in our team. *(pause)*

Playwright: That's right.

Roby Das: We share each other's dreams. When I interpret and direct, I try to highlight these invisible spots of life. My job is to express the inexpressible.

Producer: Roby Das! Why don't you throw light on the major booster of inspiration for the playwright?

Playwright: What's that major booster, you think?

Producer: Shelly Das, the heroine. Don't you need that body heater?

Playwright: Where's she? She seems to have been compressed somewhere between passion and sin, between coquetry and love.

Producer: That's again an invisible terrain! Roby Das may summon her. What do you say? You are the director of the play.

Roby Das: There's an irony involved in it. Let me ask the sound engineer to play Shelly's favorite song. The song would melt her and she would come floating in the flood of love: Sound engineer! Play the record:

Producer: Roby Das! Do you really need a song here?

Playwright: Yes! You can't delete songs from my plays under the pretext of realism or modernity.

Roby Das: Shall it be in male voice or female voice?

Producer: There's a stock song in Pranob Pattnayak's voice. Play it if you so like. But what does your realism demand?

Roby Das: Songs do not hamper realism. I will use the song to evoke a memory, a song in male voice.

Playwright: To lend a dreamy ambience to the sequence. I don't know the song rendered by Pranob Pattnayak, but the theme should be similar to Shakespeare's sonnet in

"*As you like it*". Something like: "Life is drama and the world is a stage and we human beings are actors". Shelly's movement should feel like poetry in action.

Producer: Ok, done. We'll include the song here. But you must hide somewhere. Make yourself invisible.

Playwright: Why?

Producer: Shelly will come searching for you and finally find you in a tight embrace. *(He laughs)* Ok? Now you get lost.

(The playwright quits the stage by the left wing. The producer pulls the director and they exit by the right wing. The stage is empty and the prelude of the song is played. Shelly is aged about 30, though she is decked up lasciviously to betray her age. She emerges and searches for the playwright as if they are in a hide-and-seek game. After sometime, Roby Das enters and exercises his powers as a director)

Roby: Stop playing the song! *(The song stops.Shelly freezes)* There was no song in the original script. The dramatist introduced this game now. *(He touches her body and asks)*Defreeze now! *(Shelly breaks the frozen posture)*

Shelly: Where's the Playwright?

Roby: May be hibernating in his cave. He's writing a play about you and feels sultry in your absence, little deflated. You need to pep him up. Act as a stimulator to that depressed guy. *(Takes out a bundle of currency notes)* Keep this money with you for meeting the incidentals. Use all your guile and slyness. Okay?

Shelly: *(She smiles)* I'll pump him up by my love, inject warmth in to his body.

Roby: That's right. You are capable of that Shelly! Now your job is to transport him to new heights, to propel and shoot him to a blooming creation….Okay? All the best.

(Roby Das claps rhythmically and orders)

Start music!

(The music starts, Roby Das disappears and Shelly's quest game starts in choreography. Lights change)

Song

Life is a drama
It's flawed actor I am
I've put on a blotch of blemish
Like the moon's dark surface.

I've to enact my part
With whatever is given to me as talent
Never to bother for
Small or big achievement.

No credentials will I win,
I'll calmly exit when
I'm through with the scene.
I will go unconsecrated and forlorn;
No garlands, no kudos for the performance.
They'll deface
My body with blemish and stain
Still I'd consider it a providential boon

(The song allows Shelly and Playwright to play a crude game of hide and seek in choreographed steps. Shelly, at the climax, embraces playwright and transports him to her house. The change of space is highlighted.)

SCENE-2

The Playwright is frantically searching for Shelly and hollering for her at different sides:

Playwright: Shelly! Shelly! Where're you? Are you hiding somewhere or what? Cooee!

Voiceover: *(Shelly imitates)* Cooee! You are playing hide and seek with me! Now it's my turn *(She appears laughing)*

Playwright: Oh! It's such a big apartment! So big are the halls. Is it a basement?

Shelly: Yes! It's a basement! My new house!

Playwright: Why did you hire a basement? There are no windows!

Shelly: I haven't hired it. I bought it. What are you going to do with windows? Space is stretching all around us.

Playwright: It's damp. Water seeps up through the floor. Feel, the bed sheets are damp.

Shelly: I'll put hot electric Iron on your bed.

Playwright: The walls are damp! There's mildew round the skirting. It's dirty, it's greasy. We were much better off there in my old room. I thought you were taking me to a cozier comfortable heaven! But what I find it now the bed sheets are damp and dirty! It's stinking!

Shelly: Oh, no! You are making it up! What gives you the idea the house is stinking? Don't you ever notice anything brighter? Why do you always look at the darker side? It's morbid. Your imagination!

Playwright: There are no streets, no open air!

Shelly: But I'm a professional artist you know! I am hired for theatre shows; producers call in, I get contracts for T.V. serials….I shouldn't be easily accessible to them…I mean, I should not be available on the streets and pubs…My clients should reach me through a circuitous way! Climbing down and climbing up, hidden behind curtains and frills and falls! *(she laughs coquettishly)*

Playwright: That's how you keep them hypnotized!

Shelly: Otherwise how can I fleece them? You know I'm a bad girl! *(laughs)*

Playwright: Too bad a girl! *(laughs)*

Shelly: That's the only way I survive in this material world. In the so called gentle families they search for chaste girls….ha ha! I hate them like disease. I'm born as a bad girl, misused by my father's friends as I was bad, and finally I am here-(*sighs*) a bad girl.

Playwright: What happened to your father? He was an officer in the secretariat.

Shelly: He bamboozled government money and got fired. Then he was hospitalized for cancer. That last day of summer of 1975, I had just turned fifteen-it was the beginning of real life for me, the life that separates castles in the air, and illusions and gradually I experienced fables from harsh reality. I was forced to step in to the glamour world, swayed to the rhythms of the album songs and then the producers asked me to sway my hips on the bed up an down. Father's cameo therapy was costlier than my body. We could not take possession of the dead body of my father for the funeral rituals. Then I sold myself to a theatre company. And since then I am an incorrigibly bad girl, irrecoverably bad.

Playwright: Ah! This is so cruel. It leaves no one. And now, as I look at you, you've aged already. You've developed your first wrinkles on your face. Is there a white hair on your ear? You didn't have it before. *(Shelly lowers her head)* Your head is drooping, a flower too heavy for its stalk.

Shelly: How does it matter how fast I grow? What's the difference whether it takes ten minutes or an hour, a fortnight or a year? We all get there at the end.

Playwright: Your story seems to ooze secretions of decay like your basement house. The ceiling might soon fall in. The plaster's crumbling. I can feel the weight on my shoulder already. Is all this an image of time? Everything disintegrates before our eyes.

Shelly: So long as I'm with you I'm not afraid to die. But how long shall you be with me? You are commissioned to write a play, right? How much they are going to pay you?

Playwright: Nothing! They pay for the poems, for writing fiction-not a farthing for the plays. So, I think I will write down our own story.

Shelly: Our own story? Is that so cheap? Are you going to write our story ex gratia? I'll ask the producer.

Playwright: That'd be fatuous.

Shelly: I will contact a serial producer. They pay good money. Shall I talk to one?

Playwright: Yes! Please do.

Shelly: On one condition. You'll have to stay here with me, in this basement; for eternity. I'll sit beside you, caress your body and shall of course, inspire you.

Playwright: Okay! Granted! I am ready to hazard prolonged winter in your frozen basement.

Shelly: Don't worry. I'll heat up your cold through the warmth of my love.

(She goes near and embraces the playwright)

Playwright: *(Holding her)* Thank you. But I'm afraid, you can't hold me for eternity. Look, you've already started crumbling. Your warmth may not last long. All I can see is mildew in your body.

Shelly: It seems you are obsessed with the idea of decay: we'll all decompose one day. Your play shall be dated and rotten one day.

Playwright: I submit myself before time. I'm not an author pining for a space in eternity.

Shelly: Writers are always mysteries to me. What you people do exactly when you write? Do you journey through a story that does have neither a beginning nor an ending?

Playwright: Where's the beginning? I grasp a chaos; I enter into a wilderness...Then I try to tame the chaos and the disorder.

Shelly: What do you get out of this exercise?

Playwright: May be...I don't know. May be I want to transform the world through my play...

Shelly: What sort of a "world" do you need?

Playwright: A world as it should be...That's what I mean is quiet personal.

Shelly: And that leads to a greater entropy than in your personal chaos. Every time, when you start thinking so much about a simple life, an eat-and-sleep-and…and-fuck life things shall get complicated. You'll again end up in wilderness. If you seek for pleasure or something, that is different.

Playwright: Taming the chaos is not agony, it's pleasure for me, a sort of spiritual exercise.

Shelly: Do you want to harvest contentment?

Playwright: Contentment is not enough. I hope for boundless joy…kind of ecstasy. I hope, with you beside me an epiphany may strike me; a completely unexpected and inexplicable experience. In this timeless moment my understanding and experience of the universe might be irrevocably transformed. I am waiting for some kind of a sudden manifestation. May be, some day the intuitive revelation would enlighten me.

Shelly: You amaze me, Playwright! May be, you are the only species in the world who is still waiting to experience an emotional euphoria. But I wonder how I'll help you inducing such an ecstatic moment! If you want I can call a younger girl from the Drama school. You said I'm crumbling with age.

Playwright: Ecstasy is a perilous condition Shelly! Which young girl you'll call for my inspiration? What will she do? Ecstasy leads to loss of self-control; it's a temporary loss of consciousness. I can't write the play if I'll be in a state of epiphany all the time. I must come back to reality.

Shelly: Ecstasy is very transient.

Playwright: I might attain that in the process of creation.

Shelly: But how can you create unless you blend my experiences into that of yours? First explore my interior.

Playwright: Do you insist me to dig into you physically? Or is it a spiritual interiority you are asking me to explore?

Shelly: I don't believe in this spiritual-sexual duality. Our stories should interpenetrate each other. Won't you cooperate?

Playwright: I'll call it my story.

Shelly: And so I'll call it my story.

Playwright: One day, you will be freed from the bondage of your "I-ness"

Shelly: And you'll be emancipated from your "mine"

Playwright: That will be the content of our Play about the play.

Shelly: Fine! You start writing; I'll go for the shooting of a serial. They pay two thousand rupees per day. We will manage to meet our expenses comfortably. Okay? I'll be back by 6 in the evening.

Playwright: That's okay!

Shelly: There's a henchman outside. He'll guard you from outside interferences. He won't allow visitors to meet you. At one thirty P.m. he will serve you three and half pegs of whisky and your lunch: Fried rice, salad and chicken curry. What more you need? Don't allow that hench man to pour whisky for you. That bugger'd gulp the full bottle. I've kept the bottle in the refrigerator. Go personally and consume your quota, Is that alright? So, I'm going.

(Shelly embraces the playwright registers a kiss and leaves)

After Shelly leaves, the saxophone player enters from the left playing his horn. He crosses from left to right and plays. The light dims and the background keyboard plays the counterpoint the sax player. The Playwright keeps himself busy writing. The henchman enters from behind with Nirlipta, a new comer, a young handsome bureaucrat. The sax stops playing and the player exits the stage. Silence.

Henchman: *(enters with Nirlipta)* Get in Sir! *(Nirlipta enters to Playwright)* Jai Hind! Sir! This Sir is pestering me to talk to you sir! Kindly adjust him! Jai Hind Sir! *(He exits)*

Playwright: Yes! How can I help you Sir?

Nirlipta: I want to meet Shelly Das.

Playwright: She's out for shooting a TV soap. May I know who you are, please!

Nirlipta: I'm Nirlipta Pattnayak, an administrative officer from the Odisha Secretariat, an old friend of Shelly. Who are you Sir? If you don't mind!

Playwright: I'm a playwright, working on a new project-writing a play about a play.

Nirlipta: Nice meeting you Sir *(both shake hands)* I just need a bit of information, I mean small details. What's so big about this play?

Playwright: It's a new experiment, to be precise, it's a play about a play. We are using our own life experiences as the theatrical events of the play.

Nirlipta: Life experiences? You mean autobiographies?

Playwright: I'm a character in the play. I write what I do with Shelly. Shelly is a character. She narrates her own autobiographical elements, what she has done with you.

Nirlipta: How dares she? Has she narrated about me also?

Playwright: Yes! She was with you for about four years. She supported you fiscally, slept with you physically and you could get through civil service exams because of Shelly. You promised her something-which she did not tell us.I know you before you emerged here. She told me about you.

Nirlipta: I heard something like that. That's why I wanted to check up myself personally. Are you writing the script?

Playwright: Yes. I'm writing What Shelly says. Shelly wants to include what I do in the middle. Then the director comes and the producer. The roles they play will also be included. Their dreams and nightmares shall be dramatized if it is possible. They called me for consultation. All of us shall put our heads together to build this play. DO you also want to join us? You can.

Nirlipta: I want your play to be edited and censored.

Playwright: Why?

Nirlipta: Because all that Shelly says is not true.

Playwright: We don't bother whether the story is true or not. It's a part of Shelly's life. She wanted to marry you, Is that true? And you duped her, and then flung her in to the dustbin of the society.

Nirlipta: My time is limited, Ok? So, I didn't waste it living someone else's dreams. My dreams are mine. Now, can you tell me whether you dream this play? If you don't Why do you write this play? That too, leaving your home and sojourning here in a female actor's basement? Don't you feel this is little below your dignity?

Playwright: I enjoy writing plays Mr.Pattnayak! I don't bother whether they pay me or not. I don't bother if its' Shelly's basement or not! Shelly is not only a female actor to me. She's much more than a human being to me. She is an inspiration, a harbinger of sudden brilliant ideas.

Nirlipta: I will give you a cheque of five lakhs if you stop writing this play. You will have to stop mentioning my name in connection with Shelly.

Playwright: Are you serious? What's the harm? Are you expecting some kind of a hitch? With your wife or somebody like that?

Nirlipta: No, I'm not marrued yet! But there's a marriage proposal with the daughter of a minister-in the central cabinet. They won't appreciate my link with a theatre professional.

Playwright: Why do you nurture a biased view about Shelly? She's not only a theatre star, but she also acts in films and T.V serials. She could have brought you good luck and promotions in your career.

Nirlipta: Don't encourage Shelly to hang on my neck. I am…I am slightly scared of her openness. Now keep this cheque with you *(He writes something on the cheque)*.This is for five lakhs. Please see that my name doesn't figure in your play about a play. Bye! Don't inform Shelly that I came to meet her. She might have forgotten my name.

Playwright: Nobody has forgotten nothing Mr.Pattnayak.I know you since long-as a student of English literature…in Utkal University…You were the topper in political science..Shelly was known to me since I was a Playwright. You visited her every evening, downloaded your orgy and she gave you money for paying your mess bills.

Nirlipta: That was a figment of your imagination, not a fact. Now, I am going. Please see that your play does not include my character. Otherwise I will send the police to stop your play (Exits).

Lights focus the playwright.

Playwright: *(looking at the cheque, he monologuises.Before the monologue starts the sax player enters playing horn evoking a pensive mood. Over the saxophone the playwright speaks in an over dramatic mode)*

Once upon a time there was a playwright. He wrote screenplays for films and soaps. Nobody paid him a farthing. Only they promised him big amounts. He knew nothing except dreaming big amounts. He realized that money was power…The soap producers did not pay. But the playwright became popular, grew into a star material. He wrote attractive dialogues for female heroes, invented new rhythms. Suddenly one day a young bureaucrat came and forced him to put a full stop on writing plays and he was paid a handsome amount…a cheque for five lakhs was given to him for not writing anything. Behind him was innocence. Breathing became difficult for him. The memories of the female characters pricked him. They no more visited him. He was frozen in the middle of creation.

He thought it was a jam in the middle of traffic of ideas. He scratched his intuition, nothing emerged. He searched for his old inspiration. But that was not money. It was a dead stop, a nightmare. Money equaled power, power equaled protection, but there was no protection for his wounded emotions.

(*Shelly enters with a cup of tea set on a tray and finds the saxophone player playing softly. She points at him to quit the stage. Slowly the sax player exits. She comes to the playwright.*)

Shelly: I know you are in the middle of a creative jam. *(smiles)* What are you doing here? Frozen in the middle of an idea? Don't worry. you badly need a cup of tea.*(The playwright lifts the cup from the tray)*

Playwright: Your ex-lover came to search for you, bad girl.

Shelly: Ex-lover?

Playwright: You must have lied him several times-"I love you", "I adore you".

Shelly: Yeah! That's why I never said these lies to you, good boy! In fact, I never loved anybody dear! I have lied to all of them, Always. I think the only man I have never lied on the bed, is you.

Playwright: Well, coming from you, that's a declaration of love!

Shelly: Yes and no, because love does not feed my mouth. I want money, because even though I have some kind of security I have no money to buy whatever I want! I still work for money. I still sell myself for money. Money is more precious than love.

Playwright: Well, Well, bad girl! Haven't you discovered that money is not always happiness? I have received a cheque of five lakhs for not writing the play. Do you think I am happy? No! I'm somewhere on the threshold of morbidity and depression.

Shelly: I want to elevate your mood… I want to give you a couple of pegs of black night, but I am sorry, I can't afford. So, I am trying to manage your writerly mood with this cup of green tea. Please Playwright.

Playwright: That's fine, bad girl. That Pattnayak fellow seems to be stinkingly rich; if you meet and hoodwink him, may be, he'll give you some money.

Shelly: Which Pattnayak you are talking about?

Playwright: Er....er......Nirlipta Pattnayak.

Shelly: *(amused)* Oh! Did he come here? I must meet him. But where is he now? I must find out his address.

Playwright: Nirlipta Pattnayak is the secretary and commissioner of culture department. You should meet him in his residence. That shall be an interesting scene of our play.

Shelly: In that case I shall find out his residence and meet him. Should I ask him for something?

Playwright: Yes. Submit an application for a grant. The government shall pay you twenty five thousand rupees as research grant.

Shelly: But if he'd treat me as a beggar? Won't it be an insult?

Playwright: Well....

Shelly: I may be a "bad girl" for you, Playwright! But I'm a star. I stand before the camera and I'm transformed. I mount the stage and I am in front of the stage lights, I am transformed in to a heroine. I'm not myself, I'm a star! I am in my own firmament I look at myself when I come down from the stage, and I hate myself. Buyers of drama tickets take me as an item of entertainment, they devour me as a consumer item. Yet, I hate having to eat and sleep and going to the bathroom like an ordinary biped. I hate having to live in this body, which is not a star's body. People dream me as a star....I dream myself walking in the floor as a star...I dream the same dreams like other dreamers, but I never live the dreams. What do you think a commissioner of culture is? Is he greater than I? Why should I stretch my hands for a research grant? Instead I can offer twenty percent of my grant to the Culture department and get a grant independently.

Playwright: Bad girl! You have to act humble before him. Don the role of a sufferer, show up as an afflicted person, a wretched one going through hardship and distress.

Shelly: Yes, I can role play the distressed woman…an actress growing old and getting bogged in the quagmire of poverty.

Playwright: That's right! Your conversation with Nirlipta would make a good scene in our play. I will write that as you meet him. Where shall you meet Nirlipta? Don't meet him in his office. He will not talk to you as a man. He will don the role of an officer. He will say "we are the brain of the city".

Shelly: They have demented brains. Do you know that? I will meet him at his residence. Let me go and find out from the director brother Roby Das where, exactly, the director of culture lives. Wait for that moment. *(Shelly exits)*

Playwright: Best of luck.

Lights go off…

SCENE-3

The producer enters from the left wing holding a mobile phone and talking to some officer in the directorate of culture.

Producer: Yes, I met the commissioner. He is unwilling to give us a grant for the production of the play. Why I don't know. May be he is angry. He alleges that our playwright has written the story to vilify his personal character *(pause)*.I know nothing about the story. No, I have to check up whether it is true or not! Okay! Bye! I'll meet you tomorrow in the office. *(switches off the phone)*.

Roby Das enters from the opposite side and asks

Roby Das: Oh! You've come back? How much they have assured us to pay?

Producer: Nothing! The commissioner threatened me to ban the performance.

Roby Das: Why? What's wrong with us?

Producer: Perhaps the playwright and the commissioner are at logger heads. The commissioner thinks that the playwright deliberately portrayed his character in the play as an evil character. He is, as he is characterized, madly in love with Shelly.

Roby Das: I've to check it up with the playwright. By the by who's the commissioner?

Producer: One Nirlipta Pattnayak.

Roby Das: Oh! That handsome dandy? Vanivihar hero? I know him since long-since my student days in UtkalUniversity. *(suddenlyremembers)* Ah! That fellow was infatuated with Shelly.

Producer: How do you know?

Roby Das: Do you remember that lady artist called Dolly?

Producer: Dolly Das? The girl who went with us for a picnic to Chilka Lake at Barkul dakbungalow? Yes, I remember. Dolly was hobnobbing with you for about two/three years.

Roby Das: Shelly is Dolly's younger sister.

Producer: That I don't know. But Dolly behaved like a pet cat when she was with you.

Roby Das: Yes, I was an agent for providing her with new contacts for acting in serials and theatre productions. That's why Dolly was visiting me whenever she was free.

Producer: Yes, that triggered off a kind of tangle in your family. But then what happened to Dolly?

Roby: I'm no more interested in her. She's married to a costume designer. Shelly is Dolly's younger sister. She was in school when Nirlipta Pattnayak was appointed as a tutor to Shelly. Later they were sexually infatuated for each other. Shelly earned some money as a sex worker and gave it to Nirlipta to take a coaching at Delhi to sit for the civil service exams.

Producer: And that commissioner doesn't want Shelly to act as the leading female artist of our play-wants to bungle the entire play. Okay. Now we have to talk to Shelly. Come! Two of us shall go to her house.

Roby: Shelly has left that hired apartment has shifted to a new house with the playwright.

Producer: That's right. We will find out her new house.

(Both of them exit. Lights go off)

SCENE-4

NirliptaPattnayak'sgovernment quarters.Sound of the calling bell disturbs Nirlipta. He enters and opens the door. Shelly enters with a smiling face.

Shelly: Namaskar Khoka Bhai!

Nirlipta: Namskar! *(He doesn't recognize Shelly)*I'm sorry! Do I know you? You are….

Shelly: I am Shelly! Are you alone in this big bungalow Khoka bhai? I mean are you still a bachelor?

Nirlipta: Yeah of course! Didn't find time to bring a wife. What about you? How often do you change your husband?

Shelly: You know Khoka Bhai, I'm a bad girl since my childhood! I use husbands like my panties.

Nirlipta: But you were married, didn't you? How may times?

Shelly: My third husband deserted me and went to Surat, Gujurat. I don't know whether he got married to another. No interest to spy him. He didn't give his family details; told some pious lies I ntended to disguise a childhood and adolescence that embarrassed him.

Nirlipta: What about your children Shelly?

Shelly: I can't afford to become a mother Khoka bhai! I traffic in my youth to make my livelihood.

Nirlipta: But you are nomore young Shelly.

Shelly: That's why I have come. Can you help me getting a pension or a research grant from the department of culture? How much they give? Ten thousand per month? Or, twenty five thousand from the Human Resources Department? Do it for me; I will give you five thousand per month. This is Shelly's word!

Nirlipta: How could you find my residential address? I can't think why you've come, Shelly! What do you want from me?

Shelly: I bother you, don't I? Upset you?

Nirlipta: You don't upset me. I'm fond of you, you know I am.

(Shelly shrugs her shoulders and laughs bitterly)

You don't appear to believe me, but it's true.

Shelly: It's not my fault, Khoka bhai. After you got in to civil services, you went to Massouri and then you were lost. I left chasing you. I emancipated you....gave you the license to doom the fate of some innocent girl.

Nirlipta: I was in Delhi for about five years and you change husbands. He and your address changed frequently. How could I locate you? Otherwise, I would have contacted you.

Shelly: I never understand you Khoka bhai. Not even in the past. You were a top brash, a high voltage intellectual.....and I was an obedient school girl by that time. But I understood your physical needs. I understood your body language. Sometimes I pretend I don't, so you will think I am stupid. But I understand all right. I understand everything.

Nirlipta: Then you should realize you've no business to be here! We are poles apart now.

Shelly: I have come here to pay you a visit. Is this how you welcome me? Like this? You haven't yet given me a chair to sit. Thank you. I can stand here for two hours. No one in your family looked at me with honor! They treated me as dirt. But outside I have hundreds of fans. They are strangers, but they respect me. They are sophisticated people. They kiss my hand and say, "Please don't go, do stay for dinner." But I always say no. I don't upset them. I only bother you. You hate me because I am famous. Is that right Khoka bhai? Since that's the way you feel, I shall leave. *(She turns to make an exit)*

Nirlipta: Don't misunderstand me Shelly. You came here supplicating for a pension. You've to put up an application for that; that's in the prescribed pro forma. You can do that later. Sit for a minute. I can serve you a cup of coffee with some cookies.

Shelly: I'm not hungry; thank you. I never drink coffee; never, never, never touch whisky. I've always led a sober life. My second husband was a professor in a countryside college. I wrote a thesis for him. He manoeuvred through his political contacts and entered in to the university. He owed his brilliant career to me in his autobiography. I was an inspiration to him. He boozed away all his money and left me bankrupt. Then there were lots of handsome men who came and courted me, here, in this house in the basement. I get pestered by my fans, I often have to lock my door. I don't wish to marry again.

Nirlipta: Yes. I have seen that basement. I had been there to meet you. You were not there; went for some shooting for a tele-soap. There was a pigheaded playwright sitting there. The fellow said he delineated my character in some play.

Shelly: He's not a pigheaded playwright Khoka bhai. He is a genius. I am working with him in an autobiographical project for about a year.

Nirlipta: Why has he included my name in that play? Who's he? I'd request you Shelly to delete my name and character from your play. Otherwise……

Shelly: Why so Khoka bhai? Have you forgotten those days when I was young and was forced to sleep in star hotels to send you money? You had been to Delhi to take coaching for civil service exams those days. Weren't you a part of my life Khoka bhai?

Nirlipta: Those days are over Shelly. I was nobody those days- just a vagabond, but honest in studies and in love.

Shelly: I'm also honest in love Khoka bhai. One day I also dreamt to be in your bed for my entire life. Later I felt that I was deluded.

Nirlipta: That was impossible Shelly!

Shelly: What happened to your honesty? Did you convince yourself that honesty was inadequate to keep both ends meet? You were never honest with your inner self, Khoka bhai! You know that. It was also the same case with me. I grew up with the illusion of love and finally realized that sex is the truth; love is an immature emotional euphoria, good enough for adolescents. I want to leave this message to my beloved audience. So, we have knowingly included your character; as an epitome of foxy behavior and guilefulness. The young women of our state should begin to question the word of love.

Nirlipta: That's your grudge against me, Shelly.

Shelly: But I'm honest to my core.

Nirlipta: Your playwright would portray me as a betrayer, as a villain, who knows nothing about moral value.

Shelly: That's his sharp intuitive power Khoka bhai! Honestly speaking, aren't you wild like an animal on the bed? The playwright has a master hand in painting characters; he'll put you in right place.

(There is a long ring on the calling bell and with that enters Madhav Das, aged about 60, but looks stronger for his age. He is a Minister at central secretariat. He stays mostly in Delhi)

Madhav: May I come in? Of course, I've already entered into your quarters khoka! Ha ha!

Nirlipta: Welcome, Uncle! *(He touches Madhav's feet)*

Madhav: If you don't mind Khoka... *(looks at Shelly)*...this lady..?

Shelly: I'm Shelly Das, female actor for films, T.V serials and theatre.

Madhav: Oh! An artist? What are you doing here? With the joint secretary!

Nirlipta: She had come to apply for a government pension for artists.

Shelly: And, you Sir? If you don't mind?

Madhav: I'm Madhav Das, Minister in central secretariat. I stay in Delhi, but my daughter Pratidhvani knows you. In fact, she was talking about you!

Shelly: I feel honoured to meet you Sir! But Pratidhvani? Who's she?

Madhav: She's my daughter! Also an artist of national reputation.

Shelly: Oh! I see! That Odissi dancer from Delhi?

Madhav: Shortly getting married to Nirlipta Pattnayak.

Shelly: I see! *(laughs)* That's good news!

Madhav: My daughter alleged you are trying to hook her would-be-husband!

Nirlipta: How could Pratidhvani know about Shelly hooking me up? Is she spying on me? That's bad, Uncle!

Shelly: Pratidhvani is jealous of me. She wanted to get in to films. But I was selected for that role. A dancer cannot do justice to that role, they said.

Nirlipta: Shelly has a long experience in acting. She's almost equal to a director. As the commissioner of Department of culture, I get a chance to know all about our actors.

Madhav: That's right Khoka, but Pratidhvani was also talking about a playwright. He is a writing a play about a play; a play in which you are a character Khoka! Do you know about that? He may cause severe damage to your public image!

Nirlipta: I have discussed the matter with that playwright. Let's see what happens. I will check up myself. But why is the play so important in the media?

Shelly: That will be a great promotion about you. If needed, we shall act in that play together. We will be famous and our love shall be immortalized.

Madhav: But Pratidvani might discard you Khoka. I know she was mad to marry an administrative officer. So she is extremely possessive about you. She would not allow her future husband to be brow beaten by a theatre girl. May I request you to desist from such a nightmare, Shelly?

Shelly: I'm flattered by your request Sir! But I am also not less passionate about Khoka bhai. I've loved him since I was a child. I'd love to act as his fiancée in my next play. That'd bring me luck.

Madhav: Shelly! You must refrain from such overbearing ambitions. What social status do you have to aspire for Khoka as your fiancée? After all you are a theatre girl; producers hire you for their requirement.

Shelly: Yes I do everything for money, but I don't cheat people as politicians like you do. You are selling the country for your personal benefit. I don't. I hate politicians.

Madhav: Shelly! I will smash your career, you theatre tart. Hold your tongue! You are talking to Madhav Das.

Shelly: Should I take it as a threatening sir? I care a fig for political menaces. I'm not a government officer to feel scared by a Minister's threatening! I am here not to stand in supplication before a minister!

Nirlipta: Shelly!

Shelly: I'm sorry Khoka bhai! This old man may be your future father-in-law, he may give you a huge amount as dowry: his electronic factory at Gurgaon; and his mansion on Puri beach for example.That does not mean I'll lick his shoes. I am a free lancer artist. I will see that our play is written with Khoka bhai as an anti-hero.If he holds himself back to do the role, someone else will do it. But I challenge you sir! You may take the help of the police you may take the help of the law! I don't bother!

(She exits with quick steps.Nirlipta and Madhav stare at her agape. Lights are put off.)

SCENE-5

As the lights come on to the stage, we see a tense moment between the playwright and Nirlipta Pattnayak. Nirlipta is in a violent mood and determined to attack him.

Playwright: *(shouts)* So what? I admit; you've given me five lakhs. Does that mean you have bought my head?

Nirlipta: What else is it? I've given you the money to stop tagging my story with that of Shelly. I've given you the money not to make a fuss out of our relationship.

Playwright: I've not made any fuss out of anything. I'm committed before Shelly to include her life story in my play and I'm sticking to my point! What I've written is truth; its neither exaggeration, nor a figment of my imagination.

Nirlipta: I've paid for burying that truth. Your job is to stifle the voice of Shelly.

Playwright: How can it be? This is Shelly's story and I'm portraying Shelly's dreams.

Nirlipta: You can do anything for Shelly; but you don't have the rights to disparage me. I've paid you because this is something very serious you are writing-nothing should go against me!

Playwright: Look, Nirlipta Pattnayak is a character in my play. The character has no relation with you. Moreover, it's drama, not something real and actual.

Nirlipta: Aye playwright! Whoever you are! You've to obey my orders. If you don't give in, I'll get it done by force.

Playwright: I don't care for your threatening. You're just trying to overshadow my freedom as an artist, my freedom of artistic expression.

Nirlipta: Who gave you the freedom to trespass the borders of my personal honor?

Playwright: Personal honour? What do you mean by that?

Nirlipta: You have portrayed me as a parasite grown on Shelly's body. Have I leant on Shelly to get through the civil service exams? How dare you write like that?

Playwright: You come off a lower middle class family having very high ambitions.

Nirlipta: Is that a crime?

Playwright: You were giving tuitions to Shelly when she was young. You developed sexual relations with her and encouraged her to become a sex worker. After the death of her father, she trafficked with her body and sent you money to study at Delhi for civil service exams. You got through civil service exams and you have disposed off Shelly calling her a tart. Aren't you an unfaithful deceiver? Have you not committed a breach of trust?

Nirlipta: That's your point of view. The reality was different. Shelly corrupted me, initiated me in to sexual practice.

Playwright: That was a sign of maturity. You grow up from a adolescent to a verile young man. Shelly knew everything about you except that you were an imposter!

Nirlipta: I can't afford to expose my real self before an immoral woman, whose only job was to attend to calls for selling her body.

Playwright: Shelly was younger to you, but she mothered you for two long years. You never had the courage to accept her greatness. Mind it, Mr. Pattnayak! You were inspired and nourished by her sacrifices.

Nirlipta: That's not true. I requested you not to portray Shelly like that and me as a parasite!

Playwright: What are you Nirlipta pattnayak?.

Nirlipta: *(annoyed)* I'm not a parasite you pig head of a playwright! Why don't you understand that? I won't allow you to portray me as a lecher, as a sex maniac, as a parasite. If you do so I'll punch your nose!

Playwright: *(shouts)* You are worse than a parasite!.In Shelly's experience you are an imposter, a deleterious character. This hidden part of your foxy nature requires an exposition in my play.

Nirlipta: I will shoot you down you pig head!

Playwright: You are a pig headed bureaucrat! As a playwright I have the freedom to imagine, create and distribute diverse cultural expressions as I imagine. My audience has the right to access this hidden truth of Shelly's life.

Nirlipta: Aye! You rascal! Don't show me your right and law! I have also the fundamental rights to enjoy by expressing my private feelings.I've the rights to enjoy Shelly's body when she is offering it voluntarily. You can't block my way!

Playwright: You too don't have the right to censor my drama. You can't. Neither you, nor your cultural contractor! None of you has the right to interfere. You don't have the right to pressurize me. You may go now!

Nirlipta: I haven't come here to go back without deleting that scene where I figure. *(menacingly advances)*

Playwright: I won't make any change. It's already written.

Nirlipta: Give it to me!

Playwright: No!

Nirlipta: *(Forcibly seizes the manuscript file)* I will burn your manuscript. The story you have created shall be demolished.

Playwright: I warn you Nirlipta. I also do have the strength to bring counter discourses against you. You will be sued. I shall deploy counter weights to thrash you down.

(The playwright attempts to retrieve the manuscript. There's a tussle between the two for some time. The playwright snatches the file without any damage done to the papers.)

Nirlipta: I will thrash you down rascal! What do you think of me? Where's that henchman? *(He hollers)*Boxer! Boxer! Where have you gone?

(The henchman comes)

Henchman: Present Boss!

Nirlipta: This playwright is unruly and defiant; writes diatribes against me. Fellow tries to throw mud on my face, seize that script from him.

(The boxer proceeds towards the playwright)

Playwright: No, Boxer, no! The cultural contractor has posted you at the gate to help me writing the play. I am expressing alternate visions for society in this play. And this Nirlipta Mohanty, this villain has come to bully me, has come to throttle my voice.

Nirlipta: This fellow is a radical, an iconoclast, talks to me in irreverent tone. Seize the manuscript from him *(He takes out a bundle of currency notes and gives to the henchman)* Proceed! Now it's your job to fetch me the manuscript.

(The boxer and Nirlipta attempt to take away the script from the playwright.The playwright fights with two men courageously. Nirlipta seizes the baton from the henchman and hits the playwright on his head from the back. The playwright falls unconscious and Nirlipta seizes the manuscript. The cultural contractor barges in and notices the playwright falling on the ground. He holds him.)

C.C: What's this? *Chamcha Pehliwan*! I'm asking you. Why did you hit the Playwright?

Henchman: *(apologetically)* I haven't done anything Boss! This visitor has started the brawl. He stroke the playwright on the back of his head. Go and call for an ambulance. We'll send him to hospital.

C.C: And who are you mister? Putting on a suit and a tie with a double knot? Looking like a gentle man and behaving like a hooligan? You've to explain it to me. Now.

Nirlipta: This playwright is a rogue; uses diatribes against me! I will burn this manuscript.

C.C: You can't do that whoever you are!

Nirlipta: I'm the secretary and commissioner of the department of culture. Who are you?

C.C: The only cultural contractor of the state; class one contractor. MP Madhav Das Was my assistant for three years. I'm working for introducing constant magic into theatre. This playwright was commissioned to write a play. Where's the manuscript? Give it to me.

Nirlipta: I'll burn it. When this rogue will regain his consciousness, he will find his dramatic garbage burnt into clinker.

C.C: No! You can't do that! You are not free to do anything you like. The sky may still fall on your head. *(The playwright is examined)* Take him to a safe hospital.

Nirlipta: There's absolutely no reason as to why this pig head would write about my private life. I have bribed him five lakhs to delete my character from the play. He didn't oblige; rather deceived me!

C.C: That doesn't mean you'd kill a playwright!

Nirlipta: Is he dead?

C.C: May be! Who knows? I have called for an ambulance to take him to the hospital.

Nirlipta: Do whatever you like. I'm going.

C.C: You can't leave this house. You've to stay here till the owner of the house arrives. Number two: Give that script back to me.

Nirlipta: No, I won't give you this script. The playwright has slighted my character here.

C.C: How do you know the playwright has slighted your character? Have you read the script? If so, what do you understand from a play script?

Nirlipta: I'm the secretary-cum-commissioner of the department of culture. Who are you to demand the script from the government?

C.C: I'm the cultural contractor. I've always had a taste for the arts; good music, good books, good painting, films....unfortunately I have never had much time for reading, for going to museums, libraries and to concerts or theatre. What do you do as commissioner? You are striking playwrights on their head, that too from the back! That's a crime! That means you are a criminal. You can't go out of this basement without my permission. Chamcha Pehliwan! Boxer! Hold this suited man.

Henchman: *(Enters)* Present Boss! *(He hold a stretcher)*

C.C: What are you going to do with this unconscious body of the playwright? Where's the ambulance?

Henchman: It's there outside. I've brought the stretcher. Hold it please from the other side. We'll take him to the ambulance.

(*Cultural contractor and the henchman carry the unconscious body on the stretcher and go out. Before going out the CC orders the commissioner*)

C.C: Aye Commissioner! Hold that manuscript. I'm coming back loading the playwright in the van. Don't meddle with that. Mind you! You are an actor in the play.

(The CC exits. Background music. Lights change. Nirlipta alone on the stage, with the manuscript in his hand, faces the audience. He talks to them breaking the barrier between the actor and the audience.)

Nirlipta: Now, after the playwright is deported, There's no one here except me. Since I've the manuscript with me, I can impersonate the playwright and become a celebrity, but I won't do that. The playwright has invented my character in the play; he is writing. But the Director has selected me as an actor. I was asked to beat the playwright on the back of his head and as I did so, he fell unconscious. Now I feel guilty. But who has struck him?: The "character" Nirlipta or me, the "actor" in the role of Nirlipta? Right now I don't have an answer.

(The director barges in)

Roby Das: What are you doing here on stage? Why are you dabbling with the play script? That's not your cup of tea. Give it to me. It's my property. *(He snatches the script from Nirlipta)*

Roby: I've given you the role of Nirlipta Pattnayak, right? Why did you overplay your role? The playwright has never portrayed you as a hooligan; but you acted like one. I didn't expect you'll really hit the playwright so heavily on his head.

Nirlipta: We've called the ambulance and sent him to the hospital.

Roby: That's against the theatrical norms. Your job was to act it out, not to make him bleed.

Nirlipta: The playwright wrote it in the manuscript. Nirlipta was directed to strike on the playwright's head.

Roby: Let me check *(snstches the manuscript from Nirlipta and checks)* The playwright has directed the fictional character called Nirlipta, not you. You are only donning the role of Nirlipta. Isn't it? Nirlipta was born in the imagination of the playwright. Why did you hospitalize him without any reason?

Nirlipta: Why do you say like that?

Roby: I'm the director, not he. I want the playwright now to appear on this scene. He should appear now unbattered and healthy. He'll speak his lines here. Playwright!

(Shelly enters holding the playwright)

Shelly: Yes Roby Bhai. The playwright is here. I've brought him back from the hospital. They were unwilling to discharge him from the hospital. I said, he has almost absconded from the middle of the scene.So, they left him. Is he required to deliver some lines here?

(Nirlipta advances toward the playwright apologetically)

Nirlipta: I am sorry brother! I didn't know it will lead you to the hospital.

Roby: You are supposed to deliver something to the audience. But you are injured. You have to take the makeup. Let me tie a bandage at least.

Shelly: The nurse has put a cotton pad and we can tinge it with lac dye. Won't it suffice Roby bhai?

Roby: No! You are talking as if you're the director.

Shelly: Sorry!

Roby: Call the makeup man. He has to tie a big bandage cloth round his head. Plus, there'd be a special cotton pad.

Shelly: Brother makeup sir! The director needs you for a moment. Come with your make up kit.

(he arrives with the kit)

Roby: Basu, take the cotton strip and tie it round the playwright's head.

Playwright: Excuse me! Must I absolutely wear a rounded bandage?

Roby: Yes, Of course! You are not the real Playwright. You are acting in the role of the Playwright who's injured and has come back from the hospital after dressing.

Shelly: Don't worry dear! We'll dress it softly. Make-up Sir! Please do it with care. There's deep scar inside.

(The makeup man dresses the playwright cautiously-Shelly helps)

Nirlipta: I'm really sorry playwright. But how could I have evaded it? You've written it on the script.

Roby: No! That's Ramesh Panigrahi, an Indian Playwright. But you've overdone it Sir! No one asked you to make him bleed.

Shelly: Khoka bhai! It is transparent now! You have vented out your real grudge through your action. You never liked the playwright, you didn't appreciate his idea of making you appear as one of the ardent lovers of my youth. You felt jealous of him, In fact, it's not the playwright; I insisted to incorporate it in your story. I wanted our story to be told to our audience. But the playwright immortalized you by drawing your portrait.

Nirlipta: (To Shelly) I never wanted to be your eternal lover. It was a sort of "time-pass" during my struggling days.

Shelly: I could smell such perfidy in you even when I was a teen-ager. The playwright has delineated your duplicity as a lover. May be, he has intuited in to your character rightly.

Playwright: Mr. Pattnayak is a genuine player. He knows nothing except role playing. By hitting him from the back he externalized the hooligan buried within him. Nothing else.

Nirlipta: I don't want you to be a character born out of this playwright's imagination. This playwright is an autocrat. He won't grant me the liberty to act as I wish.

Roby: Look here Mr. Nirlipta! I've recruited you as an actor, not as the playwright. The playwright has given birth to you, created you. My job is to see the Playwright's idea being theatricalized. I am a Stanislavskian Director. I believe that as an actor you have immense capacities, Nirlipta. You have an innate capacity for creativeness.

Playwright: Mr.pattnayak! I've been working with Roby Das for the last four productions. He has never misinterpreted my plays.

Roby: As an actor your job was to bring to life what is hidden under the words. As director my duty is to put my own thoughts in to the author's lines.

Nirlipta: Can't I put my own imagination in to this playwright's lines? If so, why are you making mountain of a mole? If there is deep scar because of my beating-I am ready to apologize for that. But still I say that my speech and body rhythm corresponded with the subtext of the play.

Shelly: You are behaving like a theoretical actor Khoka bhai, but we know you can never be a professional. You're just trying to exhort a mind game, on the scene.

Playwright: Let him start the mind game Shelly. I'm also an actor here, not the playwright. And Nirlipta! Being an actor is a way of life. It is separate from the work or the struggle. It's how we see the world. It's blending happiness and dark sadness. It's about feeling a lot and then feeling a lot more and then feeling a lot more.

Nirlipta: I wanted him to stop writing, but he wrote it. I wanted to burn the manuscript and the director snatched it away from me.

Shelly: Why do you want to burn our story Khoka bhai? The playwright has invented your character and immortalized you.

Nirlipta: I don't want to act according to the wayward imagination of the playwright. I don't want to obey the directorial commands of Roby Das; you don't have the capacity to create a character like me!

Playwright: What do you want? Should I change it?

Nirlipta: I want to demolish you first as a playwright. I want to burn this manuscript in to clinkers. I want to put you off from the stage.

Shelly: You can't burn my story. It has to remain immortal in mass memory.

Nirlipta: Give the script to me Roby Das.

Roby: You've no rights to do that Nirlipta! Our playwright may appear banal and medicore to you, but he's a genius creator for us.

Nirlipta: That doesn't mean he'd paint my character according to his imagination!

Roby: The playwright has the freedom to imagine, create and distribute his cultural convictions. Through the play he can disseminate socio-moral resistance and rebellion, protest and hope. This playwright may be a manifesto for our future theatre. It should be preserved.

Playwright: Thank you Roby Das for your verdict. But Nirlipta has put my play under threat! He wants to destroy it.

Roby: The play cannot be destroyed playwright! The entire play lies verbatim in the reservoir of our actor's memory. Further the play is tape recorded. We don't need a prompter to remind them the lines. So, Mr.Nirlipta Pattnayak, I'm giving the script back to the playwright. Let us resolve the virtual conflict between you and the playwright. You hug each other: You for overacting and the playwright for his tolerance. Let there be a fusion between the text and the performance.

(Both of them come forward and embrace. Appropriate blocking and lighting. Roby Das continues)

Let there be a fusion between imagination and reality, between character and actor, between the language of poetry and the poetry of space.

(The freeze and the lights go out. The back lights are on to produce a silhouette. Back ground music. Lights dim. Curtain.)

****

FORTY MINUTES

The play was premiered in Paradip Port on 17-4 2003

Characters in the play

Pradosh:	A 30 yrs old young man, Convict
Anil:	30 Yrs. Old young man, Jailor
Hadibandhu:	46 yrs, constable
Khadenga:	50/ 60 yrs, A serio-comic advocate
Bunty:	12 yrs, old, Pradosh's son
Adarsh:	55 yrs, old
Dhadia:	The executioner (45 yrs)
Leena:	26 yrs, the distantly related sister of Pradosh
Doctor:	An old man of around 50

N.B. The Director is requested to keep the production time limited to 40 minutes

There is an announcement about the cast and the duration of the play before the front screen is opened. As soon as the announcement is over, an alaap of Raag Bhairabi in male voice is heard. In the middle of the alaap the screen rolls up and the audience finds a character sitting behind the grilled door of the police lock up under a dim spot and singing the morning raaga holding a tanpura instrument. He is Pradosh, a criminal of 28/30 yrs old. If the artist does not know singing, a back ground voice should be used. After 2/3 minutes the singing fades out and a female voice recites:

This is mostly about
a life half-burnt.
Simmering dreams emit
Subdued smoke, don't search for truth
That'd end up in death,
Better call it a liberty post
it rebounds murmurs silent.

As the lights from different sources spill out the stage widely we find the jail to the mid right-stage with 7/8 vertical rails building a small enclosed chamber with fenced wells making the insider visible. Pradosh, the insider/singer puts on the uniform meant for the convicts

To the left up stage there is a small platform to stand on for the executioning. A knotted rope hangs from the top. Anil Pradhan, a 30yrs. old young jailor in uniform enters. He seems to get irritated finding a convict singing to a tanpura. He hollers in a harsh voice: "Hadibandhu"! "Hadibandhu"!

Anil: Hadibandhu! Where are you?

(*A 40 yrs, old constable reports in hurried steps*)

Hadibandhu: Yes Sir!

Anil: Who did fetch a *taanpura* to this convict, a *tanpura* in the jail? What is going on in this jail?

Hadibandhu: You told me to bring the instrument Sir!

I went to Kala Parishad Secretary and borrowed it for the convict.

Anil: Did I ask you to bring one? When?

Hadibandhu: Day before yesterday Sir!

Anil: Okay, take out that instrument from him now! And take him to the toilet. He must be bathed by someone. Make him ready for execution! It's not a guillotine... There's order for hanging him. (*Checks the wrist watch*) It's seven O'clock in the morning. He'll be hanged at 7.40 AM – exactly after forty minutes. Check the toilet: whether water is there or not! Also the fresh towel and a new cake of soap!

Hadibandhu: He is not a baby Sir! He can take the bath himself.

Anil: Take him to the bathroom. This is our duty.

(*He goes to his table and chair. Hadibandhu opens the grilled door*)

Hadibandhu: Yes Pradosh Babu! It's time for your bath; come out.

Anil: Listen. It's already seven O'clock. Forty minutes are left for the execution ritual.

(After Hadibandhu left Pradosh comes out of the lock up and moves toward the down stage)

Pradosh: Did you tell me anything Sir?

Anil: You are aware of your hanging Pradosh. You are going to be hanged after forty minutes, just at 7.40 A.M.

Pradosh: *(He does not respond. There is no change of expression. He is cool and he faces the situation calmly)*

Anil: I'm sorry I couldn't do anything for you. Finally, the execution order was received before anything could be done. I failed. Forgive me Pradosh, I am undone.

Pradosh: *(did not look at Anil, moved few steps forward and spoke casting a glance toward the audience)* No one, no one could do anything. But I could realize finally; realized that life is like a gamble. If I could have won the game...it could have been a big win. But I became a loser and here I am! But why are you apologetic Sir? Do your duty.

Anil: *(His voice breaks)* After thirty five minutes you shall be hanged right in front of me... How? How can I bear with the scene? How? I can't forgive myself, Pradosh...I can't..!*(His voice breaks and he bursts into a violent sob)*

Pradosh: Your highness should learn to metamorphose... to turn your heart into a stone Jailor Saab!

Anil: What are you blabbering? Stoicism? Why are you addressing me as "Sir", as "Your Highness" as "Jailor Saab?" Have I become so alien to you *(sobs)* Am I so distanced? Answer me Pradosh! Answer!! *(Anil goes near Pradosh, shakes him holding his shoulder and weeps loudlyPradosh is steady and stands stiff. Anil moves away from him)* Pradosh! I'm your friend. We studied together from standard four to post graduate level. We are family friends!

Pradosh: What do these cheap emotional words mean Sir? Are you trying to make me weep before I am hung? No!

I've learnt how to petrify myself, how to stand boldly in front of injustice!

Anil: But how shall I show my face to your family members? What explanation shall I give to sister-in law and to your son Bunty?

Pradosh: This world accommodates thousands of women whose husbands are dead. Thousands of children do not have their fathers, Sir!

Anil: I've told you many times, Pradosh! As a journalist you cannot afford to divulge to truth always. You must know who you are fighting with!

Pradosh: I'm a graduate from IIMS, Dhenkanal, Sir! I have a masters' degree in vernacular Odia. Everywhere they have taught me to stick on to truth. I've learnt to bring on to light all the hidden truth of the world.

Anil: No, Pradosh. Truth is nothing but a play of different forces. It is multi-faceted. It looks different from different angles. You can construct a truth by mixing up thousand shreds of falsehood.

Pradosh: I have always experimented with truth. Sir! All my life I've experimented with truth---trying to live holding the truth tightly – Someday some good can be harvested. Take the present case as a fresh experiment with truth. I'm ready to sacrifice my life for truth.

Anil: Pradosh!

Pradosh: If I've to face the hanging rope for unveiling truth – I'd understand that truth is hanging there on a rope.

Anil: You've never agreed with me, any time.

Pradosh: That's why our roads were separate Sir! You chased power and thus you've been given this uniform of power. But my mission was to unravel the hidden rackets of the society. The beauty parlour which was my target kept its exterior veiled to run the illegal sex racket.

Anil: I cautioned you beforehand not to play with fire. You didn't pay any heed to me. Do you remember that summer vacation, Pradosh? We were in final year graduation staying in he East Hostel of Ravenshaw College? That was a scorching midday with 45 degrees Celsius heat. I was coming back to my home on my bike and discovered you at Vani Vihar square sitting on a bench of a road side tea joint putting on a sweater and sipping hot tea. I wanted to offer you a cold drink and you refused.

Pradosh: I refused your cold drink because I was experimenting with the truth of heat. I transgressed all the prohibiting lines prescribed for heat.

Anil: Ha ha ha! You're vanquished, Pradosh, thoroughly vanquished. What kind of truth you were searching for amid lies with fully spread tentacles? Truth must have hidden its face behind solid avalanche of lie. You were scratching that wound and made it bleed. Why?

(*Pradosh refused to answer Anil. He moved silently to the microphone on the Apron stage and stood there silently*)

Anil: What was the necessity of scooping at that minister's dark some activities? They enjoy enormous physical and socio-legal power. Their job is to crush trust beneath the legs of the heavy throne they ride on. You hailed from that remote village called Narasimhapur and you spent your entire life either in Cuttack or in this capital city sifting the good from the bad, sieving the right from the wrong! And finally you fought with that Minister. You didn't know he was a great alchemist who transforms lies as truth! He brought the rope for hanging you as a liar not as a truth-seeker.What did you gain ultimately?

Pradosh: What could I've gained Sir? I don't see life as an account book of debits and credits. I had an idea that there's a definite sunrise at the terminal point of this dark tunnel called truth, however long it might be. I thought there's a dawn at the end of every dark tunnel.

Anil: Yes, there's a dawn, but today's morning would go dark at 7.40 AM. My heart throbs faster when I foresee what'd happen. Where's Hadibandhu? Hadibandhu!

(*Enters with hurried steps*)

Hadibandhu: Yes Sir!

Anil: What about the arrangements in the toilet?

Hadibandhu: I have put the water heater on; and kept a fresh towel and soap

Anil: Then you take the prisoner for a bath.

Hadibandu: (to Pradosh) Come!

Pradosh: Alright! (*He moves and both of them exit. Hadibandhu goes inside. Pradosh steps on the edge of the wing point. Then he moves back and walks slowly to Anil*)

Pradosh: Once upon a time you were a friend to me Sir! I've had occasions, therefore, to quarrel with you. I've quarrelled with you on the principle of living. Today is my last day of remaining alive. (*Pause, back ground music*) I'd therefore request you sir! Kindly pardon me if I've committed any wrong. Forget those quarrels of the childhood. I've told you this because I' won't be able to meet you again in this life. Good bye!

(*Pradosh extended his hand to Anil for a shake. Anil holds the hand, pulled him to his chest and embraced him. They wept for some time. The following song is rendered/ recited in female voice*)

This is mostly about
a life half-burnt
Simmering dreams exit
Subdued smoke; don't
Search for the truth
That'd end up in death.
Better call it a liberty post
It rebounds murmurs silent
(*Keyboard plays a chord in high note. Pradosh exits.*

Anil stands steady and salutes Pradosh for bidding a farewell)

Anil: Three cheers for truth! You must be realising today, Pradosh! The light you chased till the hanging rope is a misnomer... It's a mutiny in the cosmos, a priggish coup de' tat though... You are overwhelmed by bright sunlight... I noticed it on that mid-summer mid day when you put on a woollen sweater and sipped hot tea on the road side tea joint. (*Background music grows plaintive*) You could never know what we are in light, are not that in darkness. But the minister who was running a Beauty Parlour and a sex racket simultaneously knew it. He knew it well that one dons and enacts roles under bright light and one chooses to live authentically in darkness. I'm so sorry dear Pradosh! You could never learn how to enact a role. That's more important than chasing truth!

(*A middle aged advocate enters from outside. He is Mr. Khadenga. He appears very nervous and to combat the uncomfortable situation swigs intermittently from the nip bottle kept in his side pocket*)

Khadenga: Namaskar! Good Morning Inspector Sahib!

Anil: (*Changes his mood)* Hello! Good morning Mr. Khadenga! We are waiting for you. Mr. Khadenga. Your client Pradosh shall be hanged at seven forty exactly. The records must be ready and they might to be signed by you and the client.

Khadenga: That's alright Inspector. But it was 2 Am in the night when we finished the paper work. My mind is not functioning anymore! Where's the chair to sit?

Inspector: (Smiles) It's there, Sir! Right in front of you.

(Khedenga totters toward to chair)

Khadenga: Yes, yes. I'm Sorry! I'm thoroughly nervous Sir! The doctor has advised me not to undertake serious cases... I'm suffering from high B.P. I met a scooter accident while coming to your jail, Sir!

Inspector: What happened?

Khadenga: Nothing Sir! I escaped the accident narrowly. What a serious case this is! A thirty years old young man is to be hanged on a rope! Your Judge has ordered (*He swigs liquor from the nip bottle*)

Inspector: What can we do Mr. Khadenga? You are his advocate. It was your duty to defend him. What were you doing as a vokil?

Khadenga: Vookil? What Vookil Sir? He said you are his class mate in his village school (Swigs) you should have defended him.

Anil: The society we live is full of liars and they march the streets with heads high. Isn't it a Herculean task to sustain here without anything except truth?

Khadenga: That's right Inspector. Truth is like a funnel with a broad month. It is easy to enter into the funnel of truth. But you cannot come out of that narrow exit. Pradosh was drowned in the funnel like an insect *(Music)* I've tried to convince him... he didn't compromise... (*Music*) His father was known to me... was a freedom fighter, didn't enter into government service, died of heart attack last year.

Anil: I know it Sir! I've also tried to change him. What can we do! He's committed to truth.

Khadenga: I thought of his fate and I could not sleep last night.

Anil: Pradosh has to sign some legal papers before execution. Have you brought those papers?

Khadenga: Yes, Everything is ready.

(*He opens his brief case and does not find the papers. Anil looks at his watch and calculates the time*)

Anil: Just a minute Sir! Let me check up whether the executioner has kept ready all things. Give me those papers. I'll take the signature of Pradosh once he comes back from the bath room.

Khedenga: (*He does not find the paper*) What shall I do now? I don't find the paper. Did I leave them at my office room? I drafted the lines and then typed them manually.

Anil: Give me the paper Khadenga Babu. We are getting late...

Khadenga: Am I getting nervous? My throat gets parched (*He swigs*) I call it A. N. L. Sir

Anil: My names Anil. What does your ANL mean?

Khadenga: This is Anti-Nervous-Liquid.

Anil: Call it Liquid Khadenga Babu! You know it's the jailor's office and boozing is prohibited here!

Khadenga: I know it Sir! Don't make me nervous!

Anil: Give me the paper Sir! This is to (*Khadenga swigs again and keeps the bottle on the table)* be signed by Pradosh.

Anil: What are you doing Sir! This is Jailor's Office, not your Vakils' Club!

Khadenga: What can I do Sir? Nothing goes inside my head. May be there are blockages. So (Swigs again) this "Anti Nervous Liquid" is a necessity... This is because of my age. Anil Babu! Give me ten minutes, I'll go home, collect the papers and come back within ten minutes... Allow me to go Sir! After all, he's my friend's son... going to be hanged... If anything goes wrong, the ghost of his father would ride on my shoulder!

Anil: I don't know what explanation I shall give to sister-in-law Vimala.

Khadenga: Who's Vimala, his wife?

Anil: Yes. She is a lecturer in political science

Khadenga: Oh, that one? He has divorced her. She lives alone with their son Bunty!

Anil: How? Since when are they divorced?

Khadenga: Since last six months. The day Pradosh was convicted in the murder case, Vimala walked out of his house.

Anil: And Pradosh didn't meet her, didn't call her back!

Khedenga: He was shocked and awfully busy trying to prove his innocence. Vimala suddenly became rich with her UGC pay hike. Who Knows – she might have married somebody else or would have bought a new pusillanimous prig as her new husband. Who knows!

Anil: Pradosh has not told me anything about this happening!

Khadenga: How could he dare? These were secrets which can't be shared with others! Vimala thought her husband would one day come back to academia... but you know Pradosh... how irritable a character he was!

Anil: And what about that son! Bunty?

Khadenga: You know Leena, a related sister of Pradosh? She has taken Bunty to her house. I know Leena...

Anil: (*Looks at the wrist watch*) It's time now Khadenga Babu! Now rush back to your home and fetch those papers. Quick now... Hurry up!

Khadenga: Yes... I'm coming (*He exits with hurried steps*)

Anil: Oh! What a crucial day! I don't know how the day will pass... and the mind shall be lighter. (*to an absent constable*) Hadibandhu, are you through with the chores?

(*Then he goes to the telephone and dials*) Hello! Dr. Patnayak... I'm Anil Parija speaking from the central jail.. The convict shall be hanged at 7.40 AM Sir! You're to report at 7.25 AM... Oh, you are on the way? Ok? Sir! Yeah! I' m waiting for you. Bye.

(*As he turns he finds Leena with Bunty. Leena is the distantly related sister of Pradosh and Bunty, his son abandoned by his former wife Vimala and sheltered by Leena. Leena is about 26 years and Bunty is a 12 years old boy*).

Leena: Anil Bhai?

Anil: Yes, Leena!

Bunty: Good Morning, Uncle!

Anil: Good Morning Bunty! Leena, why have you brought this boy to the jail?

Bunty: My ex-father is going to be hanged today Uncle! Aunty said, I should bid him "good bye"!

Leena: Hey! Keep your mouth shut. Don't jabber gibberish.

Anil: Come here Bunty (*He goes near. Anil fondles him*)

What standard are you in, four or five?

Bunty: Standard Five Uncle.

Anil: What about your mom? Don't you meet her?

Bunty: Mummy? Oh! She's a bad woman!

Anil: And Bapa? What about your Dad?

Bunty: My Papa-Best Papa!

(*Pradosh enters after bathing. He is fresh and he has put on a now civil dress*)

Anil: Look, your "Best Papa" has come! (Bunty escapes from Anil's clutch and Jumps to Pradosh)

Bunty: Papa!

Pradosh: Bunty! (He hugs the child)

Bunty: You are going to be hanged today! Is it n't Papa?

Pradosh: Yes! I will be hanged! Just after twenty minutes... I'll go to the other side of the world.

Bunty: Wish you "all the best" Papa!

Leena: (*She's irritated*) Bunty! Come home. I'll decide how to deal with you!

Pradosh: Promise Leena! You won't keep him under any illusion. Tell him the facts – Tell him what actually has happened to his father! He should not lead a guilty life only because of me.

Leena: How shall I know Pradosh Bhai, how shall I know what is Truth? Who bothers about what has happened. I'm more worried about the dark future that I have to face after your last journey. But your son shall be an advocate when he grows up.

Anil: I'll look after you Leena, don't worry.

Bunty: Why Uncle? Papa will look after us.

Anil: Papa will be hanged today. He won't be there tomorrow.

Pradosh: I have a small request for you, Bunty.

Bunty: Yes, Papa! Tell!

Pradosh: Take a pledge that you won't speak a lie. You'll speak Truth all your life.

Bunty: That I'll do, Papa. But tell me why you are going to be hanged?

Leena: He's going to be hanged only because he divulged some hidden truth. And you'll see him after he is hanged now.... (*A sudden sob overwhelms her*)

Pradosh: No, No Leena, no sobbing here!

Bunty: What's the matter Papa? Why's Leena auntie weeping? Is it because you are getting hanged?

Pradosh: Ask Anil Uncle! (*Back ground music is heart moving*)

Bunty: Uncle!

Anil: Your Papa shall be hanged for telling the truth. I mean, telling the truth is dangerous in our times.

Leena: Never tell the truth, Bunty. We don't need truth.

Bunty: What are they talking Papa? Didn't you tell me; "Truth is like the Sun. You can shut it out for a time, but not for all times.

Pradosh: Yes, Bunty. The truth will set free, but first it may make you miserable. Never put yourself away from truth. Let what it may breed!

Leena: Don't be scared to face miseries.

Anil: An old man said: "Rather than love, than money, then fame, give me truth.

Leena: You won't be there to know Pradosh Bhai, but I can imagine. The stooges and henchmen of that Minister shall attack us one day and they'd make our life miserable.

Pradosh: Do you listen to the tragic foreboding of this girl, Sir? I'm dying after ten minutes. You've to protect my sister and this forsaken son. That's your duty.

Bunty: If truth begets so much of misery, why should one tell truth, Papa? Why invite bad luck? Again, how can I become an advocate if I stick on to truth?

Pradosh: Truth passes through three stages. First, it is ridiculed, secondly it is violently opposed. Third, it is accepted as self evident. And Bunty! Never falter in matters of truth. Three things cannot be long hidden – the Sun, the Moon, and the Truth.

Bunty: But people are afraid of telling the truth. Look at Leena Aunty!

Leena: Your Leena Aunty has seen it in Bunty. She knows the consequences of speaking out the unpleasant truth.

Anil: Look here, Bunty ... Look at the wings. There are kinds of screens behind which we can hide. People tell lies; they manufacture lies, cook lies and hide behind the screen of lies. The world does not see them. They escape law, they escape hanging. But truth has nothing to hide.

Bunty: (*Goes and holds Leena's hand and drags*) come Aunty, we'll hide behind the wings. No one can see us (*Both of them vanish behind the wings*)

Pradosh: Answer this boy, Sir! You'll have to look after him!

Anil: What "Sir"? Why should you call me "Sir"? Pradosh? You are going to die after fifteen/twenty minutes. Should you continue to call me "Sir' – till... till you breath your last? Shall you reject me as your friend and classmate? What crime have I done? You have come here and I'm the Jailor here! I'... I am just doing my duty.

Pradosh: You fellow have a job in the khaki department Anil! Learn to live with a heart of stone. I am dying. But why should you die before my death? Why do you feel so soft and sentimental for me?

Anil: What else can I do? This smallest deed done is better than the greatest intention! (Music) I'm missing one of my most intimate friends.

Pradosh: Cool down Anil. Life is as evanescent as the morning dew, as the flash of lightning. If you will die before my death, who'll guard Leena and Bunty's life!

Anil: I will, Pradosh! I' promise! I'll build their lives not as you wanted them to, but as I consider safe for them!

Pradosh: What does that mean?

Anil: They shall remain hidden and safe behind the screens and wings of lies. Tell me Pradosh! I'm not asking you as your friend Anil Parija, but as the head of this Central jail. This is an official question. You are going to be hanged after fifteen minutes. Tell me; what is your last wish?

Pradosh: Last wish? (He laughed) what wish? I wish there to be no misunderstanding about the truth I wish to uphold!

Anil: Nonsense! Don't vomit your philosophy on me. Tell me what exactly you wish?

Pradosh: What else shall I wish looking at this hanging rope? The rope is hanging like truth. Put a black screen in front of it.... Then I'll tell.

Anil: Ok! (*Hollers*) Hadi Bandhu! Hadi Bandhu! (*Hadi Bandhu arrives*) Hang a black curtain in front of this hanging rope. (*Hardi Bandhu pulls the screen rope and the black screen falls in front of the hanging rope, it might move from left to right also)*

Tell me now Pradosh. No drama. I have drawn the black curtain in front of this menacing hanging rope okay? The truth is hidden behind ... Now tell me what your last wish is. Tell me Pradosh .... I'll be looking at you and you'll die, and I won't cry! You bloody truth-speaker Harischandra fool! I won't cry when you'll die!

(*He shouts and the shout transforms into a high pitch wailing. The keyboard screams a pathetic note at high pitch, stop. Then the song or the recitation in female voice:*)

Simmering dreams emit
smoke around their humble nest.
The search for truth ultimate
ends in death.

(*Anil bursts into tears and hides his face. Pradosh shouts*)

Pradosh: Silence, you hypocrite! Silence! Your tears can't wash my sin! Remember one thing; you've betrayed me, bastard!

(*Crash sound Anil turns to front with a violent jerk*)

Yes, for you… for you only I am putting my neck into the knot of this fatal rope! You've supported that corrupt Minister and flung me into death!

Anil: I'm a poor police officer Pradosh … an insect stuck in the political web. The spider will gulp me up. I tried to convince you hundred times … requested you saying: "Pradosh! Don't draw your dagger against the Minister … He's very powerful. Don't proceed to unravel his sex racket operating in the beauty parlour…" You didn't pay any heed. You enacted the role of King Harischandra, refuted me as if I was the villain of a false melodrama. How could have I supported you? I'm a police officer taking the burden of a family of four children and a wife. Bolstering your cause would have resulted in extermination of my family…Can't you understand that? You are an idiot… You don't know what family is…

Pradosh: How dare you say that? I loved my wife and son.

Anil: "Loved my wife?" How did she desert you and flee from your family?

Pradosh: Deserted me because I am not a lecturer … I'm just a poor journalist drawing five thousand rupees and her pay was hiked five times by the UGC. She's drawing fifty thousand now. How could she stay with a poor man?

Anil: That doesn't mean sister-in-law Vimala would flee leaving a ten year old son. I'd have lifted that woman and brought her to you. But you were pursuing that Minister's sex racket madly. (*Music. Anil tries to control his excitement*) And finally you shall be hanged in my presence. (*Voice Beaks*) I'll make arrangements for your hanging! I never dreamt of such a situation

Pradosh! This is too much for me to bear with… too much (*choral humming and key board, Anil almost bursts into tears*)

Pradosh: No Sir! You are the keeper of law and order of this country. The government has vested on you great responsibility. Weeping is prohibited for you, Sir. To enter into humanitarian feeling is proscribed for you…

Anil: (*Shouts although the voice is broken*) Shut up you idiot! What do you think of me, an inhuman beast, a savage and sadistic creature?

Pradosh: (*No Reaction*) I pity you Sir! It seems you are infected with some humanitarian virus. It's not innocuous for politicians and police officers Sir!

(*Anil is overwhelmed, he distantiates himself from Pradosh and turns his face away*)

Anil: Pradosh!

Pradosh: Cool, Cool down, Anil Babu! You are going to be promoted to the post of DSP. You should be in Minister's good book … Of course I won't be there to see that promotion. My face will cease to talk after fifteen minutes. Listen to my last words Sir! You've to act as a sycophant, you can't swagger, can't live vertically. So, forget about the journalist Pradosh – forget about this nincompoop… he's… I'm a lost case.

Anil: (Irritated) Shut up you incorrigible idiot. Or, I'll stifle you! (*He moves menacingly*)

Pradosh: Calm down, Sir! These days CEOs are taught to do meditation for half an hour every morning. You should also practice it Sir!

Anil: (*Moves to distance place*) what are you up to? Sermonizing whenever you meet me? Sister-in-law Vimala left you only because of this.

Pradosh: She divorced me because I could not clear the NET; because I could not become a lecturer. But I struggled hard to act as a romantic husband… I took her to shopping malls, bought new dress and cosmetics for her… But luck didn't favour me …! I found…

Anil: What did you find?

Pradosh: I'm telling. Now, take your seat.

(Anil sits on the chair; Pradosh surveys the stage and mutters)

Pradosh: Okay! There's a black curtain at the background. This may be taken as Pradosh Mishra's house.

(He moves to the down stage curtain and addresses the music pit)

Well Mr. Hari Prasad Sir! Please play on the flute as background music. This is an evening in the Capital City. The sequence is like this: I reached home *(The flute is played. Lights change and the sound of pooja – bells fill the stage. A conch shell blows… Flute again. Pradosh goes to the wing and calls)*!

Pradosh: Vimala! Vimala Madam! Open the door: *(Leena opens the door, smiles and addresses)*

Leena: Pradosh Bhai! Namaskar!

Pradosh: You… are… *(Tries to identify, fails)*I mean... I'm sorry…

Leena: Not able to identify me? Strange…I'm Leena… Leena Satpathy … Do you recognize now? No? Jagatpur… the village after Mahanadi bridge… Your Grandfather's village? Your Sudhir Uncle… I mean Sudhir Satpathy… I'm his daughter Leena, completed my graduation last year.

Pradosh: Oh, yes, now I got you. How come you are here?

Leena: Because you are my only acquaintance at Bhubaneswar! I requested you to find a job for me Pradosh Bhai! Have you forgotten?

Pradosh: No. I mean… OK! Where's Vimala?

Leena: Sister-in-law left your home and went where I don't know. Seems she has divorced you.

Pradosh: Divorced me? How do you know?

Leena: She's left a letter for you!

Pradosh: What letter? Where's it?

Leena: Bunty! Get that letter our Mom left for Papa!

Bunty: Papa! Mama abandoned me and went away. She has left this letter for you (*Pradosh, who has come from an overnight tour to Sambalpur, reads the letter and the background music in flute transforms the atmosphere to a serious note*)

Pradosh: Why? Why did your mom leave our house? What happened to her?

Bunty: She didn't talk to me. I came back from school and she did not give anything to eat. I was hungry. I couldn't know where she went. Thank god Leena aunty came and bought some sandwiches for me.

Leena: Don't worry, Pradosh Bhai. I've come… There'll be no trouble for you. I'll cook the meal for you till your returns. Show me Bunty's school. I'll take him to his school in the morning. But you've to arrange a job for me Pradosh Bhai. I've brought all my certificates. Please help me.

Pradosh: I got a government quarters at Bhubaneswar. We'll shift there tomorrow first. But I want to know what Vimala's reaction was when you made an entry to our house?

Leena: Sister-in law was frowning at me for the last three days since when I came. But, what is my fault Pradosh Bhai? I was cleaning the utensils, washing sister-in-law's night-wear and I was doing all the daily chores. Still she was not happy. I was surprised to find her coming home at 8:30 in the night in an abnormal state.

Pradosh: What? Returning by 8:30P.M., from the college?

Leena: A young man used to give her a lift in his car.

Bunty: Papa! Papa! Mom used to come heavily boozed. She'd throw the food whatever Leena aunty cooked. I used to go to sleep with her on the bed. The stench of liquor emitted from her mouth made me overcome by nausea. *(Pradosh changes the topic)*

Pradosh: Your exams are over, I hope.

Bunty: Yes, Papa!

Pradosh: Now I have decided to shift you to the DAV school. We shall move tomorrow.

Leena: Take me also to the new quarters Pradosh Bhai. Can't I get a job with my graduate degree?

Pradosh: Let us hope for the best.

Leena: Shall I pack our luggage now?

Pradosh: Okay! *(Leena and Bunty exit. The flash back ends The lights change. Pradosh comes now to Anil who is seated on the chair)* This is the story of Vimala's exodus.

Anil: *(like a suspicious police officer)* More important is this new girl called Leena. How could she be entangled in the sex-racket of the Minister's Beauty Parlour? You said she is from Jagatpur village.

Pradosh: Leena is an innocent girl from Jagatpur. She knows nothing about the underworld crime rackets of this capital city. Before I tried the government sources, the Beauty Parlour offered her a job with a salary of five thousand per month. She stayed and dined with us and was happy with the job; used to send some money also to her parents… Then suddenly, one evening, the police arrested her and kept her in custody. I was shocked when I arrived home. I went and got her back with a bail.

Anil: Didn't you ask her about the charges? What are the sections she was booked for?

Pradosh: What could I've done? As an investigative journalist I tried to go into the details. Actually, it was the job of the police. But the police didn't pay any heed.

Anil: Then? How could you know that the Minister is involved?

Pradosh: The police didn't take any interest in my case, rather complicated the entire issue. I was keen because it involved Leena's life and career – a girl whom I sheltered in my house. Finally – one day, I asked about the details from Leena.

(The stages lights changes abruptly. The music too changes. Pradosh calls Leena loudly)

Pradosh: Leena! Leena!! Come here!

(Music is grave. Leena comes with a face showing signs of apology.) Tell me, why the police did take you into their custody?

(Leena is silent)

Pradosh: There may be some private affair work. I'm not interested to pry into your privacy. I'm asking just to know why the police... sort of... arrested you?

Leena: There's nothing to feel bad about it Pradosh Bhai! They've published my photo in the local daily

(Music starts. There' s a short silence. Pradosh could not ask her a question he wanted to ask. Finally he enquired:)

Pradosh: Tell me Leena, who were your customers? Were they political people or only business executives?

Leena: All sorts of people.

Pradosh: What do you mean by that? How many girls are working in the Beauty Parlour? What is the exact kind of work they are asked to perform?

Leena: We are eight girls Pradosh Bhai. Three of us are specially deployed for the massage room into which political heavy weights used to come for oil-bath and naked massage. Two worked for the police officers and I. A. S officers. I was discarded because I came from a rural background and was called *desi* item. I have seen those political people though I didn't know who they were...

Pradosh: Can you give me the names of some of these political heavy weights? I want to know about this high profile inter-state sex racket. Tell me the names, I'll bust them out!

Leena: I didn't know they were politicians. Later I found them hoisting the national flags on the independent day. I was shocked.

Pradosh: That means they are ministers. The crime branch superintendent of police Mr. Kashyap said that the sex racket had been operating there over the last four years.

Leena: When the police busted the sex racket all the eight sex workers were arrested. I was one among them. Then I come to know that the minister appointed a man of Uttar Pradesh who was allegedly running the brothel. The male technicians of the spa were working as pimps.

Pradosh: But how can you prove your statement? What's the proof?

Leena: That you're to find out; how can I help? Of course, that Abhoy Kishan used to take our photographs during action. Then he black mailed us.

Pradosh: Yes I understand. That's how brothels are run under the guise of beauty parlours

Leena: But now they can do no harm. All the photos are seized by the police. Why don't you go and ask the police? The culprits shall be caught red handed. Better you ask the police. I can't give you the exact data.

(*Leena exits through the mid right wings. Anil enters and occupies his chair and now the scene changes. Pradosh, who followed Leena and went inside, returns to Anil*),

Pradosh.: Anil! What's the progress regarding that beauty parlour case?

Anil: (*He was reading a file. He lifted his head and looked at Pradosh, didn't reply*)

Pradosh: (*annoyed*) I'm asking you Anil! How far have you gone in that sex racket case?

Anil: Oh! You've come 'ere in the capacity of a journalist but that's an old case, now closed and kept in cold storage. Why are you chasing that?

Pradosh: I've come to you only for that. Six months have already lapsed, but it seems you're not taking any action.

Anil: What do you mean?

Pradosh: No one has been arrested so far. How could you close the case after arresting the sex workers? They are poor victims illegally raped inside the beauty parlour. I came to know from reliable sources that ministers, IPS and IAS Officers and business tycoons are involved in the case. Could you trace them?

Anil: Look 'ere Pradosh! I've to handle several cases, more urgent and important than this Beauty Parlour case. Besides, I may be transformed to the Prisons Department. So...

Pradosh: You're avoiding me, it seems. My sister, Leena is involved and arrested Anil. I've brought her home on bail. I have talked to that Abhoy Kishan and he ridicules me saying Ministers are involved.

Anil: The police department is seriously dealing with the case. The Prison department has changed to Correctional Services Department now. Since you are involved I will take stern action against that Beauty Parlour. Believe me.

Pradosh: What shall you do?

Anil: The female offenders were arrested. Now we'll handle the male.offenders and consider about their length of detention. Now, may I ask you one more question? Who's Leena to you? How's she your sister? That bloody bitch is a broad! I'm sorry, but I suspect one thing. Do you have any illicit affair with her?

Pradosh: (Shouts) Anil! Mind your language. She's an innocent girl from the suburbs of Cuttack town.

Anil: You are an idiot Pradosh. Do you want to see the photographs and videos taken during her sex play? Do you want to see them? Do you? (Pause) No, I'm afraid you idiot may commit suicide. But Mr admirer of innocence, tell me why Vimala Bhavi was fuming after her arrival? It was during your absence.

Pradosh: I think it's because of normal sexual jealousy! But how do you use such harsh words and slangs against her?

Anil: I have seen the videos after those were seized from Abhoy kishan. I'd have shown you her activities during action. But I won't. As a sincere police officer, it's not my duty to show you anything before the case is settled. And Mr. Pradosh! Journalist, my foot! You must learn how to talk to the Officer-in-charge of a Police Station.

Pradosh: I'm sorry Anil!

Anil: Not Anil! Again, mind your language. You must address me as "Sir" or "Officer"! Mind it.

Pradosh: I'm sorry, sir!

Anil: Number two, I'm working here with severe political and official pressure. I can't act as freely as you work as a journalist. Do you know how difficult it is to maintain a balance between truth and Power?

Pradosh: I understand it Sir! You left the case mid-way because of political pressures.

Anil: That too from the Home Minister! We behave like pet dogs to the home department, do you know that? Pradosh! I have to survive as an Inspector and wait for the promotion. I have to earn for a family with four children, and old ailing parents. I can't afford to lose my job.

Pradosh: So, you can't show me the porno material?

Anil: No. How can I show our evidences to press people while the case is sub-judice? I can't even investigate the case authentically.

Pradosh: I have seen the seizure list. There is no mention about photographs. That means the photographs are here with you.

Anil: What shall we do with nude photographs in the police station? We've destroyed them… (*A telephone call and Anil responds*) Yes sir! I'm going in a minute! (*he gets up and tells*) you may go now Pradosh! There's a call from the boss. I've to go...

Pradosh: But you didn't show me the photographs! That's bad. I need proof

Anil: Don't nag and pester me, Pradosh! (*searching for an album in the drawer*) these are vulgar photos.... Don't faint. Truth is always nude. (*He throws the album. Pradosh picks it up. Pradosh is stunned to see some political celebrities in the parlour in nude condition)*

Pradosh: Oh my! He is the minister, home department. What an absurd photo (*he laughs*) this fellow puts on a grave face and lectures on human rights and duties like a philosopher. What is he doing here as a naked hero? (*Laughing*) give this photo to me.

Anil: No, I'll be fired from my job. Pradosh! Why? I will

Anil: What you'll? Can you publish the nude photo of the minister in your newspaper? Your life shall be in danger. His workers with come and murder you. Take care of your life and family first. Then you start worshipping the truth. Truth is a frightening monster, Pradosh! Don't act like a stupid.

Pradosh: Thank you for your advice, Sir! But if I won't expose the minister, it will be a great injustice to Leena's character. That girl cannot marry!

Anil: Why should you bother for that Jagatpur tart? Now try to understand under what pressure I'm working here.

Pradosh: Why can't you behave like an honest officer?

Anil: The government doesn't want honest officer's Pradosh! You are talking like an idiot despite my warning. I warn you again; your life is in danger! Take care!

(Pradosh drooped his head. Background music evokes some impending danger for Pradosh. Light fades out in dimmer. After a minute, light bangs in and Adarsh Samantarai, the minister enters with two of his fierce looking henchmen. They are two political hooligans)

Adarsh: What do you think of yourself? I have won the election and beaten my opponent by a margin of sixty thousand votes. I led my party to one of its biggest political victories in the past three decades single handed; stopping the opposition's juggernaut. I've paved the way for the chief minister for a third consecutive term. And a rascal journalist claims to topple the government for a beauty parlour slut? Can we bear with this high handedness, Dhadia? Barge into his house and abduct that bastard's wife!

Dhadia: Yes boss! I'll bombard his house! We shall operate in Bollywood style! (Back ground music).... Devastate that *Shala* journalist!

Adarsha: Phu! *(He laughs violently; without making any sound)*. Copy the action from a blockbuster action movie and destroy that journalist.... Or else, do it in local style... Simple acting... Barge into his quarters... Rape the girl if she's there… Leena Something!.... Don't use pistol! Insert broken beer bottles into her stomach... Then into his son Bunty's stomach... Finish the job within five minutes, not more than that!

Dhadia: Ok, Boss! (*He was leaving the stage*)

Adarsh: Listen! *(He takes out a bundle of currency notes and offers)* Keep it. It's not much; a million only...manage with this. Once the work is over, I'll give you two more bundles.

Dhadia: I'll demolish that journalist's family, boss. Done! I'll report to you over cell phone after fifteen minutes,

Adarsh: I called that Inspector Anil Parija to come to me. Did he come?

Dhadia: I'll remind him Sir! (He exits)

Adarsh: Bastard! Pradosh Mishra is a bastard! Getting a paltry sum from the Press and the fellow attempts to eradicate corruption from the country! Rascal thinks he is powerful.... He will drag my feet and oust me from my position as a minister. How dares he?

(*Inspector Anil comes*)

Anil: Good day, sir?

Adarsh: I asked you to report at 10.00am. This is 12.30pm, Anil. Why so late?

Anil: There was a serious case sir! Pradosh has killed Dhadia!

Adarsh: What? Dhadia has killed Pradosh? Is that poor journalist killed? Ah! What a tragedy! Arrest that hooligan Dhadia. Put him behind the bars.

Anil: Sir, you didn't hear me properly. Pradosh the journalist has murdered Dhadia.

Adarsha: What are you saying? How could it happen? Is that journalist a boxer? Who is he? Dhadia is an asset to our party. Arrest that journalist.

Hang him. I want to see that murderer is hanged!

(*The light gets dimmer and then is put off. As the lights fade in Hadibandhu brings Pradosh in prisoners' dress. He leads him to the gallows. Advocate khadenga totters fully sozzled. He mutters:*)

Khadenga: Section 354(5)! What a tension! Pradosh babu! (*gives a paper*) Put your signature here! (Pradosh goes to Anil's desk puts his signature and gives it back to Anil. Anil keeps it in the drawer. They lead Pradosh to the gallows. The doctor comes and examined Pradosh! The Executioner was ready. He mutters something into the ears of Pradosh. What the executioner says is inaudible.

(*A bell tolls for ten times in the back ground. On the tenth stroke Pradosh is hanged. A recitation from the Bhagavat Gita in background (male voice)*)

Vasansi jeernani yatha bihaya
Navani grunhati naroparani
Yatha sareerani bihaya jeernaa
-nyanyani samjati navani dehi

(Lights go off)

****

THE ELEPHANT IN THE CAPITAL

The Elephant in the Capital was premiered in Sangit Natak Academy Festival, 1986 held at Baripada, Mayurbhanj, Odisha. The play was produced by Ganjam Kala Parishad, Berhampur, Ganjam. It was directed by the author with the following cast:

Danei/Oldman: Ramchandra Dash

Ram Pradhan/Ram: Rambabu Dora

Veterinary Director/Elephant Language Interpreter: Sobhan Das

Spear Hunter/ Journalist: Achyutananda Praharaj

Scribbler Hunter/Research Scholar: Narayana Chowdhury

Elephant Money lender/Elephant Baba: Dasarathi Das

Mr. Elephant: Pradip Padhi

Kalia: Babu

Lakshmi-1/Lakshmi-2: Lata Nayak

Crowd, elephant victims and actors of the physicalized Elephant.

The director shall fix their number.

Set and costume: Kedar Apte

Music: Late Ashok Padhi

Preface

i. This is a reconstruction of a news story published in a local daily at Cuttack in 1986. The story narrated, "A wild elephant has killed a bicycle rider on the Chandka jungle road on the outskirts of Cuttack. The government has declared a cash prize of ten thousand rupees to the hunter who would seize the elephant live or dead." Two days later, the photograph of the dead elephant was published in the Newspaper with two hunters on both sides of the dead elephant and each claiming that he has killed the animal. The collector of Cuttack stood at the centre behind them.

   The news story stimulated my imagination and I thought of writing a play about the elephant. The play was staged at the Sangit Natak Akademi Drama Festival at Baripada. Later, its radio version was broadcast from All India Radio, Cuttack.

ii. I was brought up in a theatre ensemble called Ganjam Kala Parishad, at Berhampur, Odisha. The group of actors, musicians, playwrights and directors has come together out of dissatisfaction with the established trend of the contemporary theatre. The group was exploring certain specific assets of the stage, not as a production group, but as a group trying to find its own voice. The stable tenets of Ganjam Kala Parishad (Established in 1955) were (i) to create a situation in which the actors can play together with a sensitivity required of an ensemble, (2) to explore other specific powers that only the live theatre possesses, (3) to concentrate on a theatre of abstraction and illusion, as opposed to a theatre of behavioral or psychological motivation and (4) to discover ways in which the artist can find his expression without money as the determining factor.

   I joined the group in mid-1960s. Most of us were students, painter(s) singers, doctors, dancers, advocates and professors occasionally holding month-long workshops with freelancing NSD-ians. My play scripts were put on workshops, they were rehearsed clarifying the movement and line of action and working on individual acting problems. I used to sit, take notes rewrite expand and edit my script, at the same time making sure that the emotional imagery held firm. It worked to parody, irony, humor. Our strategy was in part to propose physical intimacy as counterpoint to the mechanical acting of the mainstream theatre houses of Annapurna, Annapurna B, Janata Theatres and Kalasree Theatre.

We had to go through that first period of enthusiasm about unusual ways of using the body and the voice before we could draw from experience to speak through the voice and the body. This mode of learning through physical resources was very interesting to me.

Our actors had to study something about performance; about the fact that we perform for each other all the time by trying to make ourselves understood. We taught them that the actor has to be able to wake himself up out of this mesmerized state of being where he is unable to distinguish between a person and picture of a person. However, we emphasized on the fact that the essence of theatre resides in the norm that it is a controlled experience, that it must transcend privatism and that the intuitive must remain subordinated to a central intelligence.

In the process, as a writer I was prone to theatricalism instead of being realistic and naturalistic. I wrote composite art work that attempts to synthesize drama with music, song and colour. Our set designers Bipin Sahu and Kedar Apte tried to unite the various plastic elements like light, music and scenery with the three dimensional actor to present the wholesome theatrical experience. We believed to achieve it through a theatrical intimacy between the stage and the audience, empathy by the sheer pressure of theatrical sensation, immediacy and simultaneity.

Realism, as we understood, whether it is socialist or not, falls short of theatrical needs. It shrinks it, attenuates it, falsifies it; it does not take into account our basic truths and our fundamental obsessions; love, death, astonishment. Truth is in our dreams, in our imagination. Reality does not have to be capable of imagination. Reality does not have to be capable of realization. It is only what it is to the artist and the dreamer, and the thinker is the revolutionary, it is he who tries to change the world. Avant-garde of any art is primarily a philosophical quest and a finding of truths, rather than purely an aesthetic activity. It is truism that ours is a period of extra ordinary and rapid change, with its attendant surprises and sufferings; it is no less true that in such a way all serious thought must try to find in it a pattern of sense.

I have focused upon this concept of the real, suggesting a course of action in art that is related to what is likely our experience today, as distinct from what are our habits from the past. If the play's theme and plot retain some of the traditional clichés they are neither meaningful, nor archaic. Rather I have felt the need to rediscover a sense of the mystical. The crisis of the modern, to my mind, is a crisis of belief and our theatre in Ganjam Kala Parishad had a crucial role in restoring this lost capacity. Theatre for me has only one meaning if it allows us to transcend our stereotyped vision, our conventional feelings and customs, our standards of Judgment. Then only my audience may experience the real and discover the real.

iii. Our concept of universally intelligible and timeless beauty of theatre has undergone a process of steady erosion; notions of timelessness, change and self-consciousness of the present have tended increasingly to become sources of value in an "adversary culture". If tradition of mainstream theatre is rejected with increasing violence, my artistic imagination would obviously start priding itself on exploring and mapping the realms of "Not-yet"

During the early 1970s I was drawn toward the antinomian and deliberately deviant patterns of modernist imagination since such a temper of avant-gardism became a winning phenomenon culturally and was translated into the life style of the intellectual minority. What we have today is a radical disjunction of culture and socio-political structure and such insurgency and political gangsterism can be traced ontologically to the elephant metaphor.

The elephant community's proclivity to harass and terrorize innocent people has almost been institutionalized if not consecrated by the apogees of elephantism. Such a socio political experience paves the way for direct revaluation. The post modernist temper demands that what was previously played out in fantasy and imagination must be acted in life as well. Anything permitted in life is permitted on stage. Second, the life style once practiced by a dreaming minority is likely to be copied by "many" and turn into a dominant force in the cultural scene.

Ramesh P. Panigrahi
105, Rasulgarh
Bhubaneswar-751010
India w.w.w.rameshpanigrahi.com

ACT ONE

SCENE-1

This is enacted in an open stage without a curtain. As audience is getting settled actors begin to appear, one by, one, or in pairs. They lie down on the stage. When everyone is settled there is short silence. As light begins to dim, a song is heard on tape. It may be played twice before action begins"

Song:

There's an elephant in my head
and a big one is he
He stamps his feet trampling my dreams
into nothing but debris.
There's an elephant in my head
He is too strong to see
He leaves me no peace, no sleep
Stomping on everything I can be.
There's an elephant in my head
and I want to set him free
Because deep down inside I know undoubtedly
The elephant is me.

As lights dim up, all the actors of the ensemble are discovered lying on the floor. As the song is repeated the actors' bodies form an elephant. The elephant formation stands up. Front lights dim down and back light is up on the cyclorama screen and the elephant formation is silhouetted. A shadow elephant appears on the back screen raising its trunk. The trumpet call of the elephant is heard. This signals for mayhem in the background. The crowd roars in fear and shouts: there's the elephant-there! The crowd runs pell-mell and shouts. The elephant's cry is heard intermittently. The screams and shrieks of the citizens fill as background effect for the elephant which has poached into Bhubaneswar from Chandka forest. A male voice from the All India Radio announces:

Voice over: This is all India Radio. Listen to our special feature programme about the elephant in the capital. The elephant that came floating from the 'Chandka forest in the flood, has poached in to the capital city of Odisha. The big animal has gone berserk and has trampled over thousands of shops and offices, kiosks and street vendors. Our special correspondent reports that the elephant has caused enormous damages to the capital city. The exact amount of damage has not yet been computed. Urgent and expedient steps are being taken by the government to dispatch relief material to the devastated sectors of the capital. The government has also declared an award of rupees five lakhs for the person who would seize the elephant live or dead.

(The announcement fades away and the screams and shrieks of the citizens are blown up through the microphone. The shadow elephant rampages on the back screen with its original trumpet sound of doom. The pell-mell encroach the stage and the audience. Stray people from the back of the audience come through aisles and passage ways and enter the stage. They run toward the left and right wings dashing with one another in the dim back-lit light.

An old man comes exhausted from behind the audience, climbs the stage and pants for breath. He speaks to the audience.

Old man: It's awful... an elephant would poach into the city and it'd chase senior citizens on the capital roads; that too at 10.30 in the day when the streets are busy. The elephant came from the Chandka jungles, they say. But how could it invade the city? The auto-rickshaws and totos are stopped. The town buses do not ply. What can I do? I'm a retired Head master... of the Unit-II high school. I'm seventy. How shall I go back home? Huh! Bhubaneswar's an insecure town. (He wipes his sweat and pants for breath. The trumpet sound of the elephant and the roar of the crowd unnerve the old man. He searches for an outlet to escape. A young man comes running from the other side and discovers the old man. He cautions him.

Youngman: Elephant! Elephant! It comes this side...! Go away! Go away, uncle!

Old man: Where shall I go? I am frightened! They trampled over me! The crowd and the elephant... (He attempts to step down the stage. The young man intercepts)

Young man: Ah! I've managed to come to this side Okay. You stay back here under. The elephant has diverted on to the park road!

Old man: How many elephants are there? It seems the capital city is full of elephants...Varieties of elephants: black elephants... White elephants and Pink, fairly tale elephants...! Rajdhani Rascals rummaging miscellaneous people.

Young ma: Don't be squeamish! Where do you want to go?

Old man: I'll go home, but before that, I'll collect my young girl from Unit-II, High school! I've no time to waste here.

Young man: Ah! I'm tired, how long can one survive with water? Absolutely there's no strength on my feet. Hungry for last two days

Old man: Oh, Heavens, fasting? What for? That won't help you in any way!

Young man: Uncle, I came to the capital city in search of a job and I lost everything in the elephant accident.

Old man: Where?

Young man: In the capital.

Old man: Ah! (He grimaces) where did this elephant come from?

Behaves like a foreign insurgent.

Young man: Emerged from that exhibition ground...from where there's a circus tent. It has then poached into the old bus stand...Turned two buses upside down and then encroached upon the railway station. All Communication Systems are disconnected.

Old man: It's a trained elephant; trained to destroy all communication systems of the capital.

Young man: What d' ya' mean? All communication System?

Old man: Heavens! This is not an elephant. Lord Jagannath has assumed the avatar of Kalki and caused this destruction. The capital is over-dumped with sin. So, Lord Jagannath has taken the Elephant avatar and destroys the sinners

Young man: That might be true. But do you think I'm one of those sinners? Why? I couldn't get a job in this capital city. Is that the cause that I am a sinner? I call a spade a spade. Is that the cause that I'm a sinner? But why did the elephant chase me on the road? I ran for my life. All my belongings were looted on the foot path. I was left sucked up. Why did Lord Jagannath turn into this incarnation of destruction? Kalki or something? To kill me?

Old man: Did it attempt to kill you?

Young man: Elephant Jagannath raised His trunk and hounded me so ferociously that I thought my paternal life would be blown away on the streets! Then, I ran for my life. But how can I run so fast? Another elephant of hunger ran inside my intestines. Then I came running and found you. Didn't it hound you, uncle?

Old man: Why should it? I don't own paddy fields. Neither do I possess banana orchards in my farm yard.

Young man: Then you're a holy man! I should stay for some more time with you. There'll be no danger, at least from the elephant side.

Old man: Look 'ere young man! Better you go on your work. I will get my daughter from the school and go home.

Young man: That's right Sir, let's go and bring her first. I will guide you to the school.

Old man: Why've you been so benevolent toward young girls and old men? I suspect something fishy in your help.

Young man: (feels awkward and smiles) I've decided to give my life in charity. I'll dedicate my life, here after, for social service...Now I am thinking of visiting the elephant affected slums of the city. I must supervise whether the government officers manage the relief work properly or not.

Old man: Thank you very much for your philanthropic mission. But I refuse to take your help... I will go to the school first and rescue my daughter!

(The old man exits)

Young man: Strange! The man doesn't trust me even though I extend my helping hand. There is a severe scarcity of "trust" in the capital. Lack of trust leads to multi-organ failure... Disease! It was an epidemic of humanitarian aridity, partially leading to spiritual bankruptcy. But the elephant population in the capital is on the rise. Every day a new elephant emerges in the city creating a new jungle. I'd have massacred these newfangled elephants. I could've raised a protest rally against them. But a hungry belly impedes me, I'm undone. Even in my village when I encountered another elephant, I thought of raising a protest. I couldn't, I could not fight that crinkly money lender!

Ah! It's eleven O' clock! I am ravaged by hunger.

The young man sits, and smokes tobacco.

SCENE-2

The atmosphere changes to an Odishan village. Appropriate sound effect is posted. Full lights shine on the stage. The young man transforms into a village farmer called Ramia. The elephant money-lender (EM) enters.)

E.M.: Ramia! Why are you sitting on the verandah in a depressed mood? Are you sick? Won't you go to the fields today?

Ramia: Where are the fields? All the seedlings are burnt into coal under the scorching sky. The seeds you supplied were destroyed in famine, they were rotten seeds.

E.M.: There's no rain since last two months what else would be the fate of the seeds? How can you blame my seeds?

Ramia: I didn't accuse you, my lord, did I? My fate is charred.

E.M.: Someone else accuses me if you didn't; Idiots. I helped them in their crisis, downloaded all the grains into their baskets; distributed everything I had in my granary. Did they speak a word of gratitude? On the contrary, they said I have supplied hollow seeds... rotten ones...! And finally a journalist wrote against my seed grains in newspapers! Isn't there anything called justice? What a horrible village I am living in?

Ramia: Where's justice, my Lord? Had there been any we would not have gazed at the sky for a drop of rain in the month of July.

E.M.: I've asked them ten times to go to that Telugu Ayya to conduct a fire sacrifice for invoking the rains. Did they go to him? They'd smoke cannabis and other narcotics in the evening...sing fake *Kirtana* and sleep without food. Thus ends their day.

Ramia: But where' II they get the money from? How can the villagers conduct a seven-day long fire-sacrifice celebration? Mounds of ghee would be burnt. How can we spend so much?

E.M.: Collect small donations from the villagers and bring if it me. I'll bear the rest of the expenses. Have they ever tried to convince me? Did they learn to live by labor! Huh! Work hard to earn your bread. Think of alternatives.

Ramia: What alternative? I've sold the pair of bullocks and with that money bought seeds to sow.The seedlings were charred under scorching heat. What more alternatives can be there?

E.M.: There's a way, if you've the will to do something. Your forefathers also suffered from scarcity and scantiness. But they managed with loans taken from money-lenders like us. So, you've to make both ends meet. Now you've brought a young girl as your wife, you've to feed her. Okay? But where would you get the money from? Do you need a loan? Why don't you ask for?

Ramia: I've not repaid the last loan. There is still some residue.

Land lord: That's alright. This year the crop is damaged because of water shortage. But next year your fields may yield golden crops. If you feel that I've pestered you to repay the loans...take it from the co-operative society.

Ramia: Will they allow me to take the loan?

Land Lord: Don't worry. I'll help you. Buy a pair of bullocks from the weekly market I'll give you a loan. But who am I to be so altruistic? God's in his heaven. Fetch me a glass of water!

Ramia: (Hollers his wife and tells) Lakshmi! Bring a glass of water... Put some Sugar and squeeze a lemon in it. The land lord has come!

Land Lord: There's no such big hazard that impels you to feel desperate. Just mortgage your house or land as security and draw and big loan from the cooperative society. The problem is over – If they don't give come to me. Mortgage your house and land and take a loan.

(Lakshmi enters with two glasses of sweet drink)

Give it to me.

Lakshmi: I bow down, my lord,

Land Lord: Take my blessings. I was convincing your husband. The situation won't improve if you sit on the verandah showing your beggar's face. After all, you're a strong young man. And you've such a beautiful wife like Lakshmi. Tomorrow she would beget children. What'll happen to them?

(Lashmi covers her face in coyness, collects the glass from the land lord and leaves)

That's all Ramia! What I wanted to say I have said. But I can't collect your finger prints by force. Do as you wish!

(The land lord leaves)

Ramia: Alright sir, I will meet you tomorrow. Good bye! (To Laxmi) Did you cook something?

Lakshmi: What shall I cook? The Land lord has given such coarse and rough rice. It takes hours to boil.

Ramia: I don't feel like eating that foul smelling rice. Rascal!

Lakshmi: That's true. But why don't you go to him tomorrow? He assured us to arrange a loan. Get it. We'll repay when our financial condition improves. Come... the rice is almost ready.

(They exit. Lights dim out.

SCENE-3

The stage is empty and it transforms into Elephant Moneylender's house. The EM holds a big bell in his hand and rings it in odd beats. He walks left and right in quick pace and babbles in high excitement. He's bare bodied and his fore head is painted in Vaishnava sect marks, like those worn by monks.)

Land Lord: Impossible! I can't change the make-up so fast. I can't transform into multiple roles. They don't give me any respite (Rings the bell used for worship) I wanted to sit for a Yoga session... to meditate on goddess Lakshmi (Rings The bell) but the mobile phone buzzes continuously.(buzzing of mobile phones EM holds the phone) I have to collect two hundred laborers from our Panchayat to send them to Surat. The textile mills say it is urgent. Of course, they will pay me two thousand some per head. But where shall I get them from? Everybody is a lord here. They neither study, nor go for physical work. They'd dope themselves and dream about cargo ships sitting on the verandah. Rascals.

Ramia (enters and bows down) Did you call me sir?

Land Lord: There was no other alternative. What more could I've done? You took the loan and by adding the interest it now comes to fifty thousand and odd. The cooperative society has ordered that if you don't pay the loan with interest by tomorrow, they will confiscate your house.

Ramia: I will be ruined, my lord, crack up and collapse! My family shall be bankrupt and destitute. (gulps his own spit)

Land Lord: Why's your throat getting dry? Keep patience. I'll show you the road to prosperity, show you the way for higher earnings. People go to Kolkata. People go to Gujarat, to Surat. They work there and get money filling in brass pots. They are building houses in the village. Why don't you go?

Ramia: But I'm an illiterate man. I don't know the alphabets... How can I aspire to earn pot full of money?

Land Lord: If you want to go-get ready to take the journey today... Take this hundred rupee note. Give it to your wife. She'll send you to the Railway station. The Contractor will take care of your journey... your ticket... your food and everything... when you reach there at Surat, they will pay you three hundred rupees per day...

Ramia: My wife Lakshmi would be alone in my house. How can she...

Land Lord: Everybody has a wife at home, except me. She died last year. Why do you worry for her? Aren't we there to look after her when she's in trouble? What do you say?

Ramia: Then I'll go my Lord.

Land Lord: That's like a good boy. Come, you'll pay off your loan and save the house from an auction sale...come...

(The land-lord takes Ramia. The stage lights dim.

SCENE-4

Back-ground music is somber. Lakshmi appears in a distressed mood.)

Lakshmi: One and half years have passed...He gave no information about his address and well being. He wrote no letters. How could he write? He does not know the alphabets... No money he remits to me... I don't know how shall I live? I'm hungry since last two days...requested the land Lord to send me some provisions... He didn't send the grocery as yet.

(Sound of somebody clearing his throat outside. The land lord enters with a bagful of provisions) He is drunk)

Land lord: Lakhimi.... Are you there in this house?

Lakshmi: Why did you carry this bag yourself, uncle?

You could've sent it through your servant.

Land Lord: I've promised Ramia to undertake all your responsibilities... why can't I carry this grocery bag? Am I so old?

Lakshmi: Why are your steps so unsteady uncle?

Land Lord: Why only legs? All the parts of my body are unsteady... After I see your tight body and sharp features...all the other parts are shaking.

Lakshmi: Sit here sir, Shall I fetch you a glass of lemon drink?

Land Lord: Can your water quench my thirst? Ramia has left you under my vigilance, has told me to take care of every inch of your body!

Lakshmi: But there's no news about him as yet.

I don't know where you've taken him to! Has he sent you any message?

Land Lord: Message? No trace of that fool. May be, he is dead under cold-wave! Sent no money to me (he sits, there is a pause) I sent one sari. Did you wear it? I'm not able to see it on your body.

Lakshmi: I don't know exactly what is done to him. Is there something lethal?

Land Lord: Let him die there, that bloke abandoned his newly married wife...such a cute and fleshy body and went to Surat. That's why I came here to inquire about your body temperature. Let me test your body's temperature first. (He touches under her neck) Why are you standing there like an untouchable? Does

Ramia understand the meaning of touch? Come, get close to me!

Lakshmi: You're reeking of alcohol.

Land Lord: That's nothing. A pint of brandy I've taken with warm water. I felt cold. (He touches her at odd places again. He gets closer to her and embraces) Ah! Your body is hot like an oven. Ramia, the bloke didn't take your proper care... come, hold my...

Lakshmi: Lord, you are like my father! What are you doing to your daughter's body?

Land Lord: Yes I'll act as your father during the day time...but if you ask me to be your father in the night, there'll be a great mislaying, forfeiture. Come... I am no more able to bear this orgy.

Lakshmi: My lord! (She steps back and the Land lord encroaches on her body)

Land Lord: Why do you step back?

Lakshmi: Lord, we are poor folk...If you impregnate me in the absence of my husband, it'll smudge and tarnish my repute in the village...My husband's friends will sneer at me and spurn. My domestic life would be spoiled.

Land Lord: Pooh! Nobody would come to know about this. I'll keep it a secret.

(The Land Lord makes an attempt to rape Lakshmi brutally. The strobe light blinks and dims. Lakshmi falls down. The back light dazzles and the rape scene is silhouetted. The trumpet sound of the elephant is heard and the shadow elephant rampages on the white screen. Its trumpet sound is repeated. Back ground music builds up tempo; abrupt silence after a bang. Someone appears on the scene with an imaginary whip and lashes at the land lord. The land lord screams in pain and runs away with his clumsily clad Dhoti.)

SCENE-5

(Lights become steady after the strobe effect is off. The young man is visible now.

Young man: I'm Ramia, the Ramia of the story.

May be I'm not Ramia-Ramia, the Labor-coolie of Surat textile mill put on a tattered pant. I'm in Jeans.

That Ramia set out for Surat. This Ramia is struggling here for a livelihood in Bhubaneswar. Ramia's Lakshmi was crushed by the wild elephant called land lord. But what happened to my Lakshmi? Ah! My head reels like a wheel, in this vast expanse of the concrete jungle; there's no one to fetch me a bottle of water... there's no one to ask whether I have eaten anything! The man in this house does not know his neighbor...And yet, I'm struggling on the pavement for a job since last five years!

(Ramia sits on the ramp and prepares to sleep there. An announcement from the municipal corporation vehicle passes by saying:)

Announcer: Urgent and expedient steps are being taken by the municipal corporation to distribute relief material to the elephant inflicted areas. Our rural correspondent reports that elephants have poached into villages also. The government has requisitioned paramilitary force and army soldiers to tackle the elephant crisis.

(The announcement fades off. Ramia gets up, sits on the ramp. The background music takes on a serious chord. Ramia gets up)

Ramia: I notice people in this city becoming touchy about petty things-things that one can probably laugh at a decade ago. Not anymore. We are on continuous trips to emotional blackholes...sexual black holes... bamboozled into economic and political black holes.

A lot of us like to hold on to feelings... feelings to hurt others like the rampaging elephant.

(A news paper hawker boy of about 12 years enters old with a bundle of news papers under his arm pit and a newspaper on his right hand)

Boy: The elephant mishap in the capital has led to endless torment and agony. The floating elephant from the Mahanadi floods has barged into the capital city and killed a cyclist carrying vegetables to sell in the market. The police have fired seven thousand two hundred forty two rounds of bullets at the elephant, but it is not yet injured or dead. The markets and vending zones at Bhubaneswar are closed and the consumers do not dare to make a communal encounter. The government has declared a prize of five lakhs to the hunter who'd kill the elephant *Samaj, Prajatantra, Sambad, Dharitriand SarvaSadharna*...Buy for four rupees!!

(The boy discovers the young man on the ramp)

Uncle! Why are you trying to sleep on this bench of the bus stand? It is now 8.30 in the evening, and the night buses will come now. By the by, what did you eat today?

Ramia: Nothing, as usual. I felt exhausted... So I was preparing for a sleep before someone else occupies this bench.

Boy: Would you please wait for a minute, Uncle? I am keeping these news papers here. Just browse through the paper and I'm coming in a minute.

(The boy leaves the stage. Ramia picks up a news paper and reads about historical elephant. All the other artists except the boy enact the historical events in different blockings in pantomime.)

Voice over

Of Ramia: In 1789, one such elephant entered into France. Before that in 1776 the animal encroached into America. The elephant had raised its trunk against Nicholas-II of Russia in 1917 and this big elephant barged into China in October, 1911...The bureaucrats and the politicians of Odisha, therefore, presume that the elephant that has poached into Bhubaneswar, a week ago, is a historical elephant...

(The hawker boy returns with some tiffin and a bottle of water)

Boy: Here's is your dinner, uncle. Take it.

Ramia: Why did you spend from your hard-earned money? I could have managed the night in empty stomach. What'd your mother say?

Boy: Nothing. Mother has great sympathy for elephant victims.

Ramia: Convey my gratitude to her.

Boy: Do you know Uncle? My Mama is also an elephant victim.

Ramia: Might be (To himself) The elephant does not seem to be an ordinary one. The poets say it's a metaphor for corruption. India has gone wild because of these encroaching elephants. Sometimes, it comes like a money lender

Boy: Any way this elephant is the bridge between you and me. It ravaged the city and helped us to become friends (Pause) Okay Uncle! It's late evening... I've to go home Mama will be waiting for me.

Ramia: Thank you Kalia! Good night!

(Ramia leaves the stage through the left up wings and Kalia runs to the right up and hollers)

Kalia: Moma! Moma!

SCENE-6

(He turns back and finds that Ramia is gone and in his place stands Lakshmi smiling)

Lakshmi: Ah! Kalia...my son... my darling....

(She embraces her and kisses on his forehead)

Kalia: Mama, Again I met uncle today.

Lakshmi: Was he also, hungry today?

Kalia: Yes, didn't have anything to eat... was trying to sleep on the old bus-stand bench... I fetched him some tiffin and a bottle of water.

Lakhmi: What happened to that elephant? Is it still prowling on the Rajdhani streets?

Kalia: No. But it must have hidden somewhere; may be, inside the government park!

(The trumpet sound of the elephant is heard at a distance.)

Lakshmi: May be, it's coming this side.

Kalia: Will it trample over our hut?

Lakshmi: Why're you so afraid? Hell with these elephants! Allow that bastard to come here. I will slap its trunk twice!...Sshala!....Raises its trunk shamelessly and intrudes into our private selves!

Kalia: Don't worry ma'! I'll grow up in another five years.

Lakshmi: Yeah, you'll. Otherwise, how can I live in this lane of comfort women? Teams of elephants barge into this lane every day! No one prevents them.

Kalia: Don't worry Ma'! The Odisha government has declared an award of five lakhs for the person who'd siege the elephant live or dead. I'll kill it.

Lakshmi: Huh! You're a kid. It'll squash you. How can a small boy like you kill a big elephant of this country? Come inside...Take your dinner and we'll sleep.

(Lakhmi takes Kalia inside)

SCENE-7

The back-screen is lit. the shadow elephant rampages over the screen from left to right. Its trumpet sound is heard. A bald man enters holding a giant size pen on his shoulder like Hanuman holding his club. He is full of confidence and he displays virility in his walk.

(He introduces himself as a hunter. But he is a lean man).

Hunter-I I'm a hunter employed by myself to kill the elephant. I admit I am a lean man, but...

(A flabby middle-aged hunter with a shrill voice enters from the other side like a storm. He is Hunter-II. He carries a spear)

Hunter – II: Shut up! I'm the hunter. I am deployed by the government to spearhead the movement against the elephant! (He points his spear toward the Hunter-1)

Hunter-I: How dare you? What do you think of yourself? Would you exterminate the entire elephant population from our country? That too with this spear? You look like my phys.-aid teacher in the college. Number two: spear hunters like you can't eliminate the elephant qualities from this country. You can only kill the elephant, the physical phenomenon. We're concerned here with the essence of the elephant... the media calls it "corruption", which grows in this country like an elephant....it is impervious of vigilance traps "The wildest elephant that treads the capital roads is terrorism, craze for perilous power.

Hunter-II: (Coolly) Who are you, a philosopher?

Hunter-I: I'm a scribbler-hunter. This pen is my weapon. I'll write satires and diatribes on this terrorist elephant and Kill it virtually. It's a perennial nuisance to the moral uprightness promoted by our dharma-elephants... I have killed the elephant by the column I have written today in the leading paper.

Hunter-II: Ha, ha, ha...Here is a crack...! A crack hunter who dreams of having killed elephants, by his satires! Ha, ha, ha!

Hunter-I: Why do you laugh?

Hunter-II: Because you thought yourself to be great hero with this pen... Elephants are impervious to your satires and burlesques... lampoons and spoof...raillery and ridicule!

Hunter-I: It is already dead!

Hunter-II: Why do I deplete my vital fluid, then? Why do I move with this sinister spear? Only to kill the impertinent elephant...Its impudence and cheekiness… Its rude trunkiness! You need a spear to pierce into its ugliness!

Hunter-I you're a ninny nitwit! Long ago, once upon a time, the elephant was struck in the Indus valley civilization with the artillery of mantra. Hundreds of pages of our mythologies are sodden with the blood of such elephants. I've fought five big battles with my pen...won the jnanapeeth award three times, and two lotus awards

Hunter-II: Two lotus awards for killing elephants? Which elephant? Or, did you kill them by developing a relationship with the elephant; a psychic relationship?

Hunter-I You are trying to inflict a lecture on us. There is nothing called an elephant. It is only a complex, a fear complex. No animal species called elephant live in this city according to the latest census report. So, we two siblings would hereafter cease to fight. We'll order the architect to sculpt a dead elephant.

Hunter-II: A dead elephant?

Hunter-I: Yes, a dead elephant. We two will stand on both sides of the imaginary elephant and take a selfi...Come here *(Hunter-II comes and stands) yes...smile...one...two...thank you. (Everything is done in mime action. Both stand frozen. They are held tight on a spot.*

SCENE-8

An anchor man with a microphone passes by and announces)

Anchor man: The capital city is infested with various elephants...the public is requested to maintain a safe distance from them. Beware of elephants while negotiating the city roads. The Government has announced a relief of five lakhs for each elephant victim. The elephant victims are therefore requested to report at the Municipal Corporation with their election I.D.s and Adhaar numbers.

(The Anchorman passes by; the trumpet sound of the wild elephant is heard and the Elephant enters the stage with its trunk fitted to his mouth as an appendix. With him follows a pyjama and topie clad middle-aged man who is known as Elephant Language Interpreter (ELI). He carries three flower garlands in his hand. As he enters the stage, the Scribbler hunter and the Spear hunter defreeze and come to the Elephant language Interpreter. They take two garlands from him and crown them on the Elephant's neck. An imaginary crowd claps from the back ground. The Elephant raises its trunk and trumpets. The Elephant language Interpreter translates.

E.L.I: I'm the interpreter of Elephant Languages. Mr. Elephant says that he is an image of humility. When he undertakes such melancholic migratory trips to the city, he wishes to die a martyr. The civilians have electrocuted the elephant brothers in the paddy fields. Men have deforested their habitats, built bridges, and roads, and looted their diet leaves by felling the trees. During the last six years there had been around two thousand wars between men and elephant in which 512 men have been dead against 429 elephants. (The elephant roars again) Mr. Elephant says:

"I've come to the capital city to investigate how madness is not different from wisdom and how the 'folly' of all 'knowledge' validates the transiency of all human learning. We are sorry we are not able to spend more time with you. But we promise, we'll return soon."

(The elephant and the Elephant Language interpreter exit

SCENE-9

; the old man barges on to the stage hysterically)

Old man: Where? Where's the elephant? What do you need from me; a garland? Come closer to me. (The elephant does not come) Oh, you don't recognize me. Don't you know this Danei Master?... Look at me. You've seen me thousand times. I'm Danei...Das...Former Head Master of the Capital High School... I've given you lots of coconuts and bananas... sweetened rice and banyan tree leaves and... and at the end, you devastated my little world! How could you do so Dark Elephant?... They say you're Lord Jagannatha. If so, is it the price you paid for all my lotus and basil-leaf garlands? Is it the price, price for my devotion? Aye! (*He wails loudly. The voice of Lakshmi is over heard. Then she appears*)

Lakshmi: Bapa! Bapa!!

Old man: Who called me ' father?'

Lakshmi: Bapa...I'm your Lakshmi...your daughter! Come, we'll go home!

Old man: Which home? The day Lakshmi abandoned me and went to Bhubaneswar, my home was lost...I've deserted that village, Gopalpur... and since then, there's no one with me to boil a palm full of rice for me. This Danei Master's life had passed away long ago...Lakshmi eloped with Elephant Swamy...I don't know where! And since then I haven't had a mouthful of rice! I've been roaming on the roads of Bhubaneswar homeless....Lakshmi abandoned me. (He wails again)...

Lakshmi: Your Lakshmi is standing here Bapa, right in front of you, at Bhubaneswar, but she is not dead, Bapa! Here, I'm standing in front of you. I've come to take you home.

Old man: Which home; that hut in the remote lane of station bazaar? People call it a prostitutes' den... Lakshmi does not belong there! She's the respectable daughter of Danei master! She'll go to our ancestral house at Gopalpur.

Lakshmi: Lakshmi shall never go to Gopalpur Bapa. She has become an unmarried mother. So, she won't go. (pause. Back ground music) Here's our house Bapa!... You're standing near Master Canteen cross...Look at this statue...It's near station bazaar. Come, we'll go there...you'll stay there with me. We will all make it a home, call it a sweet home. Your grandson Kalia studies in high school... sells newspapers in the market and gets a commission of thirty rupees per day...won't you bless him Bapa? Won't you teach him grammar?

Old man: Why should he be my grandson? Who's his father? Where is he?

Lakshmi: His father is a big animal, yes, a big animal, as big as an elephant...But why do you bother Bapa? Your daughter Lakshmi has delivered him... He's the real son of your unmarried daughter.

Oldman: (Nods his head) No! All of you've cheated me. I was naïve. I believed in occult treatment. So, I went to Baba. Sent you to his Ashram to bring my medicine and he trapped you. I didn't know. You were a victim.

Lakshmi: I offered my body as a yogan, Baba. I thought it was a spiritual necessity. And Kalia was born as a consequence.

Old man: (Speaks to himself) I didn't know much about the world. My life was like a simple sentence, without clauses. I dwelt at the feet of that Elephant Swamy… Trusted him… Fed him with sweets made of pure ghee...and he eloped with my school going daughter... blinded me (Music, on a melancholic note). The day I'll get the Swamy, I'll butcher him with my axe! Sshala! Poses as a god man and a goddess man? Why? Oh, of course; he cured my tuberculosis with his mantra! Shala lecher and a lewd animal, an Imposter he was.

Lakshmi: Forget about that religious Elephant, Bapa. We have committed a blunder by over-trusting him.

Old man: Leave it! You go inside and cook an indigenous meal for me. I'm hungry. Okay? I am sitting here warming my body under this blanket. (He coughs continuously. He spits)

Lakshmi: It's very cold outside, Bapa. The cold wave is active. Don't spit here...the verandah would be dirty.

Old Man: Did you inform about my cough to the Elephant swamy?

Lakshmi: I had personally been there.

Old man: What did he say?

Lakshmi: Welcomed me warmly; said, you're the daughter of that great Danei Master! Then he gave me some sweets to eat.

(Danei got up and went toward the right wings. Turned back and contacted his daughter)

Old man: That wasn't 'sweet', you fool...that was Lord 'Shiva's *prasad*...you're fortunate to get a bit of that as the daughter of Danei Master. This time you will stand first in the annual exam.

(He closes his eyes and meditates on Elephant Swamy)

Baba Elephant swamy! Have mercy on us! Even an oblique look of blessing would save my motherless daughter's life.

(Elephant Swamy emerges with his saffron costume and stands in front of them)

Baba: Did you remember me, Master?

Old man: Baba...I can't pull on much longer with this (coughs) hoofing cough! It makes me breathless. If I die, my daughter will drift away from the vortex of social life. Save me!

Baba: I'll build a barrage before she's swept away. I'll catch her with my divine protection before she slips and slides away

Old man: I'll be extremely grateful to you. I prostrate at your feet! (He prostrate on the floor)

Baba: Everything will happen by the grace of the divine Elephant. I've nothing in my hand

Old man: Recite some mantras of therapy, Swamy.

Baba: Don't be so restless. I assure you. You'll be cured.

Lakshmi: Extend your helping hand, Baba, Bapa has superannuated from his job and feels insecure. Do some special pooja to boost his confidence.

(The Baba performs some puja rituals and utters some indistinct mantras)

Baba: Danei! You're cured. By the time you come my Ashram, there'd be no trace of tuberculosis on your body.

Lakshmi: If Bapa is cured completely I'll come again to your hermitage, Baba.

Baba: Don't worry girl. If I wish, I can also emerge in your home flying in my meditation. Take care! (Baba exits.

SCENE-10

Danei Master stands there closing his eyes. Enters Rama, one of his village students and touches his feet)

Old man: Ah! My entire blessings son! But I could not exactly place you...you are?...

Rama: I'm Rama Chandra Pradhan Sir! I stood first in High school certificate examination...you taught me English grammar Sir....I used to commit tense mistakes and you were canning me! I'm that Rama, the friend of Lakshmi.

Old man: Oh! I remember! Are you Govind's son? Gobind Pradhan, the famous leftist writer?

Rama: Yes, you've rightly identified me Sir!

Old man: How's Gobind Babu?

Rama: He's dead long since. In the cyclone, when the sea water engulfed our village. He was alone at home and was incautious.

Old man: Oh my! Gobind Pradhan as a writer was implacable, highly political writer he was when he began. We were fiends. What are you doing now boy, writing something like your father? Are you also a revolutionary as your father was?

Ram: No Sir! Revolutions are outdated now. In our generation everyone is a tail-wagger. They compromise with corruption.

Old man: Did you compromise with corruption?

Rama: Corruption is like a wild elephants. It tramples over our mental roads. It crushes all truth-speakers. That's why outspoken young men are the elephant's worst victims.

Old man: It's a new era phenomenon. We were born during freedom struggle...we had more elephants in our time, but they were not so large and rampant. The most amazing matter is that the elephant was on the rampage over the city streets, demolished the slum colonies, ravaged the tiled roofs and trampled over the beggars on the foot path. The school buildings and the dispensaries are totally damaged...

Rama: And yet these white elephants of the city did not pay any heed to the debacle. They failed to provide me with a job though I have a first class degree. What can I do Sir? I have no house. I sleep on the cemented bench of the old bus stand. (Pause) Offer me a packet of food for my dinner. How can I survive in this city, Sir? I...I feel like committing suicide.

Lakshmi: (*She was cutting vegetables. She Shouts*) No! I won't allow you to commit that crime... Better you stay with us. I will give you half my food. But don't...

Rama: No Lakshmi. I don't want to be a burden on your family. I am preparing for the Bank exams now. I'll struggle. I'll take up some private tuition if available.

Lakshmi: That's alright Rambhai, You can appear the bank exam staying with us. We are childhood friends. We were playing those interesting family games, don't you remember? You played the husband and I played the wife! We were children...you were in standard eight and I was in standard five. Do you remember? In those summer mid-days... under the village mango orchard we were teasing the cuckoos (she laughs and Ram responds)... misleading them hiding under the bushes... (Ram Laughs)

Old man: After all, you belong to my village, Gopalpur and you are my friend's son.

Rama: Yes Sir! I remember, Lakshmi was a naughty young kid those days.

Old man: (Sighs) Unfortunate girl! Her mother died the same year! She was only a six years old.

(His eyes are moistened and he strikes off a drop of tear; music)

Rama: How's your health Sir? What about that chronic cough you suffered from?

Lakshmi: I'm going to the Elephant swamy regularly. He has assured. Bapa will be cured. The doctors failed. We couldn't bear the expenses.

Old man: Keep coming whenever you feel like. We are alone. Come for gossip chats. Both of you are grown up now! It's nice to see you together after a long gap. I feel so happy.

Ram: Okay sir! It is a lucky day for me. I got your residential address. How could I've known it?

Lakshmi: Keep coming here Ram Bhai. We'll go to the park and ruminate over our childhood in the afternoons. (Pause) Or else, We'll go to the Ashram...It is a lovely, lonely ashram...

Rama: So pleasant to meet you after such a long time Lakshmi I'll come whenever I'm free.

(He touches old man's feet. The old man embraces him and they exit. Lakshmi goes absent minded. Back ground music is soft and nostalgic. A classical alaap in female voice would do.)

Lakshmi: Please come like a shower to me Ram Bhai...like a drizzle on the arid fields...come like a cockatoo of winter morning...I'm only a spider's web in the village mango orchard...come like an elephant and play with me...lift me to the skies with your giant trunk...Lift me to the rainbow. Lift me as a piece of cloud...this life is more than meat and the body is more than raiment.

(The colour of the stage lights change. Back ground music changes to a classical Odishi dance rhythm. Lakshmi imagines to be dancing in multiple stop-block compositions. Ram Joins her and the dance composition is now choreographed for a duet, but again in stop-blocks. In one of the Rati and Kandarpa erotic composition the rhythm stops, the lights become steady and normal and the dancers freeze. Elephant swamy (Baba) emerges like Durvasa and shouts.

Elephant Swamy: Who are you here to defile my divinity in the Ashram premises? You're love-bombing each other at this hour of the noon.

Ram: (de-freezing from the blocking.) We are not into a whirl-wind relationship, Baba. We are childhood friends. We come here to visit the Ashram. How serene it looks…

Elephant Swamy: So...it's a kind of dating, It is no longer a metaphor for love, it is rather a metaphor for hunting. You're hunting down this woman. It's a form of repressed violence-a lethal technique to disarm this tender girl of the city. It's after effects shall be felt in the gynecologist's clinic. Who are you?

Ram: I'm Ram!

Elephant Swamy: But you're not from Ayodhya, only a pip-squeak of the city roads. Why are you playing this toxic game with this girl? Go away! I say, get out.

(Ram comes closer to swamy and touches his feet. The girl stands hiding her face in one corner of the stage)

Rama: I'm sorry, Baba!

Elephant Swamy: Never use this ashram-space for sexual abuses. Now you may go...

(Ram exits. Lakshmi stands hiding her face)

Now! Who's this girl? (Goes near) show me your face please! (*She turns. shocking music*)

Lakshmi? Danei's daughter? Oh my! You've grown up and your father has granted such liberty for lax indulgence? I never knew that.

Lakshmi: I'm sorry Baba, don't tell it to Bapa! Save my face.

Elephant Swamy: Who's this young man? I don't think he comes from a good family. Does he tell that he loves you all the time?

Lakshmi: Yes

Elephant Swamy: Is he telling you exactly what you want to hear about yourself?

Lakshmi: Yes, Baba!

Elephant Swamy: Are there too many grand gestures and compliments coming your way?

Lakshmi: I love him Baba! We'll be married here after.

Elephant Swamy: Then he is seducing you, I understand. Don't feel so excited. Come inside my room. I'll teach you how to control sexual impulses.

Lakshmi: Is there a way, Baba?

Elephant Swamy: Yes. I'll mélange behavioral science with yoga...mixing it with art of making love.

Lakshmi: And then..?

Elephant Swamy: Then we'll go for a demonstration show, come,

(Elephant swamy leads Lakshmi inside. A mysterious music of violence engulfs the mise-en-scene. With this music, Elephant Baba /Swamy and Lakshmi circumambulate the stage in different erotic blockings, with strobe effect. The music, after a short while, is superimposed by a trumpet call of the wild elephant and a crowd shouts from the back "Elephant Disaster!" This is complemented by another slogan: 'kill him', 'Kill the Elephant Baba'. This noise is cut through a sharp scream of Danei, the old head master)

Danei's voice: Lakshmeeee! Lakshmeeeee!!

SCENE-11

(*After 2/3 long-distance calls, old Danei barges into the stage angry and shouting, lapsing into abrupt mood-shifts. He acts with furious energy and agility*)

Danei: Where's Lakshmi? Where was she lost? Lost in the crowd of this unreal city... Lost in a crime of passion... My dear victim girl! You were five years old when your mother passed away. This old man raised you mingling his sweat and tears and now, when I am decrepit, how did you abandon me on the streets? How could you frisk away? (Back ground music. The old man weeps in anguish... The Veterinary director-cum-the Elephant-Language – Instructor passes by and stops near Danei. Danei does not pay any heed. He continues to weep melodramatically. Underacting and naturalism should be avoided.)

ELI: What happened to you old man? May I help you?

Danei: (Does not care to respond) Who did take away my daughter? They might've killed her. The elephant is a serial killer. It has committed nine murders within a week, might have killed more. All the statistics have been overturned in only a matter of hours. The elephant is a murderer.

ELI: No. you are bringing serious allegations I've doubts about this old man's statistics.

Danei: I'm not mad, Sir, and I'm not contradicting myself. For example, I can't be sure that my salary will be deposited in my account at the end of the month, but I don't actually doubt that it will. Do you see what I mean?

ELI: Don't talk to me in metaphors. I want to know exactly which elephant has murdered nine persons in the city. Why are you raising a rebellion here on this stage?

Danei: Rebellion? No Sir, I am not asking for an increase in salary. I'm only saying that certainties and doubts coexist in this city. I doubt that the Elephant Baba blackmailed my daughter!

ELI: Yes, he might have raped your daughter. But that elephant is blacklisted by the public. The elephant Swamy was trafficking in dopes and narcotics. He might have doped your daughter and raped her. Everything is possible these days.

Danei: How do you have no doubts about the case?

E.L.I.: Because I'm the Elephant language Instructor... The elephant is in my mind. I've cured a couple of elephants that had gone berserk! Do you know? When I went moving in Chandka forest with my pet elephant it used to lay golden eggs.

Danei: (Laughs) You belonged to the golden age Sir! That's why elephants laid golden eggs

ELI: Yes! This laughter is healthy; much better than your protest rallies. Better you laugh at the elephants.

Danei: But there must be somebody to protest and question against injustice and corruption. The power of people to question and transform elephants has been stolen from them. The changeable has been secured in this country in the interest of a particular group. These elephants are disguised as the repositories of power.

ELI: Yes, when I was the Secretary and Commissioner of Veterinary department, I gave a proposal to the government to raise "elephantries" in this state. Odisha was famous for elephants. The Odissi elephants were very much appreciated by Moghal emperors. Ha! Ha! Our elephant culture had become a universal phenomenon.

Danie: You are a white elephant Sir, and your talk is a big a bureaucratic guffaw. You know only mechanisms by which you obscure your artificiality. I refuse to talk to hypocrites... Phooh! (Goes to the corner)

ELI: What do you think of me, you lunatic of a lost asylum? Am I prestige-less? I'm the former Secretary-cum-Commissioner, a senior... class one Officer, and super class one! Don't I've dignity? Ah! I committed a mistake by negotiating this slum-dweller intellectual. Huh!

(The ELI exits in quick steps. Danei stands alone on the stage. He talks to the audience:)

Danei: This Vet. Officer is a fraud... He talks about Elephantry... as if it is fishery... Rascal! Here's a state where people die of hunger and he's talking of elephantries... Bhubaneswar is already a pound for all the white elephants of the country. They want to dissolve the distinction between surfaces and depths, the artificial and the original... Like the Elephant that ravaged our capital city... We never know whether it is a real elephant or a metaphor.

(Sudden trumpet call of the elephant is heard. A howling effect of the crowd is posted... The voice of the newspaper hawker boy is also heard)

Boy: (He enters) Elephant disaster in the city... Buy newspapers... *Samaj, Prajatantra, Dinalipi, Sambad* and *Dharitri*. The party in power says that such wild elephants have infiltrated into the city to foil their five year plans. A senior journalist says that the negligent forest officers have caused this devastation. Read newspapers to know more about elephants.

Danei: But dear boy! Where's the elephant`?

Boy: The Elephant? It is in the newspaper. I've packaged it in this bundle of papers. What a silly question you've asked Gran'Pa? But who has given you the permission to loiter alone on the city roads? Go home! Momma' would be worried… Go home.

Danei: You're also loitering. Why can't I?

Boy: No! You can't! You can't move in this elephant infested city. It is a very powerful animal... The elephant uses power as a limit set upon your freedom... it illuminates your desires and fear! You're babbling on the street like a lunatic and plunging into insecurity. Come with me... Come, I'll take you home.

(The boy drags the old man and leads him to exit the stage. From the Other side straddles Ram, the young, vagrant).

The trumpet sound of the elephant is heard. The hurly-burly of the running crowd, the scream of the poor people trampled under the feet of the elephant and the chaos in the city is heard as a background effect. The Elephant Language Instructor enters with the elephant on to the stage declaring the following, through a funnel which he holds:

ELI: *(Tests the microphone)* Hello! One-two-three! Mr. Elephant! We'll have to stop here for three minutes. You've to address the public.

(The elephant raises its trunk and trumpets:)

ELI: Mr. Elephant says that he came on a friendly tour to Rajdhani. But the media has sneeringly commented him that he perpetrated neo-liberal terrorism in the city. Of course, a great anarchy has been created. Lots of underprivileged and marginalized people were crushed. Six Slum colonies were ravaged... But Mr. Elephant says, he is not responsible for all that. Young stone pelters were shot dead, fifty of them. But he is not the murderer of the stone-pelters.

(Ram enters forcefully, stands in front the Elephant and Elephant language Instructor and protests:)

Ram: Stop this bunkum! You are a white elephant. You live in this poor country like a captive animal, incarcerated by your own wealth. You're used to getting locked and barred in gilded cages. You think you are protected from the threat of the Vulgar and unruly multitude that you've systematically dispossessed over the centuries. What rights do you have to make this peace march on the roads to preach democracy`?

(The elephant raises its trunk and roars)

ELI: Wow! You're didactic! Thank you for giving unwanted instructions. Mr. Elephant promises to give you a red tea shirt and for the present, gifts you a button from his coat! A golden button: Take it. (*He throws the button and the young man holds it*).

Ram: I am an unemployed post graduate with a gold medal. But I'm hungry. So, I accept this golden button! Instead, you could have given me a meal in the roadside hotel. I am a hungry young man of your country Mr. Political Animal!... You've massacred a thousand hungry men. What justice you're giving me with this button'? It's a mockery to my gold medal! You're hiding your cruelty under the mask of philanthropy.

(The elephant roars)

ELI: Mr. Elephant is angry on you!

Ram: So what? How do I care for an animal's anger?

ELI: Shut up! You are just a stray pedestrian in the capital and you deserve a stampede.

Ram: You are a criminal. Your elephant is another criminal. But you hide your crime in the sanctum of spirituality. Hypocrites!

ELI: (He is angry) You rural folks are narrow-minded! You can't tolerate the elephant. What your external glitz and glamour conceal is a huge inferiority complex! That I've discovered. I'll thrash you! Beat the grain from the chaff.

(He takes out his belt and menaces the E.L.I. and Elephant.)

Rama: Tell me, why did you disqualify me for the interview? Tell me, why did you deprive me of a home at Bhubaneswar? Tell me, why your children are frequenting fashionable restaurants when I am deprived of two square meals a day? How do they buy ridiculously expensive shirts when I am managing with one shirt? Are you more qualified than I?

ELI: Why do you ask such silly questions to Mr. Elephant? Aren't you silly? Don't you envy the blessed sons of god? Aren't you a jealous of others? Why don't you struggle for a prosperous living? Don't you deserve a counter-thrashing?

Rama: Why should I deserve a thrashing? You Elephants have blocked my way to prosperity. You have impeded my progress. You have exploited my naiveté?

ELI: Who are you accusing to? Why are you so artless? Are you going to get an award for your innocence? It is the system young man, the system run by white elephants. Tune yourself to the system otherwise you'll be called a duffer.

Ram: But when you've a system in which delays are frequent, speed money is a necessary counterpart. Tell me, where do I get the money to bribe for a job? I can't sell my gold medal!

ELI: Hell with your gold medal. Who bothers about that? Mend your behavior first. You're very rude and rash in your behavior. If you don't let us go forward, I'll use my power.

Ramaa: What power? I'm not afraid of power!

ELI: Mr. Elephant himself is the epitome of power. He wishes to dissolve the distinction between surfaces and depths. We don't have the time to recognize the depth.

Rama: Mr. Elephant Language! Tell your dummy elephant to learn to recognize the depth.

ELI: Cut it short! He is not a dummy. If he is a dummy elephant, you're also a dummy revolutionary...

Rama: We'll castigate all kinds of power symbols in this country.

ELI: Mind your language! All your binary oppositions, all your distinctions between surfaces and depths shall be dissolved by our play of organized power.

Rama: Do you want an Evidence of our organized power? I shall show you! (He hollers) Hey you! Nincompoops of this Elephant city! Manikins of the shopping malls and you blighted women! You work with grime and sweat on your body! Listen, you've a bomb in your cupboard... You've an elephant on rampage... Come out with your bombs and artillery... Come with your guns and pistols... come with your weapons to fight this demonic elephant committing genocide here.

(No one responds. No one comes)

ELI: Hey! Who do you think you are? Lord of the laborers? You're not the victim of... of that business of wanton killing or whatever you're complaining of! Who'll listen to your clarion call? Are you the lynchpin of the saviors of the city? If so, face the war!

(Back ground music of a folk war in Vaishnab Pani's jatra folk theatre of the early twentieth Century, Odisha. The music symbolizes the war between the Gods and the Asuras of mythological time. The ELI and the Elephant march on the stage to the rhythm of the Jatra concert. From the opposite side enter the Scribbler Hunter and the spear hunter, one with the giant pen holding like a mace on the shoulder and a pistol in his pocket and the other holding a spear on his hand.)

Scribbler Hunter: Where's the elephant?

Ram: Here it is. Thank you for coming. But who're you with this giant pen?

Scribbler Hunter: At your service Sir! I'm the Scribbler hunter. I know this elephant`s mindset, never met it though. I'll finish him now. Don't worry. A couple of limericks and a satirical play will do.

Ram: How will you kill the elephant by satires?

ELI: By writing diatribes----satires against this elephant. It would die out of shame. (The elephant raises its trumpets and blows a call.)

ELI: Mr. Elephant is impervious to satires. He has a divine identity... an identity associated with Goddess Mahalakshmi.

Scribbler Hunter: No! You sound phony! He's a border infiltrator... A Paki terrorist! We've to blast its bastion.

Ram: That you may do! But promise me not to write satires any more... Thick-skins did never care for literature... We've to turn it dispirited and dismayed... dead-beat and insipid... (Advances menacingly toward the Elephant and the ELI) I'll rip you off!!

Spear Hunter: You can rip this elephant! Leave me Mr. Ram. I'm the spear Hunter... (He raises his spear and attempts to pierce it on to its body. The ELI catches the spear and protects the elephant)

ELI: Aye! Mind your behavior! Here's an elephant! Not a pig, like you.

Spear Hunter: So, what? This elephant turned the city into a jungle. You're living now in a primordial jungle called Bhubaneswar!... It's a jungle of primitive Odias!

Scribbler Hunter: Yes, it's a jungle! Otherwise, how could Paki-elephants invade this city of civil citizens? A marauder it is! A freebooter! A disease!

Ram: We must eradicate such elephant diseases. It'll harbinger an epidemic otherwise! All the Bhubaneswarians may transform into elephants.

Scribbler Hunter: The Western Odishans have already been parading the city like elephants. They have captivated the Hirakud dam and they are selling electricity at Bhubaneswar. All these elephant pillagers must be killed.

Spear Hunter: I'll lacerate him with my spear. You've failed idiot! Miserably failed.

Ram: Don't feel intimidated by the trumpet sounds of these stray elephants. There are the normal sounds heard in a concrete jungle we won't spare them. We won't leave them free... Paki elephants Chinese elephants... They shall be hacked and burnt... set on fire...

Scribbler: I'll throw them into the fire of satire! Don't think I only carry this pen. I've a pistol in my pocket (shows it).

ELI: Hey, you rascal scribbler! Don't roll your eyes and snarl your lips with a sarcastic tone! Nothing destroys relationships faster than contempt. Don't show me a toy pistol. I'm too rough a guy to shudder at your toy!

The Scribbler hunter shows an ostensible irritation. He shoots three bullets at the elephant but to no avail.

Ram: What happened? What happened to your bullets Mr. Jnanapeeth Awardee?

Spear Hunter: Bullets of alphabets are imitations, plagiarized from somewhere!

Scribbler Hunter: They are thick-skinned brutes!

ELI: Have you seen a film captioned Spiritual Hunger?

Ram: He's suffering from a spiritual schizophrenia.

Scribbler Hunter: No schizophrenia sir! It's a bullet-proof spirituality...Can't be split into two.

Spear Hunter: Mr. Ram! Can I take a second chance to kill with my spear?

Ram: You can take a trial... a final chance. Scribblers are non-utilitarian junk.

So, I'll murder you! (He attempts to murder the elephant with the spear. He pushes the spear and it is held by the ELI. The tug-of-war continues till the lights focus on the spear that gradually advances toward the elephant, as a ray of hope that it shall die.

Scribbler Hunter: Push the spear deeper... Attack its neck point... Yes... push it deeper.

Ram: A little more! Ah! You're a genius of a hunter! Push it to its neck...

ELI: That's easier said than done!

(After a great tug-of-war, the spear hunter fails. Background music builds up and the lights dim. It is dark. As the lights come up, the old man is seen stopping Kalia from going for vending news papers.)

Oldman: No, you're not allowed to go out Kalia. You've a fever! Come 'ere! Let me examine. (Checks up) It is around hundred one! Where are you going? The elephant is injured and behaves violently!

Kalia: To vend news about the elephant. Do you know Grand Pa'! The elephant has become a disease in the capital.

Oldman: What disease?

Kalia: They call it elephantatisis. It's contagious.

Oldman: What is it?

Kalia: The disease is infectious. It spreads from one person to the other.

Oldman: That's something strange. What are its symptoms?

Kalia: A man with elephantatisis is a panjandrum, dreams greedily... He wants to keep currency notes within his bulged stomach… Wants to gulp enormous amount of food... is hungry of power... physical, political and financial... aspires to become the lord of the dogs.

Oldman: What dogs?

Kalia: I mean tail-waggers!

Oldman: Everyone in Bhubaneswar is a tail-wagger!!

Kalia: I've got an uncle in the old bus stand! He's a first class first in History... But he's not a tail-wagger... far away from sycophancy...

Oldman: Then he can't get into government jobs. He is a misfit at Bhubaneswar!

Kalia: Yes, he's a misfit... May be. He attends interviews but never gets selected...Doesn't have a house in the city... sleeps on the dirty benches of the old bus stand... doesn't get even two slices of bread for the night, so.. I buy him some tiffin and talk to him. You know Grand Pa? He's the only qualified man in the city. Others are fools.

If I don't go for vending uncle would stay hungry. So, I'm going. All my friends vending newspapers pelted thrones, at the elephant. I didn't.

Oldman: Don't behave like an oaf! You're suffering from high fever... Let's go to the doctor first. He is in our colony. If he'll permit you to go, then only I'll allow you to go to duty.

Kalia: But where shall we get the money to pay the doctor?

Oldman: Don't worry. He's an old student of mine. Dodge your vending duty for today (He leads Kalia inside).

The light fades out. There is a quick fade in effect after some 30 seconds, with dim effect of late night. A green bulb cowers at a distance in some tiffin joint in the Old Bus Stand, Bhubaneswar. Ram comes straddling to his retiring bench, where he would sleep)

Ram: (Talks to him) It is about eleven in the night and the city sleeps, under the blanket of fog. Wipe out your tears Ram. There's no one for you in this city of the elephants. What have you learnt from this long voyage into the loneliness of the roads? This small and tedious city gives me to see the horror of one thing: there is a sad oasis of ennui. Should I run away from this tedious struggle? How long can I stand this? I've to find a space on this cemented bench to spend the night; to cheat the deadly enemy called time.(Two stray dogs bark and quarrel)The newspaper boy, my young friend Kalia did not turn up today. Who'd feed me today with a couple of slices? I've to sleep empty stomach… (*Music is on a serious note on the key board*). Sleeping empty stomach is a kind of yoga...sort of perseverance... I must learn to live in crunches... Ah! But what happened to Kalia?

(The dogs bark and fight again. The sound of hurly-burly disturbs him. The cry of a child weeping loudly is superimposed.)

Ram: Is he, too crushed under the elephant's feet? I must find out his house in that dark lane behind the railway station. I must make a backward move (He starts to move backwards. Stage lights are very dim. The sound of a goods train passing through the station with a whistle blowing for a long time is heard from the back ground. Ram dashes against two strangers, whose faces are not decipherable in darkness.

Voice-1: Ohhhhh!

Voice-2: Ahhhhh!

(One of them whispers:)

Voice-1: (whispers) There's somebody, ask him

Voice-2: I can't see anybody. It's dark.

SCENE-12

(Full lights come on the stage. We see that the scribbler hunter and the spear hunter have transformed themselves as a research scholar and a journalist, with slight change of costume. They are investigating about the elephant havoc in the city. Now with full lights they see Ram)

Stranger-1: Errrr…I am sorry….You are Mister….?

Ram: I am Ram. Ram Chandra Pradhan. Who are you?

Stranger-1: I am Rakesh, a journalist from *News Weekly*. We have come to survey the damage done by the Paki-elephant.

Stranger-2: I'm Mohan! I'm a sociologist and a research scholar... Rakesh is my friend. We're conducting a field study of the elephant devastated areas.

Ram: Field study at 11 PM in the night? That too in this infamous dark lane? Do you know where exactly you have landed? You are in the midst of a comfort women's street.

Mohan: Doesn't matter. Where's Lakshmipriya Devi's house?

Rakesh: We'll take an interview of that lady. Can you help us find her house?

Ram: Lakshmi? I mean.... it won't be proper to...

Mohan: Kindly help us Sir! We are metaphorically in a dark lane!

Rakesh: Also literally we are in dark. Kindly throw on us some light.

(A spot light makes them visible distinctly)

Ram: Let me try.... Lakshmeeee!!

Mohan: Lakshmee Madam!

Ram: Go ahead. This is the house! (He steps back and leaves the way to Mohan)

Mohan: Lakshmi Madam!

Lakshmi: (Appears with a lamp and asks harshly) Who're you?

Mohan: We have come to.... I mean…

Lakshmi: Two customers at a time? But you look like babus!

Rakesh: So what? We are baboos. Aren't you Lakhmi Madam?

Lakshmi: What's there in a name? Eh? I understand, you're in search of a hole! (Pause) I've closed my business for tonight. My son is sick.

Mohan: We won't take much of your time.

Rakesh: Ok we'll just take a snap.

Lakshmi: Why? Would you lick my photo? You're silly! No snaps are allowed here!

Rakesh: We want to take your interview. Kindly invite us inside.

Lakshmi: Are you new sneaking customers here? Are you coming for the first time?

Mohan: First time..! Yes... but why should we visit you? We are not sex crazy people here. We are married. I'm a journalist. I'll only take an interview from you and publish it.

Lakshmi: What's that to me?

Mohan: Your postcard size photo shall be published in *News Weekluy*.

Lakshmi: And what shall I get in return?

Mohan: You'll harvest lots of publicity... your market would be wide spread!

Lakshmi: (aggressively) what did you say? "Widespread? Mind you! I am already a broad… widely spread... Don't pump me up further! Huh! These bastards have publicized my name when I was raped by the elephant Swamy... When I was pregnant... then you made me a cheap tart-Bastards! A prostitute you called me. Why? What was my fault? The elephant beguiled me! Seduced me! (The journalist was taking notes) The Elephant Baba bullied me. I was an innocent young girl. And now I find abortion clinics are mushrooming in the city. Are they all prostitutes who go to the abortion clinics? Is there an elephant trying to hide in every hole? Aren't you ashamed of your attitude? And you are a journalist with such gender bias! Tchchi! Get lost!

(Lakshmi spits on their face and exits)

Rakesh: Enough! this "too much".

Mohan: Almost "*three-much*". Damn your Ph.D. thesis.

Rakesh: I wanted to write a thesis on the "Presence of Elephants in Odia prostitution" chapter one: the elephants of Kendra Sahitya Akademi searching for holes, chapter two: Female Poets raped by Elephants Chapter-three: Poets back-geared by Elephant awardees etc. But my guide advised me to conduct locational studies about elephant-ridden victims. And finally this is the consequence.

Mohan: Better we should leave before the police come for patrolling. Come! Where is our bike?

Rakesh: On the main road. Have you locked it properly? Let us check whether street elephants have lifted them or not.

Mohan: You're connecting thefts with elephants?

Rakesh: There are elephant thieves in this city. You know some of them. Make haste!

(Both of them exit. The stage lights black out. Lakshmi comes again to check whether the researchers have gone. Ram, who was standing at a distance comes out and asks)

Ram: (From a distance.) Is it Kalia's home? Is he at home? Kalia…my partner?

Lakshmi: (Politely) yes sir, this is Kalia's home. (pause) Who are you sir?

Rama: Tell him, his 'uncle' has come from the old bus stand.

Lakshmi: But I'm asking for your full identity sir. How can he….

Rama: I am (not able to explain himself)... Kindly tell him 'uncle'... He'll recognize me.

Lakshmi: Kalia is sick... he caught a fever this morning... You come inside, come in sir!

(Rama goes near and mutters)

Ram: I apprehended something like that... Haven't seen him since last two days... I felt disturbed. I did not know your address... Just figured out from what he spoke sketchily...Now I got it conformed.

Lakshmi: Kalia tells about you all the time... Let me bring the hurricane lamp. It is dark over here. The street light is fused.

(Lakshmi brings a hurricane lamp, raises its wick high, and stares at Ram. Back ground music.

Lakshmi: Who're you sir?... (She identifies) Ram. Ram bhai!

Ram: Lakshmi! How come... how is it that you have come to this prostitutes' lane? Is Kalia your son?

Lakshmi: (Her voice breaks almost to the brink of a sob) Yes, Ram bhai. Ram bhai... It's all my fate (She weeps)

Ram: I've searched for you all my life... I came to Bhubaneswar in search of you... Days and nights I have hazarded for locating your residence,...Searched for you in the galaxies... Ah! How many strings I've touched in the life's orchestra! How many rhythms I've rehearsed only to sing for you! But you melted away in the thin air of time... Your absence… raised waves of emptiness in me...

Lakshmi: And you're finally consigned to the footpath... to the grimy cemented benches of the old bus stand... Kalia has told me everything Ram bhai... The society here couldn't provide shelter to a gold medalist of the university; whereas the riff-raffs became ministers in your time... You look so pathetic with this uncared-for beard... namby-pamby and mawkish!

Ram: I lived bearing the burden of a long quest... Lakshmi... All my pain, all remorse, hidden tears in the broken temple of my heart, I tried to shape the incomplete god of love, but I could not find you.

Lakshmi: (In broken voice.) Why do you call it an incomplete god of love, Ram bhai? It poised in our space of embrace... in time eternity.

Ram: Nothing happened. Nothing could we do. Life for us is a yawning sigh... an enormous emptiness for us!

Lakshmi: No, Ram bhai, I still love you! Don't make your heart an empty space. Don't fill that empty space with dregs... Come in side... (Holds Ram bhai) Embrace me as a prostitute... If you shudder, embrace me as a fairy... Let us ride on the horseback of dreams... Let us set out for the unreachable! We'll striptease from our body all logic and all reasoning. Logic and reasoning are rendered lame for us. Come! In the crystal blue of the sky, to the distant mirage we shall fly. (Music starts for a slow waltz. Lakshmi holds Ram and slowly dances round. Ram is magnetized and he moves like an enchanted angel. The voice of Lakshmi's father is overheard).

Voice Over: Lakshmi! Who has come at this hour of the night? Your favourite customer? Hang on to him Ha... Ha! That's the anchor of our survival.

Ram: Who's he, Lakshmi? Where's my respected Danei Sir?

Lakshmi: Do you want to see him? (She goes inside) Let me bring him here... (She brings the old man. He has grown unkempt beard and gone insane. The oldman holds a dried coconuts shell and tears the choirs off into small pieces. He is heedless of others' comments).

Ram: Who's this old man Lakshmi?

Lakshmi: (in broken vocie) Your Sir...YourDanei Sir Ram Bhai... He became insane after Kalia was born... asked me 'who's his father'... I said, the 'Elephant Swamy'! He looked at me day long and night long... He stared at my child... in the eyes of mud and garbage... Lots of Kalias appeared to have been born everyday like sin, Kalia was a sign of sin. He had endless births. The sin called Kalia suddenly looms limpid and I saw Bapa's Victorian values imploded... He became insane! (Lakshmi weeps) (The old man laughs).

Ram: Didn't he teach the boy Kalia English grammar?

Lakshmi: The pages of grammatology are torn into shreds – he says... What did you say, Bappa?

Old man: I am born each moment in the corridors of a new grammar; enchanted alternately by bliss and sorrow. In every door of my consciousness I discovered an elephant crossing boundaries and trampling over my values of life.

Lakshmi: Who are you talking to Bapa? Here is Ram bhai... He's come to see you, to talk to you!

(Ram goes and touches the old man's feet)

Old man: Who's this young man with French-cut beard?

Lakshmi: Your friend's son. Gobind Babu, I mean Gobind Pradhan's son,

Old man: Gobind is dead long since. He had a son. Yes. He was studying well, but he didn't nourish a beard! Who's this strange man at this hour of the night?

Lakshmi: That boy Bapa! He used to come to our house everyday... He was my friend... We used to play cat and mouse in our orchard. He came accidentally with some strangers and located me now.

(The old man staggers toward Ram and examines his bearded face staring at him intently).

Old man: Hm! Do you also suffer from that elephant?

Ram: Yes. The elephant has undone many... I could not pass across its brutal hooves. I was also crushed on the high way of life.

Old man: But you told you were appearing at competitive exams? Some bank exams?

Lakshmi: After his father's death, his landed property and house were auctioned away by the Elephant money-lender. Then he was thrown into the streets of Bhubaneswar as a guttersnipe. He spent his nights on the old bus stand bench and Kalia bought him his dinner occasionally.

Old man: Why didn't you come to my house? Lakshmi earns money by prostitution. Come inside. We have a high bed, a sofa and a refrigerator. We've a television box... But she is still unwed. She got a son on bonus. Finally she has become a strumpet.

Ram: No sir! She is seraphic and sublime. She has turned her back on filth. She was never a brat. She'll never be one.

Danei: How dare you say that? One day she openly declared herself as a prostitute. I thought she has gone mad after the Elephant Swamy raped her. But finally doctors said I have gone berserk.

Lakshmi: Yes Ram bhai! Your Danei Sir is off his nuts, after that Elephant Swamy incident.

Danei: Examine her body. She's like a shriveled orange; her customers squeeze and press her every day

Lakshmi: Dirt! It's all dirt of his mind; he down loads with old age. (She stamps her feet and goes hastily casting a vile look at her father)

Danei: Ah! And she was my daughter, once upon a time. (Music) when her mother died untimely... She used to go the village cemetery in the midnight and weep there in front of the tomb. This was the girl I nurtured. And see her today... She became an unacknowledged mother and gave birth to this bastard!

Ram: Who's that? You mean Kalia? He can't be a bastard Sir! Lakshmi gave birth to this little seraph. He is a celestial bliss... He feeds me every evening! And you call his mother a prostitute? Since she delivered a child before marriage? Why Sir? Why couldn't you become little lenient?

Danei: Do you know? She's dumped me in a cesspool of defamation and dishonor? She has blackened my face?

Ram: That's because she didn't have the money to pay the doctor for an abortion.

Danei: You are right to some extent. But owning a grandson from an unwed daughter is treated as a sin in our society.

Ram: But Lakshmi never plunged in voluptuous delights. You don't know sir, premature sex games are very common in our society. Would you call all of them brats and whores?

(Lakshmi enters like a storm)

Lakshmi: It's futile, Ram Bhai... totally inefficacious. Bappa shall never be convinced He does not believe that, the

Elephant Swamy has crushed me down. Doesn't believe that in an alien city like Bhubaneswar I became a prey to various elephants... the political elephants, the business elephants and the medical elephants... Ram Bhai was lost in the crowd struggling for a meal! My last ray of silver line was extinguished in the monotone of the black, chilly nights. I was all alone; left at the streets as a destitute. Bappa doesn't understand the insecurity and desperation of a countryside girl in a sprawling city; in a city nurturing elephants without scruples. The administration can't incarcerate them, it would neither keep them in quarantine, nor restraint them.

Ram: I was, too, wandering on the streets penny less searching for a job to sustain, so that I could appear for the competitive examinations. I never knew Lakshmi was bartering her body to earn a livelihood in the same city.

Danei: I've had a strange belief, somehow, that there's an elephant behind every debacle. The elephant has devastated our family.

Lakshmi: You, Bappa! You've unnecessarily chastised me.

Ram: We also need a counter-elephant, I mean, an elephant to counter the atrocities committed by New Capital White Elephants.

Danei: If they are available tame them and train them.

Lakshmi: Build up Kalia as a new age elephant Bappa, Train him to kill the largest tormentor.

Danei: I always offered my words of protest skyward. Surely, someone behind the clouds will listen to and understand my anguish. And finally, I got Kalia. But, where is he now? Why was he sleeping there on that tattered, shaggy mattress? (He calls) Kalia! Kalia!!

Lakshmi: Let me find out. He was sick. (Goes inside)

Danei: Ram! Kalia is the child of this, wretched century. Yet, like in every child's brain he too nurtures an elephant.

That is his ambition. He is never intimidated by the heavy weight demons.

Ram: Yes Sir, he hazarded the Rajdhani roads during the elephant rampage... He bought me breads and little curry.

(Kalia enters with his mother. He wears an elephant mask)

Lakshmi: Look here my child, See who has come!

Ram: Hello Partner! How's your health? Your mother said you were sick.

Kalia: Yes, I was sick, suffering from a new generation disease called elephantatitis. Look, I'm transformed into a miniature elephant.

Ram: What did the doctors say?

Kalia: They refused to treat me. May be, they don't have the vaccines to counteract elephantatitis. That's why the disease has turned into an epidemic. People beg for food in great hunger! (Remembering something) Momma! You give him a sumptuous meal! Uncle must be hungry. Might not have eaten anything since morning... Give him some food! Otherwise he will catch elephantatitis.

Lakshmi: Let me bring something. Ram bhai! You were lost for a long time! I'll never let you go... You'll stay with us. (Lakshmi exits.)

Danei: Then you promise me Ram, You'll raise Kalia as a counter force to check the elephants from committing mid-day crimes...

Ram: Yes, I'll train him how to wage a guerilla war against elephants of corruption. I know the war tactics I know how to check these thick skinned, bullet proof huge elephants. They crave for power. Power of any kind to dominate over others!

(Danei goes to Kalia who has put on an elephant mask)

Danei: Yes, my dear tiny elephant! You'll be the savior of all elephant-victims… You'll be the little healer of elephantatitis. By the way, what are the symptoms of elephantatitis?

Ram: It's a multivalent hunger! They crave for power in every sector. They crave to be the greatest connoisseurs of child sex... They want to play the global intellectual... and want to enjoy the status of the greatest pop singer. They grab a *"jnanpith"* award in literature and then slither their way into getting a *"padma bibhusand"* from the government. They are the elephants, Sir; they celebrate the murder of the subalterns and protesters. They grow elephantine noses, elephantine ears, elephantine hunger and elephantine physique!

(Lakshmi enters with some food in a bowl.)

Lakshmi: This is sweet porridge, Ram Bhai, not the food for elephantatitis. Take it now just to assuage your hunger! I'll bring the main course later!

Danei: Cook a big meal also for Kalia, Lakshmi. We'll nurture him as a little elephant. But where did he get the mask from?

Lakshmi: I've bought him that mask to play the elephant.

Danei: Otherwise, that demonic elephant's voice could never be silenced again; neither by bullets nor by incarceration. The animal trumpets and whispers, it sings the lullaby of death for the homeless street-dwellers. We don't need masked elephants, any more, lakshmi! We need a real counter elephant-even though he is artificial, but he should be able to doctor such invaders.

(Enters Elephant and ELI with a roar)

ELI: Mr. Elephant expresses his deep sorrow for barging into this private house at this odd hour of the night. He breached the glittering barricades fixed for protecting the ordinary citizens who were prostrating under his feet to get trampled for *salvation.* He is an incarnate of Divinity. But you call him a demonic grabber of power and a mass killer. You want to bolster the case by killing him in any way it is possible. You've handed over the case to the police. The police have filed a case under Prevention of Terrorist Act. The CBI failed. The Forest Minister could not bear with the Elephant Reality and has tendered his resignation. Mr. Elephant, therefore, displayed an unseemly sense of urgency and presented himself physically in the courtyard of this small house.

(Another roar from the elephant)

Mr. Elephant says, "I want to see the hero who has targeted me to kill."

Ram: I'm not a hero, but I intend to kill you... Want to kill you 'cause you're absolute evil.

Kalia: I'm a little newspaper vendor. I know the atrocities you've perpetrated. So, I want to kill you by hook or crook. I know, I can't kill you physically... If it is possible, I'll scrape off the terrible elephantinity that makes you wild... turns you into a diabolic phenomenon.

Danei: You can't kill this giant animal my son! The diabolic phenomenon has crushed our marrow-bones after independence. (Turning to the elephant boldly) Yes, Mr. Elephant! Mind You! I'm a freedom fighter. We've driven the British white elephants away from our country. I won't spare you. You must meet your end.

Lakshmi: You the demonic elephant! You've ravished and despoiled me... inseminated me with your elephant eggs. You've blazed me as a whore... pulled me down from the cozy blanket of my green dreams... I will never forgive you.

ELI: Look Madam! As a woman you are not privileged to put up a protest show in this Elephant Era.

(The Elephant roars)

Lakshmi: Shut up you abominable Patriarch. Do you have any idea about the collective conscience of this country?

They'd not cease to throw mud at you till the capital punishment is awarded to you!

(The Elephant trumpets again)

ELI: Mr. Elephant says he is not prepared for a skirmish now, especially with a pig-headed whore like you.

Kalia: Eh, you bull headed Language freak! How dare you call my mother a whore? You are only a profligate theatrical sign; a sign of power, kind a' an ugly nuclear bomb! Before you shatter the world with a final explosion, I would warn you to change your character! If you want to be a good elephant, don the role of a peace-keeper of the world.

ELI: What kind of peace? Are you Emperor Ashoka? Or a Gandhian fraud?

Ram: Shut up, you linguistic hoax! Listen to this young vendor first. He begs you to transform your character...He begs you to make a peace-march instead of getting the city roads on rampage. Why are you flared up pointlessly?

Kalia: Yes! I pray you my giant master! I am a tiny newspaper vendor with this tiny homeopathic bottle... Would you like to taste some globules?

ELI: How many globules?

Kalia: Only four sir!

ELI: Ha, Ha, Ha, Ha, Ha.

(The Elephant nods his head)

His Highness, Mr. Elephant has given you the permission to give him the peace medicines. This is going to be a big event in the country! Journalists and guests from the media! Kindly give a good coverage to this historical event... Mr. Elephant will take four globules of homeopathy from this self-styled mini doctor and go for a peace-march tomorrow parading the capital roads! Now Little Doctor! Don't be afraid of the elephant! Go near and drop the globules in his mouth. Start now!... One... two... three... four... start!

(With this signal begins a primitive drum beat. Kalia opens the little bottle in an exaggerated stylized action and advanced toward the elephant menacingly. Both of them attempt to hunt each other. The elephant gives a trumpet call and circumambulates the stage.

Danei, Ram and Lakshmi also circum-ambulate the stage, sometime appearing like the tangled petals of a wild flower which the elephant menaces to crush. The tempo of the hunting drum rises up. The movement in the choreographic compositions changes into various patterns. Posit Kalia separately so that rhythmically he'll cut his way and reach the elephant's mouth. The actors should perform the scene with gusto of robust fighters in separate blockings, though.

Kalia dupes the elephant and drops the globules into his mouth. With this, there is a giant explosion on the stage. The sound makes the elephant blind. The blocking(s) made by the other characters are blown into bits. The explosion reverberates and repeats. As it begins to die down, we see all the bodies exploding to the pulse of the sound. This is done in slow motion. As the sound dies away, we see everyone in a clustered death struggle. When they are motionless and dead, their bodies form the shape of an Elephant in the reverse order of the opening elephant image.

With a trumpet call the Elephant and the ELI enter and laugh like ethnic villains. Then they join the group to form the elephant image.

ELI: You can't kill the Elephant. It is omnipresent. The Elephant is within you, in your mind, citizens of the world. You can't erase its picture from your psyche. The presence of the Elephant is instinctual. (Mr. Elephant roars from behind. No BGM, silence.)

ELI: This is an explosion of self-esteem. Like a nuclear test. What you find here is a road to resurgence... It's a moment of pride! Hail to the Elephant Era! Not only can the Elephant deploy the explosion to threaten the enemy, it can use it to declare war against the unruly rebels. Such massacres, mayhems... such endless columns of broken people are like documentary film strips of World War Two. But why's there no sound track? Why's the hall so quiet. Mr. Elephant would form a committee to inquire into the historical muteness. Do they have a voice?

(The Elephant and the ELI make an exit)

(There is a sharp roll on the octopod and the scribbler and spear hunters enter the stage surreptitiously.)

Scribbler hunter: Ah! This is a genocidal massacre!

Spear Hunter: The carnage, it seems, is designed as a public spectacle, whose aims are unmistakable.

Scribbler Hunter: This could've been avoided had the administration invested an iota of trust on my capacity to save democracy.

Spear Hunter: It did neither trust on my mythical spear that killed thousands in the War of Mahabharata. I'd have lynched this demonic elephant easily... They ignored me since I had no political godfather and I come from Koraput jungles.

Scribbler Hunter: (Meditates for a while) Idea! Let's transform ourselves into mythical hunters and conjure an act of tribal necromancy to resurrect the dead.

Spear-Hunter: Necromancy? That's incredible now!

Scribbler Hunter: Some act of magic realism? After all, ours is a tribal country. We're victimized by the elephants of civilization. We'll invoke the dead Shamans and they'd blow life into these carcasses. You can do it with your mythical spear. Start your operation! You're a genius!

(Abruptly starts a primitive drum-beat and the hunters move different parts of their bodies in wild excitement. The steps are taken amid the lying carcasses, now scattered throughout the stage. The spear hunter performs some Shamanistic rituals fluffing up imaginary water on them and chanting the following bizarre words written in reverse order:)

Atahtsittu, atargaj, atahsunnarabayparp
Atiatsittu, atargaj, atahsunnarabayaparp

(With this magical/bizarre chanting and tribal rituals, the dead bodies rise up convulsing with violent, irregular movement of the limbs, contraction of the muscles and they recite the following words with much difficulty and stand erect. The Director should assign and repeat the lines till the actors physicalize the elephant image to signify the reverse of what they configured at the beginning of the play. The lines are given below randomly and the director will assign them to the actors as per his convenience and to support the bit-by-bit architectural composition. The director may choose to recruit five/six more characters as fighters from outside who join the Hunters and transform themselves in tribal dancers and would join the shaman dance of the Hunters. The exact number of actors required for the elephant formation shall be calculated by the director during the workshop rehearsal. The following lines will be distributed by the director amongst the actors who will physicalize the elephant.

Lines/words are to be distributed among actors during the rehearsals. At the end the scribbler Hunter delivers the following speech on elephants:

The Elephant is a mass-murderer. All elephants are mass-murderers. Elephants do not die. They lurk in everyone's psyche. We have two India's: One with wild elephants and the other with civil elephants. One hunter says, "Give me a chance and I'll prove myself. The other hunter says, "Prove yourself first and may be then, you'll have a chance. One elephant lives in the optimism of our hearts... the other elephant lurks in the skepticism of our minds. One boy leads the campaign against the elephant. The other members follow. One group belongs to the ghosts of the past. Another group is pulsating and dynamic. The elephant-free India is emerging. Here is our counterfeit civilization. One group chooses to become rich. The other group doesn't. They are choosing stoicism over optimism. They are choosing to be poor. It's their fault. They are weak. One group sticks to nonviolent, counter elephant movements. The other group, reduced to humiliation, flounders. They flounder in the quagmire of justice dispensation. The battle stinks of death. It's by no means petty. How can it be petty when Elephants perpetrate genocides? Within an ongoing counterfeit culture genocide becomes easy, almost natural. Here ends the essay on elephants.

(By the time these conclusive sentences are spoken the elephant formation should be completed. If it is not completed, kindly repeat the lines from the beginning again. Special effect lights on the elephant. Then there is a colored sky in the background and the physicalized elephant is seen in silhouette. The following song is heard on the tape-recorder.)

Song:

There's an elephant in my head
and a big one is he
He stamps his feet, trampling my dreams
into nothing but debris.
There's an elephant in my head
he is too strong to see
He leaves me no peace, no sleep
Stomping on everything I can be.
There's an elephant in my head
And I want to set him free
Because deep down inside I know
The elephant is me.

(The curtain does not drop. The elephant formation is deconstructed. The actors semioticize a 'goodbye' to the audience in slow motion. One by one they step down toward the auditorium in slow motion as if they have come out from a long-distance jungle called civilization. Each actor chooses an audience member and touches his hand, head, face, hair. Look and touch action continues in the auditorium and the actors lose their identity in the audience/society/civilization. It is a celebration of presence. This should be done while the song is played on the tape.

****